# THE SKILLED
# METALWORKERS
# OF NUREMBERG

CLASS AND CULTURE
A series edited by
Milton Cantor and Bruce Laurie

# THE SKILLED METALWORKERS OF NUREMBERG

## Craft and Class in the Industrial Revolution

MICHAEL J. NEUFELD

 RUTGERS UNIVERSITY PRESS
New Brunswick and London

Library of Congress Cataloging-in-Publication Data

Neufeld, Michael J., 1951–
    The skilled metalworkers of Nuremberg : craft and class in the
Industrial Revolution / Michael J. Neufeld.
        p.   cm. — (Class and culture)
    Bibliography: p.
    Includes index.
    ISBN 0-8135-1394-4
    1. Metal-workers—Germany (West)—Nuremberg—History.   2. Trade
-unions—Metal-workers—Germany (West)—Nuremberg—History.
3. Artisans—German (West)—Nuremberg—History.   I. Title.
II. Series.
HD8039.M52G365   1989
331.7′671′094321—dc19                                              88-23875
                                                                            CIP


British Cataloging-in-Publication information available

To Sheila

# CONTENTS

# FIGURES

# TABLES

# PREFACE

This study is a product of a revolution in the historiography of industrialization and labor movements. In the quarter century since the publication of E. P. Thompson's classic *Making of the English Working Class*, labor historians have extensively reevaluated the role of skilled workers and artisans in the history of Western trade unions and working-class political movements. No longer seen (for good or ill) mainly as conservative defenders of their own self-interest or craft traditions, skilled craftsmen have now been placed at the center of all labor movements—conservative or radical—in the nineteenth and early twentieth centuries. At the same time the overemphasis on factory production employing masses of unskilled or semiskilled workers as *the* Industrial Revolution has rightly been questioned, to the benefit of our knowledge of both small-scale production and the often prominent role of skilled workers in the factory. This historiographical revolution, and particularly the work of David Montgomery on American machinists and rationalization, led me to examine the fate of an important group of craftsmen in turn-of-the-century Germany: the skilled metalworkers. Out of this interest there evolved, initially as a dissertation for The Johns Hopkins University, a study of this group of workers in the city of Nuremberg from the beginning of the Industrial Revolution in 1835 to the maturation of the local metalworkers' industrial union in 1905. In the end, I found that my expectation that technological change and rationalization were the central determinants of the organizational and protest behavior of these workers was not borne out. Instead craft traditions and craft consciousness, and their interaction with class formation and class consciousness, became the central themes of this book.

For his always helpful supervision of the original version, and for his advice and encouragement then and since, I would above all like to thank Vernon Lidtke of Johns Hopkins. The inspired writing, teaching, and criticism of Mack Walker, also of Johns Hopkins, were influential in shaping this work too. For my original introduction to modern social history I am still grateful to Edward Hundert, Harvey Mitchell, and Leonidas Hill of the University of British Columbia. For their encouragement to publish this work in the present series I am especially grateful to Michael Hanagan of Columbia University and Bruce Laurie of the University of Massachusetts, Amherst. I am also indebted to them for their trenchant criticism of earlier versions of the manuscript. Finally, for criticism of various portions of this project I wish to thank Frederick Marquardt of Syracuse University, Douglas Deal of SUNY Oswego, and the members of the Modern European History Seminar at Johns Hopkins. If, after all this advice, I have stubbornly refused to see the error of my ways, the responsibility is mine alone.

For aid and advice during my original residence in, and on later trips to, West Germany, it is encumbent upon me to thank first the friendly, competent, and helpful staff of the Stadtarchiv Nürnberg, especially Dr. Werner Lehnert, Herr Albert Bartelmeß, and Herr Kurt Schreppel. Thanks are also owed to Herr Werkmann of the M.A.N.-Nürnberg Werksarchiv, and to the staffs of the Stadtbibliothek Nürnberg, the Staatsarchiv Nürnberg, the Hauptstaatsarchiv München, the Bundesarchiv Aussenstelle Frankfurt, and the IG-Metall Bibliothek in Frankfurt am Main. For help during my stay in Nuremberg, I wish to thank Prof. Dr. Michael Stürmer of the Institut für Geschichte of the Friedrich-Alexander Universität Erlangen-Nürnberg, as well as his former students, Dr. Michael Beer and Dr. Dieter Rossmeissl. Prof. Dr. Hermann-Josef Rupieper of the Freie Universität Berlin was very helpful in advising me about the holdings of the M.A.N. archives.

Without the financial help of the Social Sciences and Humanities Research Council of Canada and the History Department of The Johns Hopkins University, I could never have undertaken the original research. I am grateful as well to the Colgate University Research Council for a small grant to allay publication costs. I also wish to thank the editors of the *Journal of Social History* for permission to reprint material in Chapter 2 that originally appeared in the Spring 1986 issue as "German Artisans and Political Repression: The Fall of the Journeymen's Associations in Nuremberg, 1806–1868." Finally, I dedicate this work to my wife, Sheila Weiss. Without her professional criticism of my work, and her help and emotional support, this book would not have been possible.

# A NOTE ON CURRENCY

Until 1875 the unit of Bavarian currency was the Gulden (abbreviated fl.), which was divided into 60 kreutzer. In that year Bavaria converted to the coinage of the new Empire, the mark or Reichsmark, at a rate of 1 fl. = 1.75 M. The mark was divided into 100 Pfenning. Prior to 1914 there were 4.2 marks to the U.S. dollar. In some cases, particularly in data generated by Rainer Gömmel, earlier figures have been converted into marks.

# THE SKILLED
# METALWORKERS
# OF NUREMBERG

# INTRODUCTION

Eighteen thirty-five: the average Nuremberg skilled metalworker is an artisan working and living with his master in a small shop in the old city; his work and social life revolve around the guild and the journeymen's association of his craft; a modern labor movement has yet to be created and political activities are rare. Nineteen hundred and five: the typical Nuremberg skilled metalworker now labors in a factory, which may range in size from small to gigantic, located in the rapidly growing suburbs; strikes over wages, hours, and working conditions are common; many are organized into a large industrial union, and most vote for a class-conscious socialist party. Between these two moments in time lay a fundamental transformation of Nuremberg, of Germany, and of the artisans and workers resident in them. It is the aim of this study to examine the nature of this transformation as reflected in the fate of one group of workers.

Such an undertaking promises to tell us much about skilled workers and their organizations in Germany. It is known that the Social Democratic movement was primarily one of skilled workers in small and medium-sized firms, but the political focus of previous labor history and the relatively late adoption of the "new social history" by the German historical profession have left much work to be done in charting the history of craftsmen and their organizations.[1] (With the sole exception of masters' widows, artisans and skilled workers were by definition men in nineteenth-century Germany after the expulsion of women from the trades in the early modern period.) The very predominance of socialism and industrial unionism in Germany has led German historians to take them for granted as products of industrialization; yet the labor movement in Germany, as elsewhere, was largely a movement of skilled workers with strong artisanal traditions. The acceptance by these workers of ideologies and union structures that implied at least some measure of class consciousness is an important phenomenon.

This phenomenon is even more interesting when the contrasting example of British and North American craft unionism is considered. Particularly between the 1850s and the 1890s in Britain and between the 1880s and the 1920s in the United States and Canada, the craft union was the predominant, though not unchallenged, form of labor organization, and the traditional political parties had the allegiance of most unionists. It was not uncommon for union leaders to express condescension or contempt openly toward the unskilled, who were often excluded by the unions. In contrast craft unionism was less important in Germany, especially in the metal, wood, and textile sectors, the original bastions of industrial unionism. As Jürgen Kocka has said, both the difference between British and German union structures and the absence of a lively debate over the "labor aristocracy" in Germany indicate that the distance between skilled and unskilled workers was smaller in that country than in Britain, and the separation between the working class and the white-collar workers was greater.[2] In this circumstance a higher degree of class consciousness in Germany does not seem surprising.

This hypothesis needs empirical verification, however. To discover how and why class-conscious politics and industrial unionism arose on a craft base, few groups are better suited for study than the skilled metalworkers. By the first decade of the twentieth century the socialist metalworkers had formed the largest trade union organization in Germany, the German Metalworkers' Union (Deutscher Metallarbeiter-Verband, or DMV). In size it eclipsed both Social Democratic or "Free" unions in other sectors, and its Catholic and Hirsch-Duncker (liberal) rivals in its own. Yet the metal crafts were extremely heterogeneous, and in many of them technological change and industrialization had scarcely undermined the high level of skill, prestige, and labor-market power traditionally possessed by metalworking artisans. Only with twentieth-century rationalization measures, such as the assembly line and increasingly automated machine tools, were this skill and power decisively weakened. Why did the skilled metalworkers nevertheless come together into industrial unions that accepted at least the theoretical equality of the unskilled, unlike their Anglo-Saxon counterparts? Why did the DMV and the Social Democratic Party triumph over their rivals? And why did craft unionism, which had a tentative hold in the metal trades in the 1870s and 1880s, ultimately fade away? Answers to these questions can do much to clarify the complex relationship between craft and class.

2

But the development of the labor movement in the 1870s and later cannot be understood apart from the craft traditions and artisanal institutions that preceded the appearance of the unions, nor can the general context of economic development and class formation be ignored. It is necessary to begin our examination of the history of the Nuremberg metalworking artisans in 1835, when industrialization had not yet had a significant impact upon their world, and then to see how the expansion of merchant putting-out and the appearance of industrial capitalism affected the artisanal sector. It is also important to take into account the process by which the working class as a whole was formed. Analysis of certain factors like marriage and family, residential patterns, and geographical and social mobility that influence class consciousness and formation, however, requires detailed examination of individual trades across all sectors of the working class that is beyond the scope of this study. This work concentrates on the external manifestations of class, particularly verbal and organizational expressions of class consciousness (to the extent that it existed at all) in union meetings, union structures, political activities, and in conflicts between workers and employers.

Of course the very categories *class* and *class consciousness* are controversial and in need of definition. I begin with the following assumption, as expressed by Jürgen Kocka: "One need not accept every aspect of Karl Marx's value theory in order to find him, nevertheless, convincing in stressing the basic importance of the commodity form of work and the basic distinction of interest between wage workers and capital owners."[3] The fundamental conflict of interest that arises out of ownership or nonownership of the means of production has been and is the crucial factor that separates workers from capitalists in industrial capitalist societies. And the development of a group of people whose sole or primary income is derived from wage labor rather than property ownership is the essential foundation for working-class formation. But, following Kocka, I do not see the working class as an object, which at some point becomes "constituted" or finished, but rather as part of a process—a process of class formation or class disintegration—as loyalties, social networks, and organizational ties founded upon economic class position become stronger or weaker in comparison to other affiliations and loyalties like ethnicity, religion, and craft. Class formation is therefore not an irreversible process.[4] By the same token, "class consciousness" does not imply that there is a correct or historically necessary form of awareness or consciousness of class. Therefore there is no "false consciousness"; nor is it necessary to explain away the absence of a revolutionary class consciousness. In Kocka's most recent model there are four levels of working-class formation: the breakdown of "older patterns of inequality" because of the "rise of capitalism," "state-building," and other processes; the development of wage labor; the growth of social ties and a class identity on the foundation of wage labor; and the appearance of organizations and ideologies formally expressing this consciousness of class. Class consciousness thus has two levels: an informal social level and a formal organizational / ideological level. But the first implies neither the necessary existence of the second, nor any particular content.[5]

To explain the actual content of working-class ideologies and organizations in a particular country we also need to look further afield than the underlying social and economic foundation. Recent comparative research on working-class formation in the United States, Britain, France, and Germany has shown, as Aristide Zolberg has written, that "the single most important determinant of variation in the patterns of working-class politics . . . is simply whether, at the time this class was being brought into being by the development of capitalism . . . , it faced an absolutist or a liberal state."[6] In other words, the extent to which workers felt excluded or included in the political process through the existing systems of parties and voting (if any) was crucial to the form of working-class politics that developed. To mention one obvious contrast, although rates of capital accumulation and concentration in late nineteenth-century Germany and the United States were quite similar, in the United States the Democrats and Republicans were successful in mobilizing working-class votes and loyalty, while in Germany a Marxist Social Democratic party became the chief beneficiary of worker alienation from Bismarck's pseudo-constitutional order. The relationship between the state or political system and the working class is not the only factor that determines the political expression of class consciousness, but it is a fundamental factor.

The overall political universe in which working-class organizations functioned was also crucial to the character of the trade unions formed; as we shall see, it is difficult to explain the victory of industrial unionism among Nuremberg skilled metalworkers without taking into account the rise of class-conscious socialism. But when we examine the specific process by which craftsmen in the metal trades adopted socialism and industrial unionism, we must also examine their allegiance to craft and how it interacted with class. Until recently most labor historians seem to have assumed that craft loyalties and traditions were merely obstacles to the development of a working-class identity, and that as class consciousness rose, craft consciousness fell in a linear fashion. Recent scholarship in labor history has decisively undermined this assumption, but no single conception has taken its place. Greater clarity may be achieved, however, if we look at the interaction of craft consciousness and class consciousness among skilled workers as a dialectical process.

First, the term *craft consciousness* should be clarified. It is certainly true that allegiance by a craftsman to his trade and its traditions could prove an obstacle to the acceptance of ideologies or organizations that called for solidarity with the unskilled, with women workers, or with other crafts. But craft consciousness is more than a narrow-minded refusal to look beyond the bounds of the trade. It can also be a pride and self-confidence in the skilled worker that his occupation is socially valuable, from which can spring a desire to fight for better wages and working conditions, perhaps even for a less discriminatory and more egalitarian society. The labor market power, and therefore the wages, that *may* spring from skill also provide at least a modicum of security and access to education useful for the development of a consciousness of his social position. And artisan traditions and customs of organization, solidarity, and mutual aid may also provide the craftsman with the models for trade unions, political activities, and even the shape of an alternative future society.[7] For precisely these reasons unskilled workers are rarely found at the head of workers' movements anywhere.

Craft consciousness can thus reinforce as well as obstruct class consciousness, and in fact can have both effects simultaneously in the mind and behavior of an individual craftsman and in whole crafts or groups of workers. This can be seen as a dialectic of craft and class, in which the process of working-class formation *may* prompt the growth of working-class identity, while at the same time craft loyalties and traditions survive and change as crafts rise, decline, or are transformed by capitalism and industrialization. Out of this process of contradiction, interaction, and reinforcement between craft and class loyalties and identities—in short, craft and class consciousness—will come a synthesis. It might be a labor movement in which craft unionism and moderate anti–class conscious politics reign, or it might be a movement in which class-conscious union forms and political ideologies predominate—or it might be some combination of the two. The synthesis of the dialectic depends on the strength of the class formation process and on the character of craft traditions and economic development. In a case in which the social, economic, and political environment favors working-class formation, the dialectic of craft and class could indeed produce socialism and industrial unionism on a craft foundation.

Conceptualizing the development of labor organizations and political ideologies among the skilled as a two-sided interaction works best when no third force complicates the picture. Nuremberg fits that description well. It had an ethnically homogeneous population (the great majority of Nurembergers were born in northern Bavaria), and it was predominantly Protestant. This was significant, because the strength of the subculture that centered on the Catholic church limited and moderated the development of class consciousness among Catholic workers and later guided it toward the Christian trade unions that appeared around 1900. The Lutheran church, in contrast, was much less successful in holding the allegiance of Protestant workers, a generalization that also seems to apply to Nuremberg. The Catholic proportion of the city's population did increase from 13.6 percent in 1864 to 31.05 percent in 1910, as a result of immigration from the Catholic northern Bavarian regions of Lower Franconia and the Upper Palatinate, but a strong Catholic subculture was slow in developing. Perhaps, as happened in Düsseldorf, Catholic immigrants to Nuremberg who had left the social ties of their village behind were more susceptible to secularization and the appeals of the Social Democrats than were long-established urban Catholics elsewhere.[8]

The significance of this confessional situation, when combined with the skilled character of Nuremberg industry, with its long metalworking tradition, may be seen in a comparison with Augsburg, one of the few other industrial cities in predominately agrarian Bavaria. In Augsburg the majority of the population was Catholic, and the dominant industry was textile production in large factories. Because the textile industry required fewer skilled workers, and employed large numbers of women and children, the combination of low skill, powerful employers, and an entrenched Catholic subculture prevented the successful development of a class-conscious labor movement.[9] Nuremberg, in contrast, became the center of the Social Democratic Party (SPD) and the Free unions in Bavaria, and is thus more comparable to north German cities like Berlin, Leipzig, and Hamburg, with their large numbers of skilled Protestant workers, than to any place in south Germany. Comparisons with these cities, as well as with other countries, will be used where possible to distinguish the particular characteristics of Nuremberg.

The northern Bavarian city is thus a good place to study the development of industrial unionism and socialism among artisans and skilled workers—and particularly among skilled metalworkers, for which the archival sources in the city are quite rich. The first railroad in Germany, the Nuremberg-Fürth railway of 1835, provides an appropriately symbolic date for the beginning of industrialization and of this study. Chapters 1 and 2 will focus on the pre–trade union period from 1835 to 1868, treating the impact of capitalism and industrialization on the artisanate and the transformation of the journeymen's world. In particular these chapters will examine how economic change, population growth, and political repression led to a shift toward industrial employment, a decline in master-journeymen relations, the collapse of the guild system, and the rise of politicization and class consciousness.

The end point of this work, 1905, is also symbolic. Three events in that year symbolize the maturation of industrial unionism among the skilled metalworkers of Nuremberg. In March the local DMV, after much controversy, finally dissolved its independent craft sections and formed one unitary local. Only a few months later the socialist feminist Helene Grünberg came to Nuremberg to organize the city's female workers, which eventually helped to increase the feminine membership of the Nuremberg DMV to one-third of the whole. Finally, organizing efforts in the largest machine-industry plants, in conjunction with conflicts between the union and employers in Munich, led to a huge lockout of the Bavarian metalworkers by the employers' association in June. Although the lockout was not a success for the DMV, the implicit acceptance by the employers of the union's right to represent the workers was a significant event, as was the progress made by organizers in penetrating the ranks of both the skilled and the unskilled in the big firms. Skilled workers were still apprenticed craftsmen, but they had moved far beyond their artisanal origins. The growth and travails of the union movement and the socialist party will be the primary focus of chapters 3, 4, and 5. In these two wings of the movement one can see all the complexities of the dialectic of craft and class consciousness as expressed in the transformation of the Nuremberg skilled metalworkers. But first we must turn to the origins of that transformation: the interaction of capitalism, industrialization, and the artisanate.

# 1

## CAPITALISM, INDUSTRIALIZATION, AND THE METALWORKING ARTISANS OF NUREMBERG

Nuremberg is a Gothic city. Despite the devastations of the Second World War and the burgeoning of the suburbs since the late nineteenth century, the core of the city is stamped even today by the architecture of the late Middle Ages. In 1835, Nuremberg was little different from its size and appearance of three hundred years before. The great majority of its 45,000 inhabitants lived and worked in buildings constructed in the sixteenth century or earlier, and the city had scarcely expanded beyond the massive wall dating from the fourteenth and fifteenth centuries. Nuremberg's archaic appearance—which made it a favorite pilgrimage point for nineteenth-century Romantic poets and twentieth-century Nazi leaders— was a consequence of economic decline. After its apogee as a European center of commerce and trade in the 1400s and 1500s, the proud Free Imperial City steadily sank in importance as mercantilism and endless wars restricted trade and burdened the populace with onerous taxes and a huge public debt. To make matters worse, the city's once energetic merchant-patricians hardened into a resolutely conservative caste of landowning nobles. Independence was finally lost on September 15, 1806, when the Bavarians took possession of one of their spoils of the Napoleonic Wars.[1]

Although Nuremberg had the largest territory of any Free City, it, like the others, lacked virtually all natural resources. The city's economic greatness was founded primarily on its favorable geographic location for European trade and on the energy and competence of its merchants and artisans. At the same time that the patricians were establishing mercantile connections all over the Continent in the fifteenth century, their control over the city prevented the rapid accumulation of restrictions on artisanal production and thus promoted a blossoming of the artisan trades almost without parallel in Germany. It is one of the peculiarities of the city's development that guilds in the strict sense, that is, self-governing corporations of master artisans, were never allowed. Until the mid-1500s the city council kept many crafts open and without elaborate controls on the entry of new masters or on the mode of production. Even those trades with quasi-guild statutes, the "sworn" trades, were administered by the council. But with the turn toward economic stagnation and patrician conservatism in the sixteenth century came a rapid increase in the number of "sworn" trades, and over the next two centuries the council increasingly granted the masters most of the restrictions they wanted on innovation, entry of new apprentices and masters, and enrichment of individuals. Some trades were even "closed" *(gesperrt):* their journeymen were forbidden to wander in the hope that it would prevent the export of trade secrets and technology. This only accelerated the technological backwardness and impoverishment of these crafts in Nuremberg.[2]

In conjunction with this policy, the patriciate also restricted the development of merchant and putting-out capitalism, although this was loosened slightly in the last few decades before 1800. Manufactories (large enterprises with a division of labor but without power sources) were generally prevented from competing with artisanal production where they might otherwise have done so, and numerous decrees against the extension of putting-out (where masters were supplied with materials by, and worked on order for, merchants) were issued. The very frequency of these restrictions and prohibitions suggests, however, that the dependence of artisans on capitalist putters-out in the seventeenth and eighteenth centuries was growing. As Nuremberg's craftsmen turned away from quality production toward the mass production of cheap low-quality goods, they needed the merchants more than ever to handle the large volume of exports.[3]

These general conditions were not fundamentally changed in the early nineteenth century. In spite of the disorder and change of the post-1806 period, the quasi-guild system was retained, with the state bureaucracy taking over the supervisory role from the city council. All trades, except the so-called free trades, were organized into "trade associations" (*Gewerbsvereine*). Because these associations were normally called guilds by both artisans and local officials, and because they fulfilled so many of the functions of guilds (or, in Nuremberg, "sworn" trades), this name will be retained here despite their lack of self-governing power. To gain entrance to a guild a journeyman had to obtain a state license (*Konzession*) as well as pass his master's examination; if he failed either he could not independently practice his trade. Once promoted, the new master entered an exclusive group with control over certain products or processes that other trades were not allowed to make or use. But the unclear boundaries between crafts led to endless squabbles, which the state, like the old city council, was constantly obliged to mediate. After 1818, with the restoration of communal government, the city council again governed all guild matters, with the state bureaucracy as the court of appeal.[4] From all indications it appears that artisan customs, traditions, and daily life were little changed despite the great political changes of the first two decades of the century.

This was in large part due to the absence of economic change. No significant economic growth occurred until 1825, when the new Trades Law loosened admission to mastership and eased the granting of licenses for factories (*Fabrikkonzessionen*). The short boom in Nuremberg that followed was soon over when the violent reaction of artisan masters and small towns drove the government to tighten its policy again after 1831.[5] The nature of Nuremberg production was thus little changed in the 1830s. Factories (large establishments with central power sources) had scarcely established themselves, and although the number of manufactories continued to grow, artisans remained the dominant producers. One of the city's prominent liberals, Ignaz Rudhardt, described the situation in 1827:

> The essence of Nuremberg industry is that it is not carried out *in large factories*, but rather by many independent masters, who are and will remain artisans. . . . The shipment of Nuremberg manufactured goods is handled in fact by numerous trading houses (one hundred in the city) and by far the most transactions are handled on commission. The foreigner sends his order to the house in Nuremberg, and the firm takes care of the supply, the payment of the artisans, the packaging and the shipping.[6]

The onset of rapid industrialization came only in the early 1840s,[7] although the Nuremberg-Fürth railway of 1835 was certainly a harbinger of it. A significant machine industry, to be discussed below, appeared around 1840 and was central to the transformation of many of the metal trades. Large factories also appeared in many of the traditional crafts after 1850, but it is significant that the old methods of production and export held their own well into the twentieth century. Particularly in such industries as metal toys and gold leaf, Nuremberg specialties, small masters and domestic workers continued to compete with larger firms because their trades could not be easily adapted to machine production or lacked economies of scale that would encourage extensive mechanization. Through the exploitation of helpers and self-exploitation these small producers managed to stay afloat, though usually at the cost of dependence upon the merchant houses, who supplied them with materials and markets. Putting-out domestic industry grew throughout the century, and those masters who avoided dependence on the merchants often created large shops that were, in essence, latter-day manufactories. Gold and metal leaf production in particular could not be mechanized, and it remained almost entirely the province of a few independent large masters, plus a large number of smaller ones completely in the grip of the putters-out.

The impact of industrialization on artisans was thus highly uneven, depending on technology and demand in the particular crafts. Shulamit Volkov has distinguished among (1) those trades that were essentially untouched by big business, (2) those that were gradually dominated by it, and (3) those that existed in a symbiosis with large industry.[8] Most trades, especially the metal trades, fell in the last category and benefited, like the first group, from the expansion in population and per capita income that accompanied the industrialization process. Nuremberg alone grew from 45,000 to 300,000 people between 1835 and 1905 as a result of a massive influx from rural northern Bavaria and the incorporation of suburbs. This growth benefited the local crafts, but equally important to Nuremberg's export-oriented economy was the expansion of national and international demand, which strongly affected many traditional metalworking crafts.

## The Transformation of the City's Historic Metal Trades

The working of metals, especially brass, had always been the most important sector of Nuremberg artisanry. In the late Middle Ages the city's metalworking masters gained fame for fine scientific and mathematical instruments, watches, gold leaf, armor and armaments, and luxury and household objects of all kinds. A very elaborate division of labor arose, which was reflected in a bewildering array of distinct occupations: there were up to one hundred different metal crafts in the seventeenth century.[9] Although the situation was not this extreme in the nineteenth century, the division was still large. Table 1.1 shows the development between 1831–1832 and 1873 of twenty-two metal trades plus two (toy-makers and turners) who included metalworking artisans among them. The totals are only a low approximation of the number of craftsmen working metal, not only because of the gaps in the data (especially for 1851) but also because a few trades have been left out—most prominently the fine mechanics *(Mechaniker)*, a free (unguilded) trade. Masters and journeymen who worked in factories have also been excluded because they were not counted by the city as artisans. Of all master artisans working in Nuremberg (just under three thousand in the 1830s and 1840s),[10] those in the metal trades constituted approximately one-quarter.

A comparison of the total numbers of masters and journeymen reveals that the size of the average shop was very small. The master–journeymen ratio was approximately 1.0 before 1873, which was little changed from 0.86 in 1785.[11] The Zollverein censuses of 1847 and 1861 show ratios of 1.3 and 1.5,[12] but this may include some small factories or manufactories—the dividing line was not easy to draw. A handful of masters might have ten or more helpers; many others would have none.[13] In addition, although the number of masters in most trades was fairly stable over the forty years from 1831–1832 to 1873, despite rapid industrialization after the 1840s, a few obsolete trades like the awlsmiths and the needle makers were in drastic decline, while others grew dramatically. The increase in gold beaters, tinsmiths, locksmiths, and the two mixed trades of turners and toymakers stand out particularly, and the metal beaters are also prominent when the change in the number of journeymen is examined. The boom in gold and metal leaf manufacture, metal toy production, and construction-related metalwork for tinsmiths and locksmiths was the cause of this growth.

Numbers of artisans alone, of course, do not tell the whole story. The nailsmiths, for example, held their own, at least until 1865, but their standard of living must have declined. After the invention of a better nail-making machine by Ludwig Werder, a later collaborator of the Nuremberg machine industry magnate Cramer-Klett, the nailsmiths were hurt badly, and allegedly they even threatened to destroy the machine in

1847–1848. The real decline in numbers came after 1870, however, and by 1894 there were only four masters left.[14] Information on the income of masters might shed more light on the many trades in Table 1.1 whose numbers were relatively stagnant, but unfortunately there are no reliable data.

Capitalist industrialization, in addition to its multifaceted economic impact, had numerous effects on the organization and social relations of production in the handicrafts. No matter whether a particular craft thrived or stagnated, it was not free of considerable changes in the relationship between masters and journeymen (as will be discussed in Chapter 2) as a result of the gradual collapse of the old paternalism and its replacement by an employee-employer relationship that reflected the growing capitalist spirit among masters and the growing working-class consciousness among their helpers. This widening gap was in part the result of the adaptations more and more masters were forced to make either to compete with industry and other masters or to meet increased demand. Such masters employed female labor, mass produced a few items, tightened work discipline, and lengthened the workday.[15] But these changes were not always made; Bavaria was a backward and agrarian state, and the quasi-guild system was only abolished in 1868 (after a preliminary loosening in 1862). The availability of state-supervised guild mechanisms to resist the innovations of other masters and the encroachments of other trades undoubtedly encouraged some masters to remain stubbornly traditional. In the long run, however, this sort of resistance was doomed to fail because of the eventual acceptance of economic liberalism by the Bavarian bureaucracy and middle classes.

The process of adaptation and transformation in metalworking can be better understood through a close examination of a few major crafts. This will also provide the background necessary for later exploration of the lives, work, and consciousness of artisan journeymen and skilled workers. Three crafts or industries will be examined here: brass molding, toymaking (together with the sheet-metal trades), and gold and metal beating. All three were strongly penetrated by putting-out capitalism as a result of being export industries, but their development was diverse. Brass molding was a craft in decline because of competition from industry and other trades armed with new technology, but it did not disappear like nailsmithing and awlsmithing. It falls on the border between Volkov's categories 2 and 3. The toy industry, in contrast, falls into category 3, that is, a symbiosis between artisanry and industry. Small-scale and domestic production coexisted with large factories. The beating trades,

Table 1.1. NUMBERS OF METALWORKING ARTISANS, 1831–32 TO 1873

| Trade | 1831–32 M | 1844 M | 1844 J | 1844 A | 1851 M | 1851 J | 1851 A | 1865 M | 1865 J | 1873 M | 1873 J |
|---|---|---|---|---|---|---|---|---|---|---|---|
| Awlsmiths | 50 | 35 | 16 | 2 | 27 | 16 | 9 | 30 | 0 | 2 | 0 |
| Bellmakers | 34 | not given | | | 25 | 7 | 5 | 17 | 1 | 8 | 0 |
| Blacksmiths | 19 | 20 | 58 | 3 | not given | | | 23 | 53 | 25 | 45 |
| Brass molders | 203 | 193 | 156 | 46 | 197 | 109 | 22 | 172 | 111 | 129 | 169 |
| Braziers | 33 | 30 | 31 | 12 | 30 | 26 | 15 | 32 | 34 | 25 | 35 |
| Chain and ringsmiths | 3 | 2 | 2 | 1 | 3 | 1 | 1 | 2 | 1 | 2 | 0 |
| Compass makers | 74 | 78 | 65 | 10 | 79 | 57 | 18 | 71 | 60 | 62 | 92 |
| Coppersmiths | 8 | 9 | 10 | 3 | not given | | | 10 | 13 | 8 | 15 |
| Cutlers | 14 | 13 | 12 | 2 | 12 | 19 | 3 | 17 | 15 | 14 | 18 |
| Filemakers | 37 | 36 | 28 | 0 | 33 | 22 | 10 | 39 | 21 | 20 | 20 |
| Gold beaters | 17 | 15 | 60 | 24 | 21 | 50 | 17 | 47 | 112 | 48 | 320 |
| Goldsmiths | 51 | 53 | 39 | 20 | not given | | | 46 | 36 | 36 | 37 |
| Locksmiths | 35 | 43 | 55 | 41 | not given | | | 76 | 122 | 79 | 117 |
| Metal beaters | not given | 10 | not given | | 17 | 38 | 40 | 32 | 112 | 21 | 118 |

| | | | | | | | | | | | |
|---|---|---|---|---|---|---|---|---|---|---|---|
| Nailsmiths | 26 | 26 | 40 | 11 | 27 | 40 | 6 | 32 | 26 | 23 | 7 |
| Needle makers | 15 | not given | | | 16 | 11 | 2 | 11 | 2 | 9 | 5 |
| Panmakers | 2 | 1 | 0 | 1 | 0 | 0 | 0 | 0 | 0 | 0 | 0 |
| Stickpin makers | 55 | 40 | 19 | 7 | 30 | 14 | 2 | 18 | 8 | 9 | 2 |
| Tin molders | 30 | 28 | 11 | 2 | 23 | 11 | 5 | 21 | 2 | 20 | 17 |
| Tinsmiths | 58 | 60 | 176 | 77 | 62 | 119 | 46 | 112 | 144 | 118 | 215 |
| Toolsmiths | 6 | 7 | 4 | 2 | 5 | 4 | 5 | 9 | 5 | 7 | 6 |
| Wire drawers | 64 | 79 | 11 | 2 | 33 | 12 | 5 | 42 | 44 | 20 | 33 |
| SUBTOTAL | 834 | 778 | 793 | 266 | 640 | 556 | 211 | 859 | 922 | 685 | 1,271 |
| Toymakers | not given | 70 | not given | | | | | 183 | 168 | 188 | 278 |
| Turners | 135 | 136 | 103 | 35 | 140 | 152 | 66 | 168 | 180 | 187 | 327 |
| TOTAL | 969 | 984 | 896 | 301 | 780 | 708 | 277 | 1,210 | 1,270 | 1,060 | 1,876 |

SOURCES: Adapted from Schröder, *Entwicklung*, 232a–b. Based upon StadtAN, HR 12773 and 12780. The number of locksmiths in 1844 corrected from HR 12774.

NOTE: M– Masters; J – Journeymen; A – Apprentices. The number of wire drawers is inaccurate, because all surveys did not include all branches of the trade.

finally, can be put in category 1, as crafts without competition from big business because of the difficulties in adopting machinery. A rise in demand and competition nevertheless forced fundamental changes. Three further trades will be detailed in a later section (the iron molders, blacksmiths, and locksmiths) because of their close association with the machine industry. Let us begin with brass molding.

### THE BRASS MOLDERS

Until the 1850s the brass molders *(Rotgießer* or *Rotschmiede)* were numerically the largest metal trade in the city, in part because the guild incorporated a number of related crafts: the brass turners *(Rotschmiedsdrechsler),* the scalemakers *(Waagmacher),* and the two branches of the molders proper *(Rotgießer* and *Rotschmiedsformer).*[16] By the late nineteenth century these distinctions appear to have died out, as the term "brass and bell molders" *(Rot- und Glockengießer)* became dominant. Except for the brass turners, who smoothed and polished the molders' product with water-powered lathes in mills owned by the city, the basic technology of brass molding was uniform. Molten metal was poured into molds, which were made of clay or sand inside wooden caskets. Great skill was required both to make the mold correctly and to pour the metal so that it did not contain bubbles or cavities. Through this process a great variety of objects were made in the early 1800s: rings, faucets, weights, harnesses, household objects, and parts for trades that were forbidden by law to do their own casting.[17]

Of the decline in this trade there can be little doubt. Confirming the data in Table 1.1 are innumerable complaints from the masters. In connection with the 1837 and 1845 revisions of guild statutes by the government, the guild superiors *(Vorgeher)* of the brass molders requested restrictions on the acceptance of new apprentices that were both anachronistic and illegal.[18] This, as well as the 1845 request that journeymen be exempted from mandatory wandering "because they would carry their knowledge *[Wissenschaft]* out of the country, and would thereby take work away from the trade and the country *[der Stand und Land],*" demonstrated how little the mentality of the masters had changed since the eighteenth century. Complaining that "the times have not become better, but rather much worse," they listed two causes for their decline: the pressing of metal on a modified lathe *(das Metalldrücken)* and iron molding, which was now used for the "larger and heavier jobs."[19] In 1846, however, they admitted that a lack of innovation and a reluctance to learn new techniques were also causes—an admission confirmed by one of Nuremberg's delegates to the 1851 London Exhibition, who accused the masters of being too slow in switching from clay to sand molding.[20]

Although technological change and the rise of iron as the dominant industrial metal certainly had much to do with the decline of the brass molders, lack of initiative also contributed. The quasi-guild system, by denying masters the right to use techniques or make products of other trades, restricted innovation and put a premium on jealous backbiting within and between crafts. It became increasingly ineffective as the various levels of government became economically more liberal, or at least more indifferent to the fate of the guilds. In 1844 the city council denied the request of the journeymen brass molders (supported by their masters) that the employment of journeymen from other trades or unskilled laborers be prohibited. Apparently a few masters, out of "egoism," were trying new methods of enriching themselves at the expense of others; capitalist behavior was penetrating the artisanate.[21]

For the losers in the struggle with other masters, trades, and industries, the result was impoverishment and an ever greater dependence on the merchants and putters-out who largely controlled the sale of brass objects. In July 1843 the guild superiors requested the withdrawal of the licenses of thirteen masters or masters' widows on the grounds that they had been inactive for years. Among the license holders singled out were a tobacco factory worker, an errand runner, a church servant, a police constable, and an alms collector, all rather lowly occupations for a master. The last four had all worked occasionally for putters-out or for other masters, as had one widow who described herself as a *"Heimarbeiter"* (domestic worker) for two brass-molding masters.[22] An 1858 complaint regarding exploitation of apprentices showed that another master had to send out his apprentice as a day laborer in a brewery because business was so bad.[23] Many masters tried to manage without any employees at all or by exploiting one or more apprentices and often had a standard of living worse than journeymen.

The journeymen brass molders themselves were not particularly well paid. But an 1851 survey reveals that their average annual income of 312 marks was better than that of the dying crafts like the nailsmiths (267 M) and bellmakers (178 M).[24] In contrast to these crafts the decline of the brass molders was not absolute. New industries arose, such as the manufacture of fire-fighting equipment, which provided new sources of employment, and indeed there was an increase in the number of journeymen between 1865 and 1873 (see Table 1.1). But the craft's numerical dominance of the Nuremberg metal trades was forever lost.

THE TOY INDUSTRY AND THE SHEET-METAL TRADES

In contrast to this picture of decline, the manufacture of toys and house-hold objects from sheet metal rose from insignificance to central importance in the city in the course of the nineteenth century. Nuremberg historically had been a major toy producer, but primarily in wood. By the middle of the century, however, it became increasingly difficult to compete with the domestic producers of the mountainous regions of Thuringia and elsewhere, who had a plentiful supply of cheap wood. But new ways of working sheet metal, such as pressing on a modified lathe and stamping, combined with the rise of a mass market for cheap toys, provided a ready replacement for the declining wood toy market, and the merchant-controlled export system already at hand enabled Nuremberg to become paramount rapidly. Tops, trumpets, and rattles were the most frequently produced articles, but from the 1860s on they were joined by more complicated mechanical and optical toys, whose production had earlier been inhibited by the guild-enforced division of labor between trades.[25] The industry became quite large and diverse, employing workers in numerous shops ranging from small-scale domestic industry up to large factories. Large numbers of unskilled women also came to be employed because of the lightness of the work and the potential for simplification and mass production. They were mostly involved in soldering, stamping, painting, and packaging.

A number of traditional trades benefited from the development of the metal toy industry, but by far the largest was that of the tinsmiths (*Flaschner*). The word, which is used only in Franconia and Swabia and is identical in meaning to the more common terms *Klempner* and *Spengler*, would today be translated as "plumber." But the laying of pipes was an activity that came to the fore only with the advent of modern sanitation systems, and even today Nuremberg Flaschner carry out an older form of construction-related work: the laying of sheet-metal roofs and gutters. This latter work was also important in the nineteenth century, but of far greater importance was the toy industry. According to the guild superiors of the tinsmiths, in 1852 all but ten of the sixty-four masters in their trade were dependent on the production of metal toys.[26]

In addition to the tinsmiths, a number of other skilled crafts also benefited from the expansion of the industry. Toymaking, a free trade unfettered by most of the restrictions on the guilded trades, grew rapidly despite the fact that it had traditionally been limited to wood. That growth, accompanied by the 1847 and 1851 complaints of the tinsmiths that the toymakers were not purchasing their sheet-metal parts from them as required by custom,[27] provides evidence that the toymakers were diversifying. They formed one source for a new class of capitalists that arose after the breakdown of the quasi-guild system, a class that came from diverse origins and employed a collection of skilled and unskilled workers. Among these new capitalists were also fine mechanics, turners, metal pressers (Metalldrücker), and braziers (Gürtler), but these trades were much less prominent among toy-industry capitalists than the tinsmiths and toymakers, and the merchant putters-out who had long been in control of the export trade.

Of the crafts just mentioned, three require special explanation. The fine mechanics (Mechaniker) built complicated mechanisms and machines, and they became important not only in the toy industry but also in the electrical engineering industry that appeared in Nuremberg in the 1870s. They were never incorporated into a guild but had the reputation of being one of the most respectable crafts because of the complex nature of their work. The braziers (a seemingly arbitrary translation, but Gürtler had nothing to do with the making of Gürtel [belts]) were a small dying trade who had the right to work brass wire and brass plate. They made costume jewelry, household objects, and trinkets, but a few later became involved in the toy industry.[28] The metal pressers were incorporated with the turners (Drechsler), because they used a lathe modified to hollow out and shape sheet metal, a technique invented in Paris in the 1810s. This innovation probably reached Nuremberg by the 1820s, and by 1844 the tinsmiths were complaining of the loss of work to the metal pressers / turners who used the tinsmiths' primary tools (shears, hammer, anvil, and soldering iron) as well as the Druckbank to turn out sheet-metal objects. The turners naturally protested that they also had a right to use these tools, and the eventual decision of the city council was that all these techniques, including metal pressing, would be shared by the tinsmiths, turners, braziers, and coppersmiths.[29] Unaware of this decision, Karl Rosenhaupt asserted in 1907 that barriers between trades obstructed the use of metal pressing in toy production until the 1860s.[30] No evidence has been found to verify this claim, but it is certainly possible that traditionalism and inertia among master artisans slowed innovation.

GOLD AND METAL LEAF PRODUCTION

Another Nuremberg industry that flourished in the nineteenth century— or at least until the 1880s—was the making of extremely thin sheets of gold and pseudo-gold (a brass alloy) for gilding. The city's gold beaters (Goldschläger or Feingoldschläger), were a craft with a long and proud history. First recorded in Nuremberg in 1373, they became the most important producers of gold leaf in Germany, a position they held until the twentieth century. The essential technology of gold beating also changed little in all that time. After having been rolled with a machine into thin sheets, the gold was cut into small squares, put between sheets of parchment, and a pack of hundreds of sheets was then beaten with a twenty-pound hammer, a task requiring considerable strength and great skill to do properly. By this means the gold was greatly thinned and enlarged. The leaves of gold were then cut into four pieces, the pieces put between the leaves of a "form," which was made out of a cow's intestine, and the whole process repeated up to three more times. The final product, which was about 0.0001 mm thick, was put between the leaves of small paper books and sold.[31]

Around 1700 artisans in Lechhausen, a suburb of Augsburg, discovered how to produce leaves of a brasslike alloy that appeared much like gold. The work process was essentially identical, although slightly less complicated because no metal can be beaten as thin as gold can. This cheap substitute was viewed as a real threat by the Nuremberg gold beaters, and they succeeded in persuading the council to ban its production in the territory of the imperial city. They had no control over Fürth, however, only six miles to the northwest but inside the territory of the Margrave of Ansbach. The first Nuremberger established himself there as a metal beater *(Metallschläger)* in 1705 and from that time on Fürth became the center of the craft. In 1774–1775 the city council licensed the first metal beater in Nuremberg (despite the inevitable protests), but the city was never able to overcome the lead of Fürth. Although both trades grew considerably in the nineteenth century, the metal beaters remained the poor cousins of the elder trade.[32]

In both cases the growth of production in the nineteenth century was not primarily due to mechanization. Repeated attempts were made to mechanize the beating process, but to no avail. It took too much dexterity and judgment to beat the leaves to the desired thinness. Some preparatory jobs were eventually done with power machinery, for example, the rolling, but the real innovations were all organizational. Until about 1840 the journeymen gold beaters had a set schedule in which they did the heavier jobs of preparation and beating for two days, and on the third day rested by doing only the lighter jobs. Sometime before 1843 master Conrad Pauli started employing young women for the tasks of cutting the leaves and laying them in books when they were finished. Through this division of labor, labor costs were lowered and the journeymen could concentrate on the heavier but better-paid jobs, though at a long-run cost to their health. Through piece rates the journeymen were spurred on to even greater productivity, and because the system was set up so that they, rather than the master, paid the women out of their earnings, they were forced to spur on the women too. All indications are that the journeymen generally accepted this arrangement—Pauli claimed that they refused to join the complaint launched by the other masters against him.[33] The journeymen gold beaters were among the best-paid skilled workers in Nuremberg, a kind of aristocracy of labor aloof from the other workers until the 1890s. They fought repeatedly to retain the piece-rate system after a shift in taste away from heavy gilding and ornamentation brought the decline of the industry after the 1880s. The metal beaters acted similarly, and female labor was introduced in that craft at about the same time (1840). But they were not as well paid or as aloof from other workers as were the gold beaters, because the preliminary stages of production were more easily mechanized and the beating process itself required less skill.[34]

In a word, it was capitalism and not industrialization that transformed the beaters. As the old guild controls slowly disintegrated, a number of masters began to break with custom and compete with each other with all available means. Those masters who were unable (for lack of capital) or unwilling to imitate them were reduced to impoverished small masters, dependent on the putters-out, while the large masters rose to positions of considerable wealth. In November 1843 Pauli already had twenty women in his shop,[35] and in later decades even larger firms would appear. The destruction of traditional bonds also ruptured the links between masters and journeymen. The latter began to see themselves as permanent employees rather than as future masters, and later they even saw themselves as members of the working class. But this is a story for a later chapter. Let us turn now from the transformation of the traditional metal trades to the second major sector of employment for metalworking artisans in Nuremberg: the machine industry.

## The Rise of the Machine Industry in Nuremberg

Although some of the light metal trades were transformed by capitalism and capital accumulation into industries with large factories, others, as we have seen, were little changed in external form from traditional artisanal production. Shops were small and steam power was rare. The machine industry, in contrast, conforms more to the usual image of industrialization: long, low, and dirty factory buildings, with black smoke pouring from the steam-engine house that powered dozens or hundreds of machines through a complicated pulley-and-drive system. The building of machines did not start on such a scale, however, and even in the late nineteenth century artisanal methods of work based upon a high degree of skill survived in the largest enterprises, and skilled workers retained something of their journeymen origins. The building of machines was a complex business, and it was only in the twentieth century that rationalization and mass production became the norm in Germany.

In their beginnings the first Nuremberg machine factories remained strongly tied to artisanal work methods. Johann Wilhelm Spaeth (1786–1854), an apprenticed miller, founded a small shop in 1825, after having acquired considerable experience building and repairing mills and textile-factory machines in the Nuremberg region. In 1831–1835 he built a factory on the Dutzendteich, a lake a few miles outside the city, in order to take advantage of water power. But he did not get a factory license for machine construction until 1842. Such a license allowed him to ignore the boundaries between trades and to use any machine tools and techniques he deemed necessary to build machines. Until that time he worked cooperatively with independent masters, who were on contract to him, although they may have worked entirely within the factory. His production program was in no way systematic. He built mills, steam engines, factory equipment, and machines for the Main-Danube Canal. He also assembled the English locomotive for the first German railroad from Nuremberg to Fürth in 1835.[36]

The second machine-building firm in Nuremberg, which was founded in 1837–1838 by the merchant Johann Friedrich Klett (1778–1847), had similar origins. After a unprofitable venture in the textile industry, Klett started a shop in cooperation with artisan masters to do repair work for the railway. Soon thereafter he began planning a major factory, and after having succeeded in hiring three British technicians, he acquired a license. In February 1842 he opened the new factory in Wöhrd, a suburb just outside the eastern wall. His production program was diverse, and his workshop organization was essentially "planless" for the first few years. The machines were not grouped into rooms in any particular way that would predetermine the flow of work. Gradually the factory was reorganized into the "workshop system," something already adopted by Spaeth: machines were grouped by type, with all the lathes in one shop, the planers in another, and so on.[37] Although this system organized the work flow into a clearer succession of steps, it was far from being a unidirectional and rationalized organization of work. Such a rationalized system was impossible given, first, an ever-changing production program based upon custom ordering rather than mass production, and second, the primitive measuring instruments that made the production of identical parts for complicated machines difficult before the late nineteenth century. Machine parts were made according to the eye of the highly skilled metalworking artisan and specially fitted together for each machine.[38]

These conditions were altogether typical of the German machine industry and at least partially explain the skill and central importance of the skilled metalworkers within it. But it is fascinating that the Klett plant, under the guidance of Klett's son-in-law, Theodor Cramer-Klett (1817–1884), pioneered what was already called in 1857 by the *Augsburger Allgemeine Zeitung* "detailed mass production *(detaillirten Massenproduktion)."*[39] In 1850 Cramer-Klett took over railcar production from the short-lived Royal Railcar Shops in Nuremberg (1844–1849) and in the course of the next two decades built a giant firm. Figure 1.1 shows the fluctuation in the factory's employment levels from 1842 to 1910. From a modest firm of the size of Spaeth (which had about one hundred workers in 1850), Klett rapidly expanded into one of the largest firms in Germany. At its peak in 1872–1873 the Nuremberg factory was producing about thirteen railcars a day.[40] But with the coming of the Great Depression of 1873–1896, which brought to a sudden halt railroad construction in Central Europe, the firm found itself with massive excess capacity and was plunged into a severe crisis. In the wake of this crisis Klett (which became part of the Maschinenfabrik Augsburg-Nürnberg, or M.A.N., in 1898) shifted to a more diverse production program typical of the industry.

Unfortunately very little is known about this early example of mass production or its effects on the workers engaged in it because of the destruction of much of the firm's archive in World War II. It is clear, however, that the standardization of railcar types allowed the development of specialized machine tools and further refinements in the division of labor, which in turn allowed the employment of large numbers of unskilled and semiskilled workers. Because the cars were largely made of wood, huge shops for drying, boring, planing, and sawing wood were created, and many of the unskilled were employed there.[41] Woodworking tolerances were also not as demanding as in metalworking, which required more skilled labor. Some kind of assembly line must have been created, but certainly nothing as sophisticated as a moving conveyor was used. Cars were probably pushed or pulled between work stations.

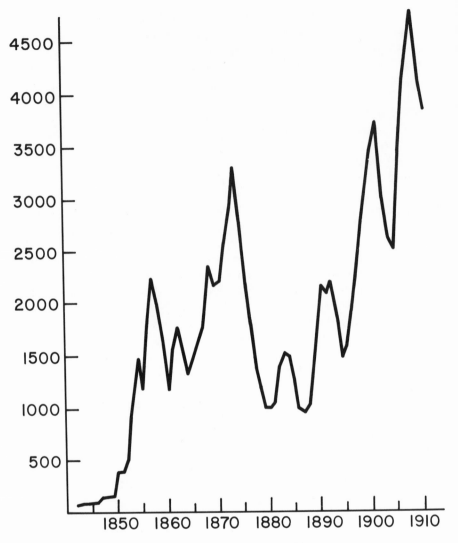

FIGURE 1.1. Employees of Klett/M.A.N.-Nuremberg, 1842–1910

Source: Eibert, *Maschinenbauer*, 331–332. For 1867–1910, these figures are for the fiscal year ending in that year, e.g., 1867 is the fiscal year 1866–67. Employees of Klett/M.A.N. in other locations are not included.

In its employment of large numbers of unskilled workers directly in the production process, Klett was quite unusual. As David Montgomery has said: "Production in the nineteenth century is carried on by skilled workers, and unskilled workers pick things up and bring them to the skilled and carry them away again."[42] Such a characterization applies better to the machine industry than to virtually any other. The unskilled were generally called "day laborers" *(Tagelöhner)* and were hired on a daily basis to do the work of lifting, carrying, and cleaning. In social status and pay they were far below the skilled: they were typically paid only about one-third to two-thirds of the wage of a journeyman, although the gap tended to close later in the century. For example, at Klett in the 1840s day laborers received 36 kr. (about one mark) a day versus skilled earnings of 42 kr. to 1 fl. 36 kr. (about 1.25 to 2.80 M) a day.[43] Day laborers were a kind of underclass with impoverished, often rural backgrounds and virtually no expectation of advancement. Job security was low, turnover was high (190 percent per year at Klett in the late nineteenth century),[44] and they often moved from one type of work to another. This instability of occupation and lack of skill caused the apprenticed workers, who developed a strong sense of self-worth and self-identity from their craft, to treat the unskilled with some distance or occasionally even disdain.[45]

Between the two main groups of workers were the semiskilled, who often came from the ranks of declining trades, like tailors, shoemakers, and others. They were trained to operate only one type of machine and were employed as specialized machinists on drills, planers, and milling machines.[46] Cramer-Klett also employed a number in railcar production, but our knowledge is again quite limited. In 1860 sawyers and wood planers earned just under 1 fl. per day (1.75 M), while skilled metal turners *(Dreher)* were making around 1 fl. 25 kr. (2.5 M).[47] Their relations with the skilled were probably friendlier; a common background in artisanry would have helped. But because the semiskilled were such a heterogeneous group they possessed little solidarity or common identity, and as Wolfgang Renzsch has noted, their reactions to their new work environment would have varied greatly depending on their attachment to their old trades and traditions. Many undoubtedly found their jobs an improvement over the poverty and insecurity of their old trades.[48]

The same could be said for many of the skilled workers. There is little evidence that snobbery among artisans toward factory work, which had been prevalent in the eighteenth century, was still important in the mid-nineteenth century.[49] Wages were higher in Nuremberg factories after 1845 because of the need to attract skilled labor, and in the machine

25

industry the gap opened even sooner and became very large. In 1851 the average yearly income of a journeyman in fourteen metal trades was 298 M, while the average income in machine building was 491 M.[50] This differential allowed industrialists to draw almost their entire skilled labor force from artisanry. Very few skilled workers apprenticed in factories. Even in 1905 only 18 percent of Nuremberg M.A.N. (Klett) workers had taken their apprenticeship in a factory, despite the opening of an apprentice training school inside the works fifteen years before.[51] Thus machine-industry craftsmen had almost all shared the important formative experiences of apprenticeship and employment under small masters. The only exception was iron molding, a craft without an artisanal past, at least in Nuremberg.[52]

With their superior skills journeymen also brought into the early machine factories a greater adaptation to work discipline than their unskilled counterparts. Yet it cannot be said that the acceptance of greater punctuality and less absenteeism, relaxation, and drinking on the job was easy. The 1844 shop rules at Klett threatened to lock out anyone more than ten minutes late in the morning and stipulated fines or firing for those caught talking, drinking, or idling. The workweek was sixty-six hours, a few hours more than what the average artisan worked. Even if these rules were not strictly enforced, they represented a significant problem to many artisans who were accustomed to less restrictive working conditions. Along with the impersonal atmosphere of the larger enterprises and their typically smaller variety of tasks, this adaptation problem made skilled work in the machine industry qualitatively different from working in a small and informal artisan shop.[53] As artisanry gradually accommodated itself to increased competition and as relations between masters and journeymen deteriorated, this became less and less the case. But even late in the century the jump from the artisanal to the industrial work environment was not trivial.

These common experiences did not weld together journeymen employed in the industry, however. Craft consciousness was the natural outgrowth of pride in particular skills, strong and centuries-old artisanal traditions, and the socialization processes of apprenticeship and wandering in each craft. Compounding the division between trades were the workshop system, which inhibited contact between different trades, and the organization of work, which in some areas was carried out by individuals rather than by cooperative groups.[54] Overlaying all of this was the heterogeneity of the work force. At Klett the work force was especially large and diverse, and the patriarchal relationship established between Cramer-Klett and his workers as a result of social welfare measures (see Chapter 3) added yet another obstacle to solidarity and protest. The rise of class consciousness in the machine industry was a slow process, but nowhere as slow as at Klett. Only at the beginning of the twentieth century was even a large minority there organized into unions.

To better understand the divisions between trades, the nature of the work process, and the impact of the machine industry on metalworking artisans, it is useful to examine a few important crafts individually. Within the workshop system of machine construction (including those sectors of Klett not concerned with railcar or bridge building) work was divided into three main areas. The basic parts for the machine were either cast in pig iron in the foundry by the iron molders or forged in wrought iron in the smithy by the blacksmiths. From there the parts went to the mechanical workshops for reworking: holes were drilled, faces were planed, the shape was refined on a lathe. Finally the various parts were delivered to the assembly room for fitting into a finished machine. This could be a complex process in itself because, as mentioned previously, interchangeable parts were very difficult to make because of the fine tolerances demanded and the lack of suitable measuring instruments before the late nineteenth century. Perhaps nowhere outside of iron molding was as much skill necessary as in assembly; each machine was essentially specially fitted together.[55]

THE IRON MOLDERS

If there was an aristocracy of labor in the machine industry, the iron molders *(Former* or *Eisengießer)*, and the pattern makers *(Modellschreiner)* who helped them, were probably the artistocrats. The pattern makers built wooden models of the parts or objects to be cast in iron, a task requiring a wide knowledge of woodworking techniques and a thorough understanding of blueprints and the technology of metalworking.[56] The models they built were sent to the iron molders, who imprinted the shape of the model into the sand or clay mold used for the casting—a complex task, because the preparation and "ramming" of the sand with "iron-shod poles"[57] required skill, intuition, and a knowledge of the properties of different kinds of sand. Improperly made sand could easily ruin a casting, because a certain consistency was needed to give the casting a smooth appearance while at the same time allowing gases from the molten iron to escape. The iron was then poured into the mold, a task which could not be done too quickly or too slowly, because the metal might contain bubbles or might become too viscous before the pouring

27

was finished. Once the iron was cooled the casket was opened and the piece was knocked out of the mold (which could be used only once). It was then cleaned and its roughness and protuberances were removed by the casting cleaners *(Gußputzer)*, who were unskilled.[58]

The work process was carried on cooperatively by groups of iron molders, helped by unskilled laborers to do some of the fetching and carrying. Although the distinction between molders (Former) and founders (Eisengießer), that is, between those who made the molds and those who poured the metal, was occasionally made, this division of labor never became permanent and the term Former was paramount. Apparently both kinds of work were done by the same people. In the larger foundries, however, there often appeared a less skilled group of coremakers *(Kernmacher)*, sometimes recruited from the unskilled workers. They specialized in the making of hard-baked sand cores used to form cavities inside the castings, an activity that had formerly been carried out by the iron molders.[59]

Mechanizing these jobs proved to be almost as difficult as in gold beating; only in the late 1880s and 1890s did the molding machine arrive in Germany, and its application was very limited because of its inherent imperfections and its suitability only for mass-produced objects. The craft of iron molding thus remained almost completely unmechanized labor throughout the period we are examining here. But it was also dirty, dangerous, and heavy work. Smoke and dust filled the large, drafty, and poorly heated foundries, and despite the help of day laborers, a great deal of physical work was necessary in making molds and pouring iron. Respiratory diseases and other health problems were common.[60]

Because the iron molders had no guild tradition in Nuremberg and no trade union organization before 1886, the information available on their early history is extremely meager. The foundries of both Spaeth and Klett were opened in early 1842, and this can be considered the beginning of the trade in the city. Where they found their journeymen and masters is unknown; presumably they advertised in other parts of Germany. Klett even found it necessary to hire Wharton Rye, an Englishman from Manchester, away from his employer in Zurich to become master of the foundry.[61] The rapid growth of the industry spurred the rapid growth of iron molding. The total number of foundry workers (including helpers) listed by the Bavarian Royal Statististical Bureau in 1861 was 237 at three foundries. Spaeth would not have been included in this total, because it was then outside the city limits. A further 65 foundry workers in two plants are mentioned under the total for Middle Franconia—Spaeth along with Engelhardt in Fürth are undoubtedly the two firms.[62]

As in many skilled crafts, the journeymen iron molders often wandered long distances. The molder Peter Kalsing, arrested in 1852 for revolutionary activities, came from Spabrücken near Koblenz, but in the previous five years had worked in Nuremberg, Mecklenburg, Vienna, southern Austria, Venice and northern Italy, Munich, and then again in Nuremberg.[63] An informal network of journeymen's organizations like those in the guilded trades (see Chapter 2) may have existed to help those wanderers. In his travels in 1866 the locksmith and future leader of the Nuremberg Social Democrats, Karl Grillenberger, met an iron molder who collected travel money from the molders in factories they passed.[64] There is no evidence of organizational ties in Nuremberg before 1886, however. The only glimmer of the social life that may have existed appears in the records on Blue Monday drinking (also treated in Chapter 2). Apparently the iron molders at Klett held a ball in a Wöhrd pub in November 1858.[65]

The lateness of unionization in this craft was in all probability the result of the molders' privileged position, good pay, and isolation from other workers. At work they were physically separated from other workers in the foundry, and they thus encountered only their unapprenticed helpers, who did not possess their bargaining power or pride of craft. Wage lists from Klett in the mid-1840s show that the molders were better paid than any other workers except for foremen and the occasional metal turner. Most made about 1 fl. 30 kr. (2.5 M) a day.[66] Wages were about the same at Spaeth in the mid-1860s (the cost of living was little more than that of twenty years before), but the pay records show great variations in income because of piece-rate rather than day-wage payment. Some employees of the foundry (probably the unskilled) were making about one fl. a day, but a few were making almost twice that much.[67] The wages of a highly skilled and productive iron molder were very good by working-class standards, and the difference in incomes undoubtedly reinforced the hierarchy of skill in the foundry. The iron molders were workers, nevertheless, and their standard of living was poor in comparison to the middle and upper classes. When they finally did join the labor movement and accept an identity as workers they became one of the bulwarks of unionism in the metal trades.

THE BLACKSMITHS

In contrast to the molders, the blacksmiths *(Schmiede, Hufschmiede)* had a strong foothold in both artisanry and industry. As artisans they carried out the traditional activities of blacksmiths: horseshoeing and ironwork related to harnesses and wagons. Because the nature of this work changed little before the decline brought on by the automobile, blacksmithing also remained one of the most stubbornly traditional trades. In spite of strikes in 1872 and the late 1890s, at the turn of the century many journeymen were still working fourteen hours a day, and living and eating with their masters—essentially the same conditions that had been laid down in the guild's journeymen's ordinance of February 1853.[68] A factor that likely contributed to this backwardness was the continuing influx from rural areas, where blacksmiths were numerous. These raw recruits seem to have had very little solidarity with their fellows and proved very difficult to organize.

This traditionalism carried over into the factories. Blacksmiths were latecomers to the union movement and displayed a "caste spirit" *(Kastengeist)* often bemoaned by unionists. This spirit was undoubtedly rooted in their experiences as artisans, but like the iron molders, physical isolation from other skilled workers in the smithy probably reinforced a feeling of separateness, as did the work process, which was cooperative, hierarchical, and highly skilled. Each piece of iron was pulled from the fire and held by the group leader, an older blacksmith who strictly controlled the working of the metal. The others had to quickly and deftly hammer it into the shape required—a process little changed from that of the artisan shop. Even the coming of the steam hammer did not fundamentally change things; it simply allowed the working of larger objects.[69] Related to the blacksmiths were the boilermakers *(Kesselschmiede)*, who worked and riveted the boilers for steam engines. They appear to have been apprenticed blacksmiths too, although not as well paid as those working in the smithy. At Klett in 1860 they made about 1 fl. a day versus 1 fl. 20 kr. for the blacksmiths (one-third more).[70]

THE LOCKSMITHS AND METAL TURNERS

Of all the trades in the machine industry, the locksmiths *(Schlosser)* were almost invariably the most numerous. The translation of the name itself presents problems because by the late nineteenth century locksmiths had very little to do with the making of locks. Despite the loss of this business to factory production, they thrived as artisans (see Table 1.1) because of the boom in construction that followed industrialization; in this area they were primarily involved in the installation of door handles, locks, stove pipes, and ornamental ironwork.[71] Locksmiths were prized in the machine industry because they were versatile. They could operate most machine tools, could usually use the blacksmith's forge, and could draft and read blueprints. Because of their industry role a better translation might be "machinist," especially for various hybrid words like *Maschinenschlosser* that were coined later. But the original name will be retained here because it reflects the importance of traditional trade names and trade boundaries in Germany. Unlike in Britain and North America, where new words like "engineer" and "machinist" were applied to machine-industry workers, the German equivalent *Maschinenbauer* was used less frequently.

The strong competition for journeymen from Klett in particular brought frequent complaints from the master locksmiths. In 1843 they were already complaining that they were locked in a "life and death struggle" with industry and that their helpers were hired away by astronomical wages—up to 18 fl. a week *(sic)*—at Klett.[72] In 1852 the masters complained that all journeymen "who are somewhat useful" were drawn to the factories by high pay and an "unrestricted life" free from a master's supervision.[73] And in 1861 the guild superiors unsuccessfully intervened with the city to prevent the moving of the journeymen locksmiths' hostel *(Herberge)* to a pub close to Wöhrd. They remarked sarcastically that "one might as well move it right into the Klett factory," since no master would be able to keep a helper anyway.[74]

As a result of their wide employment in the industry the locksmiths did not form a coherent group. They worked in all parts of the mechanical workshops, including assembly, and were paid a wide range of wages depending on training, skill, and experience: from less than one fl. to 1½ fl. per day at Klett in the mid-forties, and from one to 1⅓ fl. per day in 1860.[75] This work brought them into frequent contact with other workers, especially metal turners and semiskilled machinists, and locksmiths were prominent in the early labor movement. But because of the fragmented nature of locksmiths as a group, a strong organization was difficult to sustain.

Closely related to the locksmiths were the metal turners *(Dreher;* the translation is intended to distinguish them from the *Drechsler,* here translated simply as turners). This craft also demanded considerable skill, at least before the increasing automation of the lathe in the twentieth century. Only one year before the First World War metal turners at M.A.N. still had control over the cutting speed, choice of tool, and progress of the cutting.[76] Alf Lüdtke has outlined what a complex set of decisions this might involve:

> The preparation of the lathe was relatively time-consuming. In order to achieve the optimal speed during the turning process the gears had to be adjusted, i.e. calculated (using fractional arithmetic) and each time composed anew. Then the slug had to be centered; sometimes it became necessary to put it onto the lathe and trim some splinters by hand-filing. After having started the lathe, or more precisely after connecting it to the transmission-shaft of the workshop, the turner had to switch to a mostly passive watchfulness: simultaneously having an eye on the transmission belt and the clutch, the speed of the lathe and the part of the lathe which carried the cutting or turning tool. The turners had to employ and develop skills involving manual dexterity, knowledge of the good and bad points of worked metals, experience with the speeds and gears of the transmission belts and of "their," that is the factory's, lathe or even two or three lathes, which they had to operate. Sometimes they had to be able to read a blueprint and to translate its figures and symbols into the mechanics of the lathe.[77]

Given the skill necessary to make these decisions, it is surprising that the metal turners did not, at least in Nuremberg, possess a strong craft identity. In all likelihood this stems from heterogeneous craft origins, because there is no evidence of a strong connection between the Dreher and the Drechsler. Undoubtedly some did apprentice in that latter craft, especially under masters working metal, but others may have been locksmiths or even semiskilled machinists who, through experience, became experts at working the lathe. Given the dearth of evidence, one can only speculate. In any case the metal turners did not form independent organizations in Nuremberg; they were invariably found in the "locksmiths' and machinists'" (Schlosser und Maschinenbauer) unions.

Although Spaeth was the first and Klett was by far the largest, other machine-building firms sprang up in the forties and later. The third was founded in 1848–1849 by the Scot (and former technician at Klett) J. Edward Earnshaw, and many others soon followed. There were ten firms in 1861 inside the city limits alone,[78] with probably some 2,000 employees, of whom 1,500–1,600 worked at Klett. Late in the century two major new sectors were also added that further contributed to the growth of the industry: electrical engineering and bicycles. One firm, that of Sigmund Schuckert, rose from artisanal origins in the 1870s to prominence as one of the major electrotechnical firms in Germany, with 8,000 employees in 1900, including 4,000 to 5,000 in the city. Not long thereafter, in the 1890s, Nuremberg became one of the centers of the bicycle industry, with some 1,500 workers at the turn of the century.[79] These rapid developments fed a continuous expansion and revolutionization of the city's machine industry, which in turn contributed considerably to the growth of labor organization and working-class consciousness, to be discussed in Chapters 3–5.

## The Impact of Capitalism on the Artisanate

As this review of the major metalworking trades has suggested, the impact of capitalism on the artisanate was complex. Capitalism as such was not new; merchant putters-out had intruded into the export trades at least since the seventeenth century, and manufactories had appeared no later than the eighteenth. But the nineteenth century was qualitatively different. Capitalist industrialization not only created a virtually new industry—machine construction—to power its own growth; it also revolutionized artisanal production by wiping out obsolete trades, by introducing factories to others, and by accelerating the development of putting-out in still more. The growth of industry and the needs of capitalists also contributed to the dismantling of the quasi-guild system, the old legal system that had protected artisans from unfettered competition and that in Nuremberg had been unchanged in its essentials for centuries. Although this transformation of the legal relations of production did not cause an immediate and drastic change in the character of artisanal life, it was a powerful symbol of the slow but relentless transformation of the whole economy and society.

As a result of the slow breakdown and eventual abolition of the guilds and the rise of competition from factory and manufactory production, artisan masters were forced to make important changes in their behavior. Faced with increasing competition in both product and labor markets, masters were forced either to sell or service factory goods, or to increase the efficiency of their production through the use of new technology, cheaper labor, and more attention to organization. If they did not, they might be doomed to a marginal existence. Yet the rate and nature of this transformation varied greatly, depending on the importance of competition from industry and the nature of the market. The expansion of population and per capita income that accompanied industrialization sometimes benefited artisans more than competition hurt them—and the pull of this demand could prove to be as powerful a motivation for some masters to accept capitalist business methods as was the push from competition. The net result was often, as in the case of the gold beaters, a growing differentiation among masters. Some became much more prosperous; others experienced increasing poverty and dependency and sometimes drifted off to employment elsewhere.

The impact of these changes on the journeyman was often quite different, as we shall see in the next chapter. Industry opened up new avenues of employment for many metalworking journeymen, and the level of skill required was often little lower, and occasionally even higher, than that in artisanry. Although in industry they had to give up virtually any hope of becoming independent masters and had to submit to a more rigorous work discipline, the artisanal sector was no longer fundamentally different. The crisis and transformation of artisanry also decreased the chances of achieving independence and also imposed a greater work discipline on journeymen, while at the same time undermining the social institutions of artisanal life (guilds and journeymen's associations) and the patriarchal relations between masters and those below them. Master-journeyman relations slowly became capitalist-worker relations, and journeymen began to see themselves as workers, albeit skilled workers with strong trade identities. To examine these processes and the origins of politicization and class consciousness is the purpose of the next chapter.

# 2

## THE TRANSFORMATION
## OF THE JOURNEYMAN'S WORLD

Between 1835 and 1868 the old artisanal order in Nuremberg entered its
terminal phase. Capitalism and industrialization, in conjunction with
rapid population growth and political repression, had powerful solvent
effects on the quasi-guild system, on the bonds between masters and
journeymen, and on the organizations and traditions of the journeymen
themselves. The net result was an increasing alienation and politicization
of both masters and journeymen, as well as a growing consciousness of
the conflicting interests which divided the two groups.

These complex processes may be examined through the discussion of
four topics: the difficulty in becoming a master and the resulting impact
on master-journeyman relations; the repression and dissolution of the
journeymen's associations; the repression and transformation of so-called
Blue Monday drinking; and the growth of politicization and class consciousness. These four aspects illustrate important features of the gradual
transition of journeymen in the Nuremberg metal trades from artisans to
workers: the increasing probability of lifelong journeyman status and the
resultant effects of this, the transformation of parts of the subculture of

journeymen into skilled-worker culture, the acceptance of a new work discipline in artisanry like that in industry, and the appearance of the first tentative signs of political radicalization. Together these processes effected a transformation of the journeyman's world.

### "Overfilling" and the Growing Gap between Masters and Men

In the first chapter I noted some of the divisive effects of the intrusion of capitalism into artisanal production. Good journeymen were lured away to better jobs in the machine industry, some masters adopted capitalist methods such as piece-rate payment or the employment of women to increase production or stave off decline, and others became dependent on putters-out and were forced to exploit their journeymen and apprentices in order to eke out a living. Although the effects of capitalism and industrialization were not one-sided, in general these forces gradually tended to divide artisans into employees and employers.

Before the 1850s, however, the impact of capitalism was weak, and the alienation between masters and men apparent prior to that time must be attributed largely to other factors. The most important of these was the increasing difficulty in ascending to mastership because of population growth, economic stagnation, and restrictive laws. The continuous expansion of the population, a process that began in Germany around 1740,[1] gradually overloaded the guild system's ability to absorb new masters and thereby lengthened the already considerable time a journeyman had to wait before he was accepted as a full member of a guild. By the 1830s and 1840s this situation had become a crisis. Even in Nuremberg, with its modest economic growth during the forties, complaints of the "overfilling" (*Überfüllung*) of the trades with too many journeymen were rife. Economic expansion could not keep pace with in-migration from the small towns and villages of northern Bavaria, and the general subsistence crisis of the mid-forties could not be fended off. More rapid industrialization in the 1850s may have eased the demand for master's licenses, but it did not eliminate it. The repressive political climate, which was worsened by the aftermath of the revolutions of 1830 and 1848, further exacerbated this problem by giving the upper hand to those who wanted to restrict the granting of master's licenses and marriage and residence permits. In Bavaria the reactionary 1834 and 1853 revisions to the 1825 crafts law imposed very narrow limits on the ability of the Nuremberg city council to create new masters.

This blockage of vertical mobility undermined two important supports of the old artisanal system: the self-identity of journeymen as future masters, and the patriarchal authority of masters over their men. As the chances of achieving independence decreased, journeymen naturally chafed at their quasi-adolescent status, which heretofore had been tolerated as temporary. The prohibition on marriage and living outside the master's house gradually fell apart, and conflicts with masters over discipline and authority increased hand-in-hand with the sense of a separate identity as workers. By the mid-nineteenth century master-journeymen relations were already considerably strained. It took only the acceleration of capitalist industrialization in the 1850–1873 period to produce a fundamental division.

To understand this problem of access to mastership more thoroughly, it is useful to survey the laws that governed these matters in early and mid-nineteenth century Bavaria. As briefly discussed in Chapter 1, in the quasi-guild system master artisans were organized into guilds with monopolistic rights over certain products, but without full self-governing power. Entry into the guilds was conditional upon the completion of a proper apprenticeship, a period of years as a journeyman, including a wandering period, and a successful master's examination. But there was no automatic passage to independent status with the completion of these requirements. The state had to grant an individual a license to pursue a particular trade, and the acquisition of this prized possession was further complicated by the simultaneous necessity of receiving, in most cases, the right to reside in a particular community and the right to marry. In some trades it was also necessary to purchase an expensive private license *(Realrecht)*, which was bought and sold on the open market, in order to practice one's craft.[2]

All of these matters were regulated by three laws passed in the fall of 1825. The crafts law pertained to the quasi-guild system and access to mastership. Its intent was liberal (particularly as interpreted in the implementation instruction of December 1825), that is, to loosen the bonds of the old guild restrictions as far as possible. The residence and *Heimat* ("hometown") laws of 1825 created the first unified legal system of residence for Bavaria east of the Rhine. (The Palatinate was excluded from all these laws because of its liberal legal framework inherited from French occupation.) Every individual had a Heimat, which he or she inherited from his or her parents (or mother, if illegitimate). In practice the Heimat usually corresponded to a person's birthplace. Outside of one's Heimat one could be expelled for being dependent on poor relief or for a brush with the law. Even for those living in their hometown, this right did not confer the right to marry and be accepted as a member of the community. This could only be accomplished through the granting of settlement *(Ansässigmachung)* by the town council. For those settling outside their hometown, the new residence superseded the old as Heimat.[3]

Because the intent of the 1825 laws was mildly liberal, the barriers to mastership were low and the acquisition of a license was not necessarily linked to settlement, although it was customary. That loophole and a number of others were soon closed, however, when the hostile reaction of small towns and artisan masters drove the government to tighten the laws considerably. Nuremberg masters joined the storm of protest in 1831 and 1834 with two petitions demanding restrictions on the number of apprentices and licenses because of the "overfilling" of their trades. They wanted property qualifications as well as evidence of technical competence as prerequisites for a master's license, an end to licenses without settlement in the same community, and a consideration of the impact of each new competitor on the living standard of artisans already established in the trade. Virtually all of their demands, except the last, were granted in the revised implementation instruction of 1834, and the last was eventually granted in 1853, although it had in many ways already been taken into consideration between 1834 and 1853. A new law on marriage and settlement in 1834 also made that process more difficult by raising the qualifications needed for a successful application; it thus enabled communities to exclude outsiders and anyone considered likely to become dependent upon poor relief. Local authorities even received an absolute veto over any application, and applicants had no chance of appeal to the state bureaucracy.[4]

The net result was that most journeymen had to go through the difficult, time-consuming, and expensive process of simultaneously applying for a license, settlement rights, and the right to marry, only to face probable rejection. Many suffered multiple rejections and never achieved mastership. Although reasons were not normally given, a lack of sufficient savings or other property, previous criminal convictions, or the reception of poor relief were often the cause of refusals. Even for those who were lucky enough to be accepted, the fees owing to the guild and the city could amount to many weeks' wages, and the conferred rights did not include political rights. A settled resident *(Insasse)* was not a citizen *(Bürger)* of either the community or the state. The right to vote was reserved for those with more money and status.[5]

Without adequate statistical sources it is difficult to evaluate the real dimensions of the problem of "overfilling."[6] It is not even clear whether the problem was significantly worse in the mid-nineteenth century than in the late eighteenth. In the eighteenth century there were already many complaints, many mechanisms for delaying the achievement of independence (such as a waiting period of some years after the master's examination), and many conflicts between journeymen and masters brought on by the economic crisis in artisanry.[7] In all probability there was a period of mild improvement early in the next century, especially after the liberalized laws of 1825. In Nuremberg the ratio of independent proprietors to employees in industry, artisanry, and trade rose slightly between 1823 and 1833 before falling relentlessly thereafter. After the early thirties the situation undoubtedly worsened as a result of overpopulation, slow economic growth, and the legal revisions of 1834. The total number of employers in Nuremberg was more or less stagnant between 1833 and 1861, a pattern confirmed for the metalworking trades by the data in Table 1.1. The number of masters in twenty-two metal trades appears to have stayed between 820 and 860 for a third of a century between 1831–1832 and 1865, if reasonable guesses are made to fill in the gaps in data. The number of journeymen does not seem to have risen much either, but many may have been absorbed temporarily or permanently by the machine industry or by other jobs, without necessarily giving up their desire to become independent artisans. Another indication of the generally poor situation in the city during the 1830s and 1840s is the high unemployment estimated by Rainer Gömmel for those years. The rural influx was too large for the economy to absorb, especially during the mid-forties, when crop failures produced extreme food-price inflation and a corresponding drop in demand for other products.[8]

There were alternatives to the usual path to mastership, of course, but they were limited. Short of emigration (15,332 artisans left Bavaria between 1853 and 1859),[9] a journeyman could, for example, try his hand in one of the free (unguilded) trades—but a license for a free trade was only easy to obtain if settlement rights were not requested. He could attempt to establish himself in one of the villages around Nuremberg—but the growth in the number of suburban masters brought protests from Nuremberg artisans, and there were two directives to restrict this growth from the Middle Franconian government in 1844 and 1850.[10] He could become a factory worker and eventually receive marriage and settlement rights without mastership—but the stability of employment and the savings needed to obtain settlement through factory labor were not easy to achieve. With the expanding opportunities available to metalworking journeymen in the machine industry, especially after 1850, this last route may have been easier for them to follow than for other artisans, but it only strengthened the separation between masters and men. Journeymen increasingly had more in common with other workers than they did with masters in their own trade.

Although the general effect of the blockage of vertical mobility was to create a large number of "eternal journeymen" who began to see themselves as workers, many undoubtedly clung to the traditional ideal of mastership as the natural culmination of their training and as a status-giving moral, patriarchal, and social institution. In July 1855 Tobias Weinberger, a journeyman locksmith from Nuremberg, sent a cringing letter to King Max II after six successive rejections of his application for a license. He had expected as a son of a Nuremberg locksmith master and "Bürger" to follow in his father's footsteps and enjoy in his "later years, as a useful citizen, the society of my fellow citizens." But now, in his forties, with a wife and four sons, he was too poor to support his family as a journeyman, and therefore he threw himself at the feet of His Majesty for mercy. With characteristic bureaucratic indifference the letter was filed away as a "formless, as well as illegal . . . presentation" without ever reaching the eyes of the King.[11]

Others may have resigned themselves to their fate more easily, but their status was not conducive to upholding the patriarchal authority of their masters. The appearance of married journeymen who, like Weinberger, probably received settlement rights under the provision for factory workers, was especially disruptive to the old order. They inevitably felt little inclined to live in the master's house or to tolerate his authoritarian behavior. When the master metal beaters applied in 1850 to be incorporated as a guilded trade, they drafted a set of regulations for journeymen that drew a vigorous protest from those they intended to regulate. The journeyman superior (*Altgeselle*) said to the police: "We journeymen metal beaters are in part fathers of families, and cannot be arbitrarily ordered around by the masters."[12] Even many unmarried metalworking journeymen would have agreed, because they often had families out of wedlock. As a result of the difficulties in obtaining licenses and settlement, the illegitimacy rate in Nuremberg from the 1830s to the 1860s hovered around 25 percent, and prosecutions for illegal cohabitation were common. Marriage and settlement applications by partners with one or more illegitimate children became so normal that they could no longer be rejected on those grounds alone. This collapse of traditional morality only reinforced the impact of married journeymen upon centuries-old artisanal institutions. Masters constantly complained of the difficulties in enforcing their house rules, or as in the case of the locksmiths, of the desire of their men for an "unrestricted life." The old rules forbidding marriage and living out seem to have faded away in the nineteenth century.[13]

It is apparent that the direct and indirect effects of the "overfilling" problem on master-journeymen relations were generally quite divisive. These effects, when combined with the capitalist penetration of artisanry, also exacerbated long-standing conflicts in other areas. The enforcement of work discipline and control over the labor market, that is, the rules governing hiring, firing, and quitting, were major sources of contention and will be discussed in the next two sections. One further possible effect should be noted, however. The direct conflict of interest between masters and men over the closing off or opening up of opportunities for mastership may have deepened the gulf between the two groups. Although little evidence of direct confrontation has come to light, the two groups were clearly saying quite different things during the Revolution of 1848–1849 and after. Journeymen consistently demanded automatic promotion at the age of thirty, or something similar, whereas masters, or at least the majority of them, constantly cried out for more restrictions to protect them from excessive competition.[14] This can only have underlined the growing differences inside the artisanate. The Revolution and its aftereffects will be more thoroughly discussed in the final section of this chapter.

The Dissolution of the Journeymen's Associations

A second major aspect of the transformation of the journeyman's world was the decline and eventual disappearance of the traditional expression of their subculture and self-identity: the journeymen's associations *(Gesellenvereine)*. The dissolution of these institutions represented in part a loss of traditions and customs, and even a loss of internal cohesion and solidarity among the journeymen of a particular trade. In that sense this development ran counter to the process of working-class formation reflected in the separation between masters and men. At the same time the decline of these bodies removed some of the barriers between the crafts, and thereby furthered the growth of commonality between metalworkers, skilled workers, and workers generally. This contradictory legacy was also complicated by those elements of the old traditions that did survive the process of repression and dissolution. Important features of the journeymen's associations and subculture reappeared in the early union movement of the 1870s and 1880s, and that movement bore within it the contradiction of its origins: the unionization of the various trades—particularly the metal trades—was both helped and hindered by the remnants of the exclusiveness and solidarity of the old associations.

Formed in the fourteenth century as the distinction between masters and journeymen began to crystallize, the journeymen's associations were created to defend the interests of their members within the guild structure as well as to provide a network of self-help groups for young artisans on the tramp. Until the mid-nineteenth century these bodies survived as informal institutions without statutes because they fulfilled such important functions as finding traveling and unemployed men jobs, providing travel money *(das Geschenk)* to those leaving town, giving sick money to those who became ill, and maintaining hostels as lodging places for wanderers and as meeting places for the members of the trade. Prior to 1805–1806 the associations were also linked together into loose networks or brotherhoods *(Brüderschaften)* organized along craft lines. (In function the French *compagnonnage* was quite similar, but it was peculiarly divided into three feuding cross-trade "rites"). These brotherhoods displayed considerable power, particularly in the eighteenth century, in strikes and struggles against both masters and local authorities, but they were dealt a fatal blow when the Napoleonic reorganization of Germany ended the fragmentation of police power and allowed the systematic repression of their activities. Only furtive contacts could be maintained among the associations after 1806, although they did survive locally because the useful social welfare functions they performed might otherwise have had to be paid for out of public funds.[15]

But even at the local level the power and independence of the associations were also curbed because of the various repressive measures taken by the state and municipal authorities. The first of these was the strengthening of the power of the masters, a continuation and extension of earlier cooperation between the state and artisan masters against rebellious journeymen. Masters were often given supervisory power over the meetings and affairs of the associations, as in the case of the Nuremberg brass molders, who not only watched over the quarterly meetings of their journeymen but even controlled the records and funds of the association. The journeymen locksmiths seem to have been under similar, though slightly more lax, controls, but in both cases these controls were dropped after the Revolution of 1848–1849, when the masters decided they were no longer worth the conflicts with their men.[16]

42

Another source of conflict and object of control was the process of matching unemployed journeymen with employers needing help *(das Zuschicken)*. This function was usually controlled by the journeymen because it was a natural extension of the association's role in supporting wanderers with travel money, lodging, and assistance. But in some trades, masters in league with the authorities took over the process. Instead of having delegated officials of the journeymen direct newly arrived or newly unemployed men to masters with open positions, the master locksmiths succeeded as early as 1808 in getting a blackboard put up in the trade's hostel that strictly limited those looking for work to the next master on the list. Boycotts against masters were thereby thwarted. The imposition of a similar order provoked the protest of the journeymen metal beaters in 1850 mentioned previously. Although the master brass molders did not attempt to have the old system thrown out in their trade, the drinking that usually accompanied encounters between job seekers and association officials caused numerous complaints and protests between 1846 and 1851.[17]

Much more debilitating for the functioning of the journeymen's associations was direct official repression. Fear of revolution and fear of the secret societies of exiled radicals in Switzerland, France, and Belgium led Bavaria and the other members of the German Confederation to cooperate in suppressing almost all of the traditions of the associations, whether harmless or not. Because of the attempts of the secret societies to influence artisans, wandering journeymen were feared as the "cheapest, most secure and fastest messengers" of the revolutionaries as well as the "best tools for the preparation of a general revolution."[18] Wandering to Switzerland, and later to France, was banned, and old prohibitions of journeymen's customs were reinforced between 1832 and 1847.[19] After two years of relaxation during the Revolution, the postrevolutionary reaction renewed the oppressive conditions of the thirties and the forties. Only at the beginning of the sixties did the political climate begin to ease in Bavaria.

This assertion of police power seems to have been fairly effective in undermining the discipline and cohesion that had been the backbone of the eighteenth-century associations. Recent research has shown how strong the brotherhoods and associations were before 1800, when regional and national communication networks allowed the punishment of strikebreakers and deviants and the boycotting of offending masters, guilds, or even whole cities. In spite of increasingly severe internal conflicts in the final decades of that century caused by the economic crisis in artisanry, this strength enabled the associations to enforce a solidarity and display a combativeness unequaled by the trade unions of the late nineteenth century.[20] In Nuremberg alone there were ninety-seven strikes between 1786 and 1806, at a time when the rulers of the Free City were quite weak.[21] In contrast there is evidence for only three strikes in Nuremberg between 1806 and 1871, an astoundingly low number in comparison to north German cities, let alone British and French ones. Only one of the three strikes was in a metal trade. On May 1, 1835, the journeymen brass molders refused to work in protest over the imposition of a new medical insurance fund for journeymen, workers, and servants. They wished to defend the viability of their own association, which already provided money to the sick. The threat of armed force intimidated them into giving up within a few hours, although the city then decided not to carry out its plans immediately because of the widespread hostility to the idea among artisans.[22] Despite this concession the authorities clearly demonstrated their ability to suppress strikes, an ability that must account in large part for the very low strike rate of the pre–trade union era.

The near impossibility of striking undercut one of the most effective disciplinary weapons of the associations: the old-style boycott of a transgressing journeyman, which mandated that all those who worked in the same shop or even the same trade with the man who had been declared "dishonorable" would refuse to work until he was expelled or had atoned for his breaking of the rules. Among Nuremberg metalworking artisans after 1835 no cases of such a boycott have come to light, although investigations of the compass makers in 1842 and the filemakers in 1852 revealed that those who did not pay their dues and participate in the customs of the associations might find it difficult to get a job in their trade.[23] Clearly something was left of mandatory membership in the associations, and the city still enforced the rule that all journeymen working with a master in a guilded trade must pay their dues as an association member.[24] But even that vestige of disciplinary power was undermined as more and more artisans in the fifties and sixties began to work in industry or with masters in the free trades.

Discipline was further undermined by the attacks on the remnants of the old communication networks designed to aid and control wandering artisans. Although the Napoleonic-era assault on the brotherhoods had effectively suppressed most intercity contacts, journeymen in the nineteenth century found a new way to enforce discipline among those on the tramp: "journeymen's passes" (*Gesellenscheine*), which certified the bearer as having fulfilled all the obligations to an association—the usual condition for receiving assistance and travel money elsewhere. These documents were successors to the so-called *Kundschaften*, which were issued by the guilds and associations before 1805 as proof that the bearer was properly apprenticed and had maintained his good standing in the places he had worked. During the Napoleonic Wars Bavaria, like the other German states, had abolished the Kundschaften and replaced them with state-controlled "wander books" *(Wanderbücher)*, an idea borrowed from the French Empire. These books were issued after the completion of apprenticeship and provided an excellent means of controlling—or harassing—wandering artisans. At each stop, or on demand, a journeyman on the tramp had to present his wander book to be inspected and stamped by the police, and he could be fined or jailed for not doing so. German artisan memoirs of the period are filled with examples of police harassment of journeymen, and an English goldsmith who traveled in Germany in the 1850s wrote that "the German artisan is ruled in everything by the state. . . . he becomes numbered and labelled from the hours of his birth and the gathering items of his existence are duly reorded not in the annals of history but in the registry of the police."[25] But the wander book naturally said nothing about whether the traveler had been initiated into, and paid his dues to, an association. Thus unsanctioned passes were often issued to certify that fact.

Always frightened by the supposed revolutionary threat presented by contacts among artisans, the police in Nuremberg, as elsewhere in Germany, sought to suppress the passes. In the middle decades of the century searches in Nuremberg and other areas turned up evidence for the issuance of documents by the city's compass makers, filemakers, toolsmiths, and coppersmiths, and hints of the same appear among the brass molders and tinsmiths. Until 1841 the journeymen compass makers issued an attractive printed certificate with a lithographed portrait of Nuremberg, allegedly in ignorance of its illegality. After they were informed of the new prohibitions of that year they began issuing, in cooperation with their masters and in a the belief that it would circumvent the ban, a "testimonial" *(Zeugnis)* that the bearer had paid his dues faithfully. They felt that it was absolutely necessary that tramping artisans carry such a document because, as one said, "without it one could not wander at all [auf der Wanderschaft gar nicht fortkommen]" for lack of travel money and help in other cities. This statement was confirmed by two letters from the late 1830s found in the association's trunk *(Lade)* in which records, money, and documents were stored. One from the journeymen compass makers in Munich was a reply confirming validity of a pass issued there, and another was a desperate request from a Nuremberger in Graz for a new one, because the compass makers in Austria thought he had forged his and refused to give him aid. The passes of the filemakers from 1839 and 1851, the toolsmiths from 1840, and the coppersmiths from 1859 were not so formal: they were merely handwritten documents created upon request, and signed and stamped to make them look official.[26]

Many other passes were undoubtedly issued, but all in all it appears that the Bavarian authorities were quite successful in suppressing them, especially in contrast to the north German states. Literally dozens of passes were confiscated from north German artisans by the Nuremberg police in the 1850s, whereas ones from Bavaria were very rare.[27] This success undoubtedly damaged the viability of the associations in Nuremberg. They were robbed of one more disciplinary instrument, for the investigations of the filemakers and compass makers show that receiving a pass was usually dependent on being formally initiated into an association and keeping up with one's dues. Enforcing mandatory membership thus became even more problematic, and maintaining contacts with other associations, and excluding those who were disloyal or indifferent elsewhere, became nearly impossible. To add insult to injury, those local craftsmen who wandered to cities where passes were still flourishing were faced either with hostility and the refusal of travel money or with the necessity of being initiated anew to acquire one. These problems must have raised the question in the minds of many journeymen of why they should continue to pay dues to support every newly arrived man when the favor was not always returned, and the issue certainly drove the masters and journeymen of the tinsmiths in 1848 and the filemakers in 1859 to ask for legalized passes to ease wandering.[28] Both requests were granted, because of the improved political climate of those years. But the breathing space during the Revolution was short-lived, and the relaxation of the sixties came at a time when the associations and the whole guild system in Germany were already on the verge of collapse.

Repression also touched the positive traditions that bound the members of a trade together. Convivial drinking fests paid for with association funds were banned, although not always with much success. The journeymen braziers, brass molders, and blacksmiths were all caught celebrating between 1846 and 1853 and were forbidden to hold such festivities again.[29] The locksmiths, in contrast, held an anniversary celebration (*Jahrestag*) in 1858, in which the craft's flag was paraded to and from the hostel by journeymen in coaches, but they were not punished, a good illustration of the inconsistency that often plagued city rulings on artisanal customs. The account book of the locksmith journeymen's association for 1849–1863 also reveals expenditures for celebrations on all the major holidays.[30] Since casual and customary drinking pervaded so many aspects of the life of journeymen, restrictions on the social life of the associations were probably the least effective of all measures directed against them.

Of more impact were bans on initiation rituals for journeymen. Elaborate rites of passage had been central ceremonies to the eighteenth-century brotherhoods, because they symbolized the crucial transformation from apprentice to journeyman. Apprenticeship was, and remained in the nineteenth century, a three-year test of endurance. The apprentice was practically without rights and stood under the paternal authority of the master, who could beat him if necessary. Apprentices were also often mistreated by journeymen, who refused to accept them as equals. Only with the passage of the initiation ritual (*Gesellenmachen, Gesellensprechung*) did the former apprentice gain the right to use the familiar *Du* form of address and socialize with other journeymen. This radical change of status from servant to equal, and from boy to man, was represented before 1805 in ceremonies with extremely complex symbolism. Among the blacksmiths, one of the highly skilled "elite" trades with rigid and extensive ritual, for example, the initiate was symbolically "cleansed" of his transitional and therefore potentially unclean and deviant status, ceremonially mishandled to symbolize death and rebirth, and ritually shaved of a charcoal "beard" to represent the transition to manhood. After washing, the new journeyman was then instructed on the proper behavior with masters and fellow journeymen.[31]

Those few nineteenth-century rituals uncovered by the police in the Nuremberg metal trades, however, were lacking in such elaborate symbolism. The most complex was also the earliest—that of the nailsmiths in 1828. The eighteen-year-old initiate, Wilhelm Wolf, was called into a room of the hostel where the two master superiors of the guild, the journeyman superior, and a number of other journeymen were present. In front of the open trunk of the journeymen's association the masters asked him his wish, and then read the rules of correct behavior on the tramp to him. He then had to pick two "godfathers," a "sacristan" (*Meßner*) and one other helper from among the journeymen before the ceremony ended with a brief reading by the "sacristan" of good luck wishes to the initiate for his progress through the stages of wandering, mastership, and marriage.[32] This ceremony thus contained both remnants of its early modern religious (or pseudo-religious) character and an expectation that the new journeymen would attain the respectable status of master, citizen, and father—an expectation increasingly at odds with reality, as we have seen.

All other ceremonies I have found come from the period after repression was stepped up in the 1830s. They include no participation by masters, and are simpler. The compass makers allegedly only announced the new status of the initiate at the hostel. The brass molders and filemakers made a similar announcement, but also customarily read the rules of behavior to him. According to filemakers questioned in 1852, these rules contained instructions on "how to behave during the wander period" and "the behavior of journeymen in the workshops, especially that they behave well and make no debts, etc."[33] But also revealed by the former journeyman superior of the filemakers was the following vestige of the old custom of ritual mishandling. In 1851 two journeymen had arrived at the hostel, and they were formally inducted as new journeymen because they had not belonged to an association before. After reading the rules, the journeyman superior was reminded by another "that I should not forget the usual box on the ears, and then I gave each of the journeymen a quite weak punch, after which they were then regarded as members of the filemakers' journeymen's association."[34] The indifference with which this whole ceremony was carried out (the journeyman superior was drunk) is an illustration of how much of the intricate ritual governing artisanal life had been lost since the beginning of the century as a result of the repression and dissolution of the traditional journeymen's subculture.

What really remained of the initiation ritual was drinking. The custom of having the initiate pay for beer and food for those present was well entrenched among the compass makers, gold beaters, filemakers, and locksmiths and probably among others as well. In the case of the gold beaters the old "journeymen's dinner" (*Gesellenbraten*), which allegedly could cost the enormous sum of seventy or eighty Gulden (three months' wages), had been abolished, however, in favor of a straight payment of 24 kr. (two-fifths of a Gulden) to each journeyman, which meant a cost of some twenty Gulden in all. But this rather prosaic custom was also abolished in 1846, soon after it was introduced, when the police found out and banned it, just as they had banned other forced payments for food and drink.[35] Of course no prohibition could effectively stop the celebration of acceptance into the association and the drinking that went with it, because it remained a symbolically important occasion, especially for newly graduated apprentices like the later Social Democratic leader Karl Grillenberger, who paid five and a half Gulden for beer in 1864.[36] Drinking also accompanied eighteenth-century ceremonies, but there was an important difference: the ritual itself was much more crucial and it was mandatory that it be carried out for the status of the journeyman to be accepted. Mid-nineteenth-century ceremonies were more informal.

The decline and eventual disappearance of the formal initiation rite was only a symptom of a wider loss of ritual in artisanal life. Andreas Grießinger has revealed the extent to which rigid rules governed every aspect of the lives of journeymen in the eighteenth century. These rigid rules were based on the partially magical-superstitious concept of "honor" *(Ehre)*. It was dishonorable, for example, to come into contact with something "unclean" like a dead cat, a prostitute, or the daughter of the hangman, and the resulting damage to the honor of the trade might have to be expunged by a strike, as a cleansing ritual. Since the besmirched person contaminated the shop or the whole trade, only stopping work could restore the lost honor of the craft. Another example is the 1791 strike of the Nuremberg journeymen nailsmiths, who quit work because a master told them to go to the gallows—a polluting insult that had to be expunged.[37] But the nineteenth century saw the disappearance of this strike form and with it the concept of honor in its traditional form. Among the Nuremberg metalworking artisans it appears only in an 1837 letter from the master brass molders, who appealed for leniency for the leaders of the 1835 strike because their jailing damaged the honor of the craft.[38] Clearly a great deal of ritual was lost, and much of this must have been due to state repression, which made strikes almost impossible and the maintenance of old customs very difficult because of the constant threat of arrest, punishment, and, for that considerable proportion of journeymen resident outside their Heimat, deportation. This repression not only forced the elimination of some traditions out of fear of further police intervention but also undermined the entire substance of the old subculture by eroding the discipline and cohesion of the associations. In the decades after 1806 the meaning of the old customs and the concept of honor must have gradually been lost as the means to defend them and the context in which they operated faded away.

Of course repression alone cannot explain all of this fundamental change. The decline of popular religion, superstition, and magic may have been a factor, as was the growth of municipal institutions that threatened to supplant some of the welfare functions of the associations. The Nuremberg city council eventually revived its plan for a mandatory hospital insurance fund, and in 1850 an officially sanctioned Association for the Support of Traveling Journeymen was created in an attempt to reduce the amount of begging by tramping artisans.[39] The influx of more journeymen from the countryside and the new employment created by the expansion of industry and the free trades were also solvents of tradition. In spite of this, it is clear that the journeymen's associations did survive into the 1860s and that remnants of their heritage were preserved in the union movement of the 1870s and 1880s. Two factors in varying degrees were primarily responsible for this continuity: the survival of many crafts as fairly closed and homogeneous groups, and continuance of wandering as a significant artisanal institution.

The first factor was largely a function of apprenticeship, skill, and the impact of capitalism and industrialization. As mentioned in Chapter 1, the artisanal apprenticeship remained a crucial institution in the metalworking trades even after the rise of industry and was a central experience in the formation of craft consciousness or a pride in the particular skills of each craft. Most journeymen/skilled workers identified themselves first as locksmiths, blacksmiths, and so forth and continued to do so in part because of the lack of a rapid process of deskilling in most metal trades. The snobbishness that could result only became visible in the 1870s (the subject of Chapter 3), when general metalworkers' unions tried to bring the trades together.

The minimal impact of industry upon some crafts, like filemaking, further contributed to the survival of group homogeneity. Because of isolation from other crafts in the workplace, the cohesiveness of the journeymen's association was still reinforced by a unique craft identity and by a natural inclination to socialize with one another. Even for heterogeneous trades like the locksmiths, the power of a common identity and the movement of journeymen back and forth between artisanry and industry may have partially counteracted the loss of contact with those who went into the machine-building factories. An 1861 entry in the account book of the locksmith journeymen's association shows a contribution of 5 fl. 36 kr. "from the factory journeyman [*vom Fabrikgesellen*]."[40] Nevertheless, rivalry and hostility between the construction and factory branches of the trade were visible into the twentieth century and show how variegated work environments could undermine craft solidarity.

The second factor, wandering, bolstered the associations because it mandated the continuance of those institutions that had supported wandering for centuries: hostels, job-finding services, and the provision of travel money. A mandatory wander period as a prerequisite for mastership was abolished in Bavaria in December 1853,[41] but the tradition appears to have survived in many trades at least into the 1890s, when it lost its distinctive character as a training period for skilled artisans and gradually melted into the general mobility of the national labor market of mature industrial capitalism. In the 1860s many young journeymen like Grillenberger still looked forward to a period of adventure, sightseeing, and work experience on the tramp, and the number of travelers still justified the maintenance of hostels in most trades.[42] Although evidence is scanty, the custom of giving travel money undoubtedly also continued as long as the guilds existed, which in many Bavarian trades was until the spring of 1868. Even after 1870 some traditional crafts like the filemakers, braziers, and tin molders created new organizations to support wanderers that were more like the old associations than unions, and the unions themselves often provided travel money as a benefit. Five hundred years of tradition did not disappear overnight.

The journeymen's associations did themselves disappear, however, no later than with the dissolution of the last guilds in 1868. Others disappeared earlier, when guilds with extralocal markets were dissolved in 1862 in a preliminary move toward occupational freedom. But even before that time the signs of dissolution were also visible in a few trades. The most prominent case is that of journeymen gold beaters, where records of a long controversy over creating a formal set of statutes for the association lay bare the internal difficulties suffered by many of these bodies. When the city abolished the custom of having a newly initiated journeyman pay each of his colleagues a fee, a number of gold beaters dropped out because the dues were no longer outweighed by the fees gathered from each ex-apprentice. Since the gold beaters rarely wandered,[43] and those remaining in the association had no desire to bear the burden of supporting the few who did, the association had no function in that regard, and in the absence of any of the other old customs it had become merely a "local private illness insurance fund," as one of the members put it.[44] By this time the city had already revived its plan for its own fund with mandatory contributions, and many journeymen decided that this coverage was enough and quit the association. Only some of the married journeymen, of which there were allegedly quite a few in the trade, stayed in because they wished to have extra protection. By 1854 only seventeen of some sixty journeymen were still paying dues. In 1846 a few leaders had attempted to stabilize the declining income of the association by instituting statutes to prevent further arguments. A desultory sixteen-year controversy ensued in which this attempt became stuck in bureaucratic red tape and quarrels between the masters and the leaders of the association. The attempt to create statutes finally lapsed when the guild was abolished in 1862.[45]

Although perhaps an extreme case, the controversy among the gold beaters is significant because it illustrates many of the salient features of the dissolution of the journeymen's associations in the wake of official repression and social change. With the association stripped of its initiation ritual, and with its insurance function increasingly displaced by a municipal institution, it gradually lost its ability to hold journeymen together or to discipline them. Because the factor of wandering was not significant, the dissolution proceeded even faster. In the end, those who remained even tried to transform it into a formal institution with rules—something unimaginable to the eighteenth-century brotherhoods, in which "face-to-face communication," rather than officially sanctioned documents,[46] and an intimate knowledge of and respect for centuries-old unwritten tradition were the very basis of their existence. This step, which was taken only by one other trade, the brass molders (who were also infrequent wanderers),[47] reveals the infiltration of bureaucratic and middle-class conceptions of the *Verein* (voluntary association) as a body with a written constitution. As if to demonstrate their transitional status, the journeymen gold beaters started the first quasi-union in Nuremberg in 1865: the Association for the Improvement of the Gold-Beating Trade.[48] But it disappeared very rapidly for lack of a clear purpose. It was neither a union nor a journeymen's association, but it was nevertheless a harbinger of a new age. Within four years, journeymen in the Nuremberg metal trades, like those in other crafts, would begin to organize themselves into unions.

Work Discipline and Blue Monday Drinking

One further custom common among Nuremberg metalworking artisans needs to be examined, but its history is so curious it deserves separate treatment. The habit of taking all or part of Monday off from work to drink was almost universal among European artisans. In Germany this custom was called the "Blue Monday"; in Britain, "St. Monday." Its origin and early history are a matter of controversy, but it is clear that the Blue Monday became entrenched as a means of shortening the theoretically very long work hours of the early modern period. By the eighteenth century the power of the German brotherhoods was sufficient to have the Blue Monday at least partially enshrined in the rules of many of the crafts. In the Nuremberg metal trades an early Monday quitting time was still the rule in the mid-nineteenth century: the nailsmiths stopped at 2:00, the metal beaters at 2:00 or 3:00, the compass makers and black-smiths at 4:00, and the locksmiths at 6:00. By comparison, on other days the locksmiths usually quit at 7:00, the blacksmiths at 6:00, and the others probably between 6:00 and 8:00. Until 1840 the braziers also held their as-sociation meeting every fourth Monday, but a complaint in that year had that custom abolished. More common was the illegal celebration of a full holiday, something repeatedly but rather ineffectively banned. "Taking a Blue Monday" *(das Blaumontagmachen)* was the most frequently punished artisanal infraction in eighteenth-century Nuremberg, and every indica-tion is that the custom was still common in the early nineteenth century.[49]

The most interesting and perhaps the most mystifying aspect of the Blue Monday in Nuremberg is, however, the enormous increase in the number of convictions for this misdemeanor between 1854 and 1865. A major reason for this phenomenon was a new and more energetic cam-paign by the city council to stamp it out, but why the city's dominant social classes chose to launch a campaign at that time must remain some-what a matter of speculation. Even more difficult to assess is whether an actual rise in the frequency of Blue Mondays was in part responsible for the increased vigilance and enforcement. Certain trends, such as a rise in work hours in artisanry and growing alcohol consumption, hint at a real increase in incidence as well as enforcement.

The verifiable facts are summarized in Figure 2.1. The number of con-victions for Blaumontagmachen found in certain files in the Nuremberg City Archive varied between zero and ten from 1841 to 1854 for all trades, but the numbers thereafter increased to a maximum of eighty-one in 1858 before dropping again to a low of nineteen in 1861. For the period after 1861 the situation is further complicated by a sudden change in the char-acter of the records because of the judicial reform of 1862 in Bavaria. The city council, sitting as the "police senate," had much of its power of administrative justice removed, and Blue Monday cases were thereafter pursued in the courts. As a result, from then on only cases of nonresi-dent journeymen referred to the city for possible expulsion appear in the documents. This change explains the sharp drop in 1862, which is

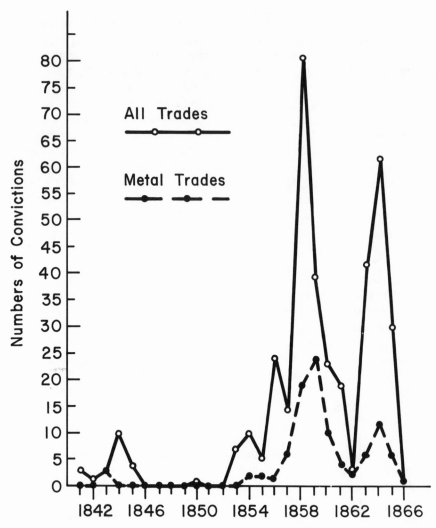

FIGURE 2.1. Blue Monday Convictions Found in the Nuremberg City Archive for 1841–1866

SOURCE: StadtAn, HR VIb7, Nr. 27, Nr. 63, Nr. 64, and Nr. 68, supplemented by Nr. 356, M Nr. 86, M Nr. 87, M Nr. 90, S Nr. 90, S. Nr. 91, and S Nr. 94. Because the M and S files are devoted specifically to various metal trades, the sample slightly over-represents these trades. The ambiguity of some cases means that the data might actually vary by about one to three convictions for the peak years. For further explanation, see text.

illusory. In fact there were 162 convictions in the second half of that year alone, and a further 323 between January 1 and November 12, 1863.[50] Obviously the number of convictions shown in the graph is only a small proportion of those sentenced after 1861, and there may be significant though smaller, underrepresentation before that time because of the haphazard way the records were collected.

Figure 2.1 also shows that journeymen in the metal trade and workers in the machine industry formed only a small percentage of those convicted before 1857. The three locksmiths sentenced in 1843 were the only cases found for the period 1841 to 1854 (the records begin suddenly in mid-1841). Even so, cases turned up in files devoted specifically to various metal trades cause some overrepresentation of those crafts, although the effect is not too strong. Of 382 convictions shown in Figure 2.1, ninety-seven or 25.4 percent were of those working in metal. Sixteen of those cases were gleaned from metal-trades files, leaving eighty-one of 366 cases or 22.1 percent coming from the general files on Blaumontag-machen, which were presumably a random sample. This percentage closely approximates the proportion of metalworkers among Nuremberg industrial and artisanal employees at mid-century,[51] so the unusually low proportion of convictions from 1841 to 1856 may be purely a random effect resulting from the statistically insignificant total number of cases, especially before 1855.

Only two women are included in the totals: two helpers in the metal-beating trade, which seems to have suffered from particularly severe problems of turnover and discipline among both men and women. Nine other individuals worked in the machine industry: four iron molders, four unskilled laborers, and one blacksmith, all at Klett. The company's 1844 shop rules stated that Blue Monday drinkers would be turned over to the police, but nothing was ever done in that regard; all nine were arrested in tavern raids in the fall of 1858. Since Klett undoubtedly had disciplinary problems stemming from the adaptation to work discipline (see Chapter 1)—and the doorkeeper's record from 1863 apparently had numerous notations of those who were "blue" that day—these problems must have been handled entirely through firing and internal discipline.[52]

The city's campaign against the Blue Monday appears to have begun rather suddenly in the spring of 1858 with orders to check hostels and other pubs on Monday because the custom was "again getting very much out of hand."[53] Earlier prohibitions, which were often included in general orders against "journeymen's abuses," do not appear to have been enforced very energetically, and an 1852 complaint about the excessive number of Blue Monday celebrants by the city commissar, a state official appointed to limit the independence of the city administration, appears to have gone largely unheeded.[54] But the new measures were more effective, especially after the regional government of Middle Franconia prodded the city to step up its campaign. Innumerable journeymen and workers were arrested in the pubs on Mondays, whether they had legitimate excuses or not. Although a number had to be let off, the conviction rate skyrocketed until 1859 when the vigilance of the police began to decline. Pressure on masters, including fines for those who did not report offenders, also succeeded in increasing the rate of reporting. After a relative lull in 1860–1862, the anti–Blue Monday crusade was renewed in 1863–1864, when general raids were staged and dozens of nonresident journeymen were expelled from the city, again with the claim that drinking on Mondays was getting out of hand. Only in 1865 did the campaign begin to slack off permanently, although occasional convictions occurred in the 1870s. Bavaria had the dubious honor of being the only state in the new Empire that retained this medieval law after the Imperial Industrial Ordinance came into effect.[55]

Further research may eventually reveal the reasons for the sudden anti–Blue Monday fervor in 1858, but the answer is at the moment rather obscure. For the second peak in 1863 the background is a bit clearer. Public drunkenness, fighting, and disorder at parish festivals (*Kirchweihen*), which often caused extended drinking into Mondays, resulted in cries of outrage from respectable citizens in the middle-class liberal newspaper *Fränkischer Kurier* and in pressure from the Middle Franconian government and city commissar for action against parish festivals, Blue Mondays, artisanal celebrations, and other popular customs. Perhaps not coincidentally, late October and early November 1863, the peak of the crusade, also saw anti–Blue Monday raids in Munich, but no evidence for central direction of the campaign from the Bavarian government has yet been found. It is probably also significant that the late 1850s and early 1860s were the period when the new liberals, who in March 1863 formed the Progressive Party, first gained a strong foothold in the Nuremberg city council, prefatory to dominating it from 1869 to 1918. Their political base included more factory owners and wealthy masters than did the old-line liberals and conservatives. A rising concern on the part of those social groups for better work discipline and a stronger work ethic must have been a factor behind the campaign, but the link is not easy to prove despite the enthusiastic support of the party paper, the *Fränkischer Kurier*. In related moves, Monday parades to mark movement of hostels from one pub to another were also banned in 1863, and parish festivals and yearly artisanal celebrations were banned in 1867.[56]

The great increase in arrests between 1858 and 1865 must thus be largely a product of increased vigilance and enforcement, but the question remains: was there an actual increase in the numbers of artisans and workers celebrating the Blue Monday? No set of arrest statistics, no matter how accurate, could answer this question, so we are left with hypotheses and circumstantial evidence. The rise in the number of convictions from 1854 to 1857, *before* any effective measures were ordered by the city council, and the complaints of increasing Blue Monday drinking coming from the council and the city commissar in 1852, 1858, and 1863, indicate that a real rise might have been taking place. These indications are reinforced by the two trends mentioned above: rising alcohol consumption in Germany, especially from 1850 to 1873, and increasing work time and work discipline in artisanry as a result of growing competition among masters and between masters and industrialists. Each of these trends potentially increased the probability of drinking and absenteeism on Mondays.

The consumption of beer and cheap spirits *(Schnaps)* rose almost continuously in nineteenth-century Germany, but its period of fastest growth was during the Industrial Revolution proper, from 1850 to 1873, a period of relatively unbroken expansion and rising real and money wages. Between 1850 and 1875 there was an overall increase in per capita consumption (measured in volume of pure alcohol) of 112 percent for beer and 44 percent for Schnaps. In Nuremberg per capita beer consumption rose from 260 liters around 1850 to 343 liters around 1870, while the average family spent a very high 10.5 percent of its income on beer in 1857.[57] Although the majority of those convicted of Blaumontagmachen were definitely either drunk or hung over on the day in question, a direct link between increased drinking and increased absenteeism cannot be shown. It does, however, seem likely.

A second likely stimulus to more Blue Monday drinking was an increase in work time in artisanry, which was symptomatic of an increased work discipline necessary to compete with industry or other masters. Rainer Gömmel estimates that up to about 1845 the average normal workweek was sixty-one hours for Nuremberg artisans, whereas industry had a sixty-five- to sixty-seven-hour week. The latter figure changed little before 1871, but hours in artisanry, in contrast, climbed steadily after 1845 to a peak of sixty-seven in 1869–1870, slightly exceeding the average work time in the industrial sector.[58] Since the regulations of most artisanal trades specified at least that many hours, if not more, this increase could only have come about through a stricter enforcement of the rules regarding starting and stopping times, Blue Mondays, breaks during work, holidays, and so on. This in turn may have provoked more absenteeism as compensation.

Evidence for this is not entirely lacking. Three braziers were convicted in 1857 for taking Monday and even Tuesday off, allegedly because their master worked them so hard they even had to go in on Sundays. They did not think anyone would care if they took a day or two to relax.[59] The reasons offered by others were seldom so explicit, but it seems probable that increased work discipline may have lain behind the propensity of many to get up late, quit early, or not show up at all on Mondays. At the very least, the nonchalant attitude of most Blue Monday drinkers toward punctuality and absenteeism suggests that there was no strongly internalized work ethic, a lack that made the imposition of work discipline difficult. Just as in the machine industry, instilling consciousness of time and steadiness of work was a slow and painful process.

The likelihood that demands for better time and work discipline may have sparked more Blue Monday drinking is increased by certain countervailing trends that undermined the authority of masters just when it was needed most. Added to the decline in paternal authority occasioned by marriage, living out, and "overfilling" were the effects of the penetration of capitalist behavior into the artisanate. Piece-rate payment, for example, made journeymen almost casual employees of masters. This allowed flexibility of employment levels but undercut discipline. The journeyman nailsmith Wilhelm Happach, arrested in a tavern raid in 1858, explained that he had drunk too much on Sunday and quit work at ten on Monday because "it did not go well, and I work by the piece anyway, so I let it drop and went to Wohlfahrt's pub."[60] The very high proportion of metal beaters convicted (over a third of the known convictions of metalworkers before 1862)[61] may also be due to the universality of piece-rate payment in that trade. Day-wage payment may have had a similar effect. Among the locksmiths the machine-industry custom of hiring journeymen by the day without any required notice period for either side was apparently adopted by some masters, which may help to explain why locksmiths were second only to the metal beaters in numbers of those sentenced for Blaumontagmachen.[62]

One final factor exacerbated the work discipline problem: the state of the labor market. The industrialization boom of 1850–1873 was interrupted by only two short recessions, and the shortage of skilled labor that resulted from the rapid expansion of productive capacity was only heightened for masters by the magnetic effects of higher wages in industry. In its July 2, 1858, letter to the city council, the regional government of Middle Franconia stated: "The shortage of journeymen in many trades has been given as an obstacle to the cooperation of the craft masters [in repressing Blue Mondays], because they feel themselves to some extent forced to turn a blind eye to this nuisance in order not to cause the journeymen to quit the shops."[63] This was not a new problem, and certainly both journeymen in the eighteenth century and workers in the twentieth also used a favorable labor market to gain leverage when possible. But the prolonged good times in the 1850s and 1860s, when combined with the pressure for greater punctuality and hard work and the growing alienation between masters and men, must have created especially severe problems for artisanal employers in controlling their labor force.

Ultimately the question of whether the incidence of Blue Monday drinking increased cannot be answered here, but it at least seems probable that greater work discipline and the anti–Blue Monday crusade widened the gap between the two main groups within the artisanate. The many masters who turned in their men to the police for drinking and absenteeism cannot have been popular, and efforts to enforce guild rules more strictly would have increased friction. The only open conflict occurred among the blacksmiths, where a new ordinance issued by the masters in January 1853 ordered a fourteen-hour day from 4:00 A.M. to 6:00 P.M. The guild superiors of the blacksmiths refused to admit that a 4:00 P.M. quitting time on Monday had been customary "for an unimaginable period," as the protesting journeymen put it. A struggle also arose out of the imposition of notice-period regulations in the ordinance. These allowed journeymen to be released virtually at any time, while requiring them to give two weeks' notice if they decided to leave. The city council backed up the authority of the masters, and the journeymen were left only with plaintive protests.[64]

Just as perplexing as the question of whether a rise in convictions meant a real rise in the frequency of Blue Mondays is the question of whether the rapid fall in convictions after 1865 indicates a true fall in the number of celebrants. It would not be surprising if the energy of the crusade in 1863–1864 at least intimidated many into taking fewer free Mondays in the short run. In the long run it seems likely too that the disciplinary measures of artisanal and industrial employers, and the acculturation processes of schools, churches, and other institutions of the dominant culture, would induce a greater internalization of the work ethic on the part of journeymen and other workers.[65] Drinking on the job and off remained a serious problem, of course, especially before the turn of the century, and there are scattered reports of the Blue Monday in the 1870s and 1880s and even later. Allegedly it was still a custom among the Nuremberg tin molders—whose work had scarcely changed from the preindustrial period—in 1899.[66] Nevertheless, certain clues indicate that the Blue Monday gradually lost its distinct identity and slowly declined in frequency.

A subtle change in language may be the best indicator of altered customs among artisans. Blaumontagmachen became simply "Blaumachen," meaning to be drunk, or to be absent from work to drink. The word *blau* (blue) acquired a slang connotation of drunkenness that it had hitherto not possessed in the German language.[67] The dropping of Monday from the word was connected to a decline in the importance of that day as *the* day to take off, although the effects of weekend drinking would continue to be a cause of absenteeism on Mondays. Like the custom of wandering, the Blue Monday did not disappear suddenly; rather it was transformed or overwhelmed until it lost its distinct identity as an artisanal tradition. As the old artisanal culture fell apart with the repression and dissolution of the journeymen's associations, and with the suppression of customs like early quitting times, parades, parish festivals, and artisanal celebrations that sustained Monday drinking, the Blue Monday disappeared too—but only gradually. Some of its spirit lived on in the common problem of drinking after paydays and during the week, and this would continue to bedevil employers, social reformers, and the labor movement alike. As with so many other aspects of working-class culture, the contribution of the journeyman's distinct culture was long visible.

The transformation of the journeyman's world was, as we have seen so far, an extremely complex process brought on by social change, state repression, encroaching capitalism, and growing alienation between masters and men. Not only loss but also preservation of tradition marked this transformation. But new elements were also added. One of these was the slow rise of politicization and class consciousness, which marked the very weak and tentative strivings of the nascent labor movement. In Nuremberg that movement was almost exclusively one of journeymen/skilled workers.

The Rise of Politicization and Class Consciousness

Eugen Weber has defined politicization as "an awareness that alternatives exist, that choices are possible, that 'political' activities are not about irrelevant abstractions but are closely related to social and economic concerns that are local, personal and immediate."[68] This realization came only very slowly to Nuremberg metalworking artisans, as was the case for all artisans, because of the survival of traditional concepts of the place of masters within an estate society and because of the power of the Bavarian state to prevent change and even to repress the discussion of change. The Revolution of 1848–1849 was a crucial break in this pattern because it allowed the open discussion of politics and the formation of organizations—something otherwise impossible before the 1860s. As a result, both masters and journeymen became much more politicized—but not necessarily in the same direction. The split between the two groups over the reform of the quasi-guild system and access to mastership grew throughout the Revolution, and the weak beginnings of working-class consciousness appeared among journeymen and foreshadowed the later rise of the socialist labor movement that would decisively divide the artisanate.

It should not be thought, however, that artisans (including the few skilled factory workers that existed at that time) were a political *tabula rasa* in 1848. In Nuremberg, as elsewhere, craftsmen were sufficiently alienated by threatening social change, economic crisis, and political repression to support the Revolution and its liberal leaders enthusiastically from the beginning, albeit often for very different reasons. Earlier political activities, including nationalistic anti-Napoleonic demonstrations by the brass molders in 1814 and support for the middle-class opposition during the first radical upsurge of 1830–1832, were also not entirely lacking. Journeymen formed most of the crowd that tried to demolish the house of an unpopular Nuremberg Landtag deputy in 1832. But the events of that first wave of radical sentiment seem to have left few marks. The state and city police were never able to turn up any evidence of the presence of democratic or socialist secret societies among Nuremberg artisans in the 1830s and 1840s, and only a handful of Nurembergers, including one brazier, were identified as members of these sects in foreign exile. North German cities, for example, Hamburg, had much more secret society activity.[69]

Artisans and other members of the lower orders also possessed traditional forms of protest, which, if not explicitly political, could at least implicitly question the validity of established authority. The previously mentioned brass molders' strike of 1835 was the last example of the kind of journeymen's strikes often waged in the late eighteenth century to defend the autonomy of the associations vis-à-vis the city government. Other forms of protest common to west European popular culture also survived into the nineteenth century. Only one year before the Revolution there was a major charivari/food riot in April 1847 against grain dealers during the last major subsistence crisis in Germany. Journeymen and workers formed most of the crowd. And as late as 1866 there was a similar riot against hikes in the price of beer.[70] The label "preindustrial" may be too condescending for these protest forms, but their eventual disappearance was one more sign that older conceptions of the just price, the "moral economy," and the estate society had faded away and that new avenues of protest had become available—particularly political parties, elections, and trade unions.[71] Of course popular violence did not disappear, especially from bitterly contested strikes, but it became a minor and highly unpopular weapon that even organized labor tried to suppress.

This fundamental reorientation of popular protest toward politics, organizations, and ideologies, which is one of the most important aspects of the transformation of journeymen from artisans to workers, reflects the evolution of Germany from an estate society to a class society in the wake of capitalism, urbanization, and industrialization. Nuremberg's metalworking artisans eventually had to discard their belief in the artisan estate's honorable but fixed place within a static urban society and accept instead that their inferior position in the city's social structure was both unjust and changeable. The causes are manifold, but the most crucial were the pre-revolutionary economic crisis, the penetration of capitalism and industry into the artisanate, and state repression and bureaucratic interference. These resulted in "overfilling," the separation of masters and men, the impoverishment or restructuring of most trades, and a sense of alienation from the city and state ruling elites. Masters had a more difficult time adjusting, because they had more to lose if the social system that gave them a modest amount of status and prestige and the legal system that protected them from unfettered competition fell apart. Journeymen, in contrast, faced with the probability of lifelong wage labor and with discriminatory harassment of their customs and organizations, had an easier time divorcing themselves from the traditional conception of the artisan's place in urban society.

These slow processes of change were far from complete in 1848, but the Revolution clearly revealed that they were under way. The upheaval began quietly. After peaceful public meetings in the first week of March, the news that the king had given into the demands of the Munich uprising on the sixth was greeted with jubilation in Nuremberg. Freedom of the press and a liberalization of the constitution were hailed by massive crowds, mostly carrying the Bavarian colors. In April a moderate liberal was elected to the Frankfurt Parliament by the city's ruling elite and higher bourgeois in a poorly attended and indirect election. But things did not remain moderate for long. In mid-April, the Political Association, the organization of the city's middle-class democrats and republicans, was the first formal political group to organize. It rapidly gained a large base, particularly among journeymen.[72] Loyalty to Bavaria also weakened rapidly as the state and southern Bavaria turned more conservative, while the traditional loyalty to the Reich in Franconia manifested itself in liberal and democratic nationalism. The incipient radical spirit was clearly visible in a petition of the journeymen superiors of the joiners, tinsmiths, compass makers, turners, and combmakers, which was sent on March 31, 1848, to the Munich government. It asked for a decisive easing of restrictions so that access to mastership would be opened up. The policies of the city council and state bureaucracy were scorned as narrow-minded and backward.[73] The master locksmiths, however, asked one month later for much more protection from competition, and later petitions to the Frankfurt Parliament from many trades confirmed the stubborn opposition of a considerable segment of the masters to any possible loosening of the quasi-guild system.[74] Neither side had given up its attachment to the basic system, but the journeymen were certainly drawing different conclusions about what should be done.

The contradictory combination of radical politics and relatively conservative economic opinions is typical of journeymen in 1848. On the one hand, as Nuremberg gradually became the center of radical democratic activity in all Franconia, the most politicized journeymen formed a Workers' Association (Arbeiterverein) at the instigation of the middle-class democrats in May 1848. Although the term "worker" was often used loosely to include small masters, its employment was an important political act signifying the rejection of the exclusivity of the old crafts and the acceptance of solidarity with all artisans and workers, whether skilled or not. On the other hand, the Workers' Association only distanced itself from the quasi-guild system with difficulty, and at times it supported automatic promotion to mastership at a specified age. This ideological mixture was well symbolized by the decorations at an association ball in February 1849, which included the bust of the democratic martyr Robert

Blum and the names of Benjamin Franklin, George Washington, the French democratic socialists Louis Blanc and Ledru Rollin, and the theorist of the renewed guild system, Karl Winkelblech. It was only with the greatest pressure that Stefan Born, the national leader of the Brotherhood (Verbrüderung) of workers' associations, was able to push through a resolution for limited occupational freedom at the conference of Bavarian workers' associations held in Nuremberg the following April.[75]

Unfortunately solid information about the Workers' Association is very difficult to obtain. No membership lists are extant, so an occupational analysis that might reveal the role of the metalworkers within it is impossible. Of six journeymen and workers arrested in June 1849 for secretly arming association members with long-handled scythes in preparation for a revolutionary uprising, three were from the metal trades: a stickpin maker, a tinsmith, and a locksmith (who may also have worked in a factory).[76] The most prominent leaders were a tailor and a glazier, however, and the executive committee of the successor organization, the Workers' Educational Association (September 1849–June 1850), contained only one metalworker out of seven in February 1850—the same stickpin maker. The Workers' Association had 364 members when it was dissolved in August 1849 for the "scythe affair," and the membership of its successor allegedly rose as high as 550 in the spring of 1850. At that time there were some 6,500 artisan journeymen and factory workers residing in the city out of a total population of a little over fifty thousand. The older assumption that the association must have been made up of factory workers because of its name may be fairly dismissed as a myth.[77]

Although the number of journeymen and workers organized was thus only 5 to 10 percent of the total, considerably bigger crowds could be drawn to crucial demonstrations by the combined forces of the democrats and the Workers' Association. The two biggest gatherings, during the campaign to save the Frankfurt Parliament and its draft constitution in May 1849, drew five to fifteen thousand and twenty to thirty thousand respectively, although admittedly they also attracted many peasants and artisans from surrounding towns and villages. These demonstrations marked the apogee of the politicization process that began rather slowly in the spring of 1848 but noticeably accelerated and radicalized later in the year. The Political Association became the dominant organization in the city, even exercising much influence over the People's Association (Volksverein), which was the more moderate organization of artisan masters and some segments of the middle classes. Some radical masters were also involved in the Political Association, but they were outnumbered by journeymen and workers.[78]

All this does not imply that politicization drew the great majority of the artisanate and the incipient working class into any sort of regular political activity. As at all times, there were undoubtedly a considerable number of artisans and workers who remained apathetic or politically moderate. Journeymen also signed the masters' anti-occupational freedom petition to Frankfurt in January 1849, although it is noteworthy that almost all the metal trades signatures came from crafts suffering severe economic decline, such as the filemakers, nailsmiths, and brass molders.[79] The meaning of this is somewhat ambiguous, because of that common contradiction between liberal democratic politics and attachment to the old economic system, but it would not be surprising if at least some journeymen in hard-pressed trades and those with greater chances of becoming masters might share the opinions of their employers.

These reservations aside, it is fairly clear that those members of the incipient working class, including journeymen, who were active politically fell almost universally within the democratic camp. Nevertheless it cannot be said that political positions were plainly divided along class lines the way they became in Nuremberg after the 1870s, when the working-class Social Democrats and the middle-class Progressives faced each other across a nearly unbridgeable gap. Because the class formation process had not proceeded very far, working-class consciousness was very low, notwithstanding a small elite who, like the iron molder Peter Kalsing, counted themselves members of the "working class [*Arbeiterklasse*]."[80] There also seem to have been no deviations by the Workers' Association from the subservient role it played under the leadership of the Political Association and the middle-class democrats.

Another strong indicator of a low level of class consciousness or at least a low level of opposition to the employers was the surprising weakness of trade-union activity in the city during the Revolution. The harsh laws on the books against striking and organizing were more or less in abeyance, but outside of some preliminary efforts to form a union on the part of the elite book printers and one meeting of the construction trades, there is no evidence of activity.[81] This is in stark contrast to two vanguard cities of the labor movement, Berlin and Leipzig, where the machine-industry and printing-trades workers developed extensive organizational links and struck frequently. Even unskilled workers were drawn into unions there. As the work of Frederick Marquardt and Hartmut Zwahr demonstrates, most journeymen in those two cities had at least a vague sense that they belonged to a socially distinct working class and that they could organize to improve their lot.[82] Nuremberg, in contrast, does not seem to have traveled as far down this road. The machine industry was as yet quite small, and a large number of journeymen were still in trades only weakly affected by capitalism and industrialization. Political repression also appears to have been successful in robbing them of their memory of their combative eighteenth-century strike tradition.

An even clearer indication of the weakness of class politics in the Revolution is the degree to which masters and other members of the middle classes were not concentrated into clear parties. Although members of the established ruling order—city and state bureaucrats, officers, rich merchants, and patricians—were represented by the tepidly liberal Constitutional Association, middle-class professionals, intellectuals, and industrialists seem to have been strewn across the broad spectrum of opinion contained in the People's and Political Associations.[83] True democratic or republican radicalism was much more prevalent than it was to become later. By comparison, the Progressive Party, the successor organization of the middle-class forty-eighters in Nuremberg, had by the 1870s turned its back on democratic ideas and ruled the city as the voice of the propertied classes through a restricted city franchise.

As for the masters, I have already noted that there were left-wing masters, although there were many more who were against occupational freedom. The ongoing division of masters as a result of capitalism caused some, probably the economically most innovative or successful, to favor a laissez-faire economy. Others, particularly owners of the expensive private licenses necessary in some trades for mastership, were hard-core conservatives because they wished to protect the value of their paper assets.[84] Most politically active masters fell somewhere in the vague and contradictory middle represented by the People's Association. They were against occupational freedom, but they were nationalistic and in favor of the Revolution, because, like Mack Walker's small-town masters, they thought of themselves as the real "people" *(Volk)* and they opposed the intervention of the states and their bureaucracies on the side of economic and social change, however modest and authoritarian.[85] Thus despite their anti–laissez faire position, the majority of masters long followed the lead of the middle-class liberals because their rhetoric promised more power to the common people. It would take some decades before those masters who could not accept their status as small capitalists in a society dominated by industry would reject the leadership of the liberals and become antimodern and hostile to both labor and capital.

Whatever their opinions, masters and journeymen certainly became much more politically involved and aware as a result of the events of 1848–1849, and they retained some of that interest in spite of the renewed repression that began in May-June 1849 with the failure of the Revolution. But the jailing, censorship, banishment, and military occupation that began then undoubtedly disheartened many and destroyed many of the fruits of two years' efforts. After the collapse of the campaign for the constitution and the failure of the uprisings elsewhere, a "small war" ensued between the Bavarian troops who occupied the city in June and the crowds of journeymen and members of the lower classes. In August the Workers' Association was declared illegal but was reincarnated only weeks later as a purely educational and fraternal society. It was then banned permanently in June 1850. Other attempts to reorganize were crushed from the beginning, and the Political Association disappeared by early 1852. A tiny conspiratorial cell of Marx's revived Communist League was organized in 1851, but it lapsed without accomplishing anything.[86] The police continued to record incidents of open or disguised hostility toward themselves, the army, or the monarchy well into the 1850s, but politically all was deathly quiet after 1852. Many, like the former chairman of the Worker's Association and one-time journeyman locksmith Köchert, likely lost interest because of either the threat of repression or the opportunities offered by the new economic boom. A political prisoner after the "scythe affair," he testified in 1853 that he had withdrawn from all politics because he was doing very well as a master fine mechanic (a free trade) and had no extra time. Besides, he saw that "it is idiocy, when *individuals* make propaganda," a statement that hints, however, at continuing left-wing sympathies.[87]

When the liberal-dominated Workers' Association was created again in October 1861 the names of Köchert and other former leaders were missing, but some of the spirit of 1848 lived on. Since the entry of the Nuremberg left liberal Karl Crämer into the Bavarian Landtag in 1859, the local democratic and liberal agitators had revived support among workers and artisans with their lively campaign for abolition of the guilds and political reform. With the economic boom, the turn of many of the German states away from the old system, and the obvious oppressiveness of the 1853 craft law revisions, journeymen and even some masters seem to have lost what faith in the guilds they still possessed during the Revolution. No revival of demands for automatic mastership during the 1860s are apparent, and the Workers' Association seems to have backed its leaders enthusiastically on the issue. The association was soon able to draw four hundred to its meetings; one meeting of two hundred in 1865 was described by the police as consisting of "for the most part young unmarried journeymen." Of twenty-nine founding members only one locksmith, one blacksmith, one brass molder, one brazier, and two watchmakers were included. Among nonmetal trades, the joiners *(Schreiner)* were dominant with thirteen.[88]

Leadership by the middle-class liberals, and in the association itself by prominent masters, seems to have held until about 1867. The rise of Ferdinand Lassalle's socialism in northern Germany after 1863 made little impression in Nuremberg, probably because the pro-Prussian statism and authoritarian character of his organization, the General German Workers' Association (ADAV), had little appeal. After the popular Schleswig-Holstein war of 1863–1864, the Nuremberg Workers' Association and much of the south German liberal movement inclined toward a democratic *großdeutsch* solution to national unification (that is, one including German Austria but without Habsburg domination). They also favored private cooperatives for artisans compatible with the principles of laissez-faire economics. Thus ADAV found little support. Instead, the transitional People's Party (Volkspartei), the embodiment of this loose and often contradictory left-liberal movement, grew in size as Bismarck's maneuvers alienated south German and Saxon opinion in 1865 and 1866. The Nuremberg Association, like the most prominent liberal leader, Crämer, briefly left the Progressive Party in 1865–1866 and aligned themselves with the People's Party.[89]

But soon thereafter came the shockwaves from Bismarck's "revolution from above," which followed Prussia's crushing of Austria and the other German states in the war of 1866. German liberalism was confronted with perplexing dilemmas as national unity was provisionally begun and universal suffrage was decreed in north Germany, in a period of social upheaval and class formation.[90] In Nuremberg the local liberal leadership quickly returned to the Progressive Party fold, influenced by the model behavior of the Prussian troops that occupied the city in 1866 and by the threat of Austrian-sponsored French intervention. The Workers' Association followed suit. But as was the case almost everywhere in Germany, the attitude of the politicized segment of the working class rapidly soured because of the Progressives' failure in Prussia, their lack of enthusiasm for universal suffrage and democracy, and their disinterest in social programs that would violate their "Manchesterist" economic principles. Although the formation of the Workers' Educational Association (Arbeiterbildungs-verein) in June 1866 by dissident Workers' Association members seems to have been occasioned mostly by conflicts over funds and administration, this new organization quickly became dominated by journeymen alienated from the local liberal leadership.[91] They inclined politically toward the People's Party, but the mostly lower-middle-class leadership of that group also refused to consider socialist answers to the poverty and distress of workers and artisans. At the very important fifth national congress of the liberal workers' associations held September 1868 in Nuremberg, the Workers' Educational Association followed the lead of August Bebel (Leipzig) and the congress majority in accepting the socialist principles of Marx's First International. A number of members joined the International shortly thereafter. In response, the Nuremberg liberals in the older Workers' Association created a breakaway national organization, but it was abortive. Although the liberal labor movement remained a viable competitor of the socialists in Nuremberg into the early 1870s, the city was by 1869 already well on its way to becoming a stronghold of the Eisenachers—the Bebel-Liebknecht branch of Social Democracy that had its roots in the People's Party. The latter party soon collapsed into insignificance in Nuremberg, as it did almost everywhere.[92]

Although this turn to the left marks the emergence of working-class consciousness in Nuremberg as a political force, the number of workers involved was still very small. The Workers' Educational Association began with only fifty-seven members. Of these, seventeen, or about 30 percent, came from the metal trades (four brass and bell molders, three tinsmiths, three locksmiths, two tin molders, one polisher, one watchmaker, one wire drawer, one toolsmith, and one gold beater).[93] At least one tinsmith was a master, as undoubtedly were a few others. A few radical masters could always be found in the ranks of the labor movement —usually small masters with few or no employees. Judging from the seventeen occupations, almost all came from the artisanal rather than the industrial sector. The membership of the association later rose to over a hundred, but its significance was still obviously not great. Organizing even a large minority of Nuremberg metal- and other workers would take decades. In the 1860s, only a small minority were politicized thoroughly —a few hundred in the Workers' Educational Association and the Workers' Association—and a somewhat larger number may at least have seen the relevance of political activity to their lives. But this level of activity was scarcely higher than that during the Revolution. The 1860s were mainly a period of revival and recovery from the effects of a decade of heavy-handed repression after 1849.

As in the revolutionary years, the 1860s had little trade-union activity, except a printers' wage movement in 1863, a tailor's strike in 1865, a bakers' wage movement in 1866, and the ambiguous gold beaters' association of 1865 mentioned above. Since unionism developed very slowly in Germany before 1868–1869, this is not surprising. Further reasons may be sought in the threat of police action (the tailors' strike was summarily crushed by the city), the attitude of the Nuremberg liberals, and the apathy of the majority of journeymen. Until 1861 organizing and striking remained criminal acts in Bavaria and were punishable, at least in theory, by jail or corporal punishment. But the abolition of this law seems to have had no effect, and until 1869 the possibility of forming a union that would not be immediately closed down as politically dangerous was very small.[94] For those strongly influenced by the liberal labor movement, the clearly subsidiary role they played there and the liberals' conception of the associations as purely educational organizations for creating good citizens and obedient followers hindered the development of class consciousness and the realization that wages, hours, and working conditions were changeable or connected to their inferior class position. For the apathetic majority, the absence of any idea that their conditions might be altered was fundamental; the acquisition of trade-union consciousness had to precede all conceptions of class and social position. Many obstacles, such as employer and state repression, a narrow craft consciousness born of relative privilege, or conversely, an apathy born of exploitation and lack of bargaining power, stood in the way. From the birth of the trade unions in Nuremberg in 1869, organizers of the metal trades faced innumerable problems—problems that reveal more about the peculiarities of the various metalworking crafts, the transformation of journeymen, and the nature of their consciousness than do the weak strivings of the labor movement before 1869. The next chapter will examine these difficulties more closely.

A World Transformed

In the thirty-four years from 1835 to 1868 the world of metalworking journeymen, like that of all journeymen, was decisively transformed, producing a decisive transformation of consciousness—if mostly *after* 1868. The decay and eventual abolition of the quasi-guild system in 1868, the impact of capitalism, industry, and work discipline, the negative repercussions of rapid population growth and rural migration to the cities, the damaging effects of decades of political repression—all combined to undermine the cohesiveness of the artisan estate and the viability of the old journeymen's subculture. Traditions of solidarity, craft consciousness, and mutual aid survived, but new elements were also added—above all a limited awareness both of the injustice and changeability of the journeyman/ skilled worker's inferior social position and of the relevance of political activity in support of the liberal reformers. The first hints of class consciousness also appeared, a consciousness springing from the slow class formation process that would eventually cut off most Nuremberg workers from their former leaders and bring Social Democratic dominance of city politics, if not city hall. Although the 1870s did not see the culmination of working-class consciousness in Nuremberg, that decade certainly did see a fundamental change. Metalworking journeymen were rapidly becoming workers—if relatively well-off skilled workers. The old journeymen's world, which had survived centuries of change and struggle, was rapidly disappearing.

# 3

**THE HESITANT BEGINNINGS OF TRADE UNIONISM**

"As a sign of the times," the Nuremberg city chronicler recorded the following incident in mid-August 1869:

> The bell molder Braun gave his workers a festive meal in honor of the marriage of his daughter. At this meal one worker toasted the young married couple and another the master. At that point the worker Faas [*sic*], who had earlier sent out the call for the international [metal]workers' congress, rose and replied that the workers and not the master actually deserved the toast, because they made the masters rich. At that the Braun family got up and left the table. The next day, when Faas appeared for work, he was sent away, and despite the earnest pleading of his wife was no longer accepted. The other workers also declared themselves against rehiring him, so he and his wife lost weekly earnings of 20 fl. [*sic*].[1]

Johann Faaz's radicalism, and his isolation, are well symbolized by this event. Only four months earlier he had organized the first metalworkers' union of the nascent Bebel-Liebknecht wing of the Social Democratic movement. By so doing he captured for Nuremberg the honor of being one of the most important centers of the early union movement in the metal trades. But his creation, an industrial union—here defined as an organization open to all workers in an industry, skilled or unskilled, regardless of the union's actual membership composition—was not successful.[2] The power of craft tradition and employer repression and the inability of the union to deliver concrete benefits to its members kept its size very small before its dissolution with the coming of the Socialist Law in 1878.

Nevertheless, in spite of this ultimate frustration, the year 1869 marks a significant turning point in the history of the Nuremberg skilled metalworkers. The appearance of the first unions and the Social Democratic Party in that year was the beginning of a slow and tortuous evolution toward an eventually quite powerful socialist labor movement in Nuremberg. That year also marks the conclusion of significant legal and political reforms begun the previous year by the Bavarian government. Those reforms not only helped to encourage labor organization but also completed the transformation of Bavaria into a state based upon liberal economic principles. Before we turn to the appearance of unionism in the metal trades, we must first examine the ambiguous nature of this social, economic, and political transformation.

### The Reforms of 1868–1869 in Bavaria

The 1868 law abolishing the guilds, and with them almost all restrictions on apprenticeship or mastership, was probably the most thorough-going and symbolically important reform passed by the liberal ministry of Prince Hohenlohe in 1868–1869. With its passage capitalism was no longer restrained in its development by legal obstacles. Yet the concrete impact of this law, especially in Nuremberg, was rather slight. Since the relaxation of the old law in 1862, new licenses had been handed out rather liberally in the city, and many of the guilded trades had become free ones.[3] Of greater impact in 1868–1869 were related changes in the marriage, settlement, citizenship, and local government laws. These reforms were significant not only for what they did but also for what they did not do, since their moderate nature left the creation of a liberal political system far from complete. Legal and political discrimination against workers and other members of the lowest income groups remained a central fact in Bavarian society, as it did elsewhere in Germany.

To finish the work of the Trades Law of January 30, 1868, that eliminated the guilds, a Heimat law was necessary to change the marriage and settlement laws. The new law, passed on April 25 of that same year, abolished "settlement" and, most significantly, the power to deny marriage applications. The immediate results were not surprising: the marriage rate shot up and the city's illegitimacy rate dropped from 23 percent in 1868–1869 to 16 percent in 1875. The concept of Heimat was not abolished, however. Every Bavarian continued to have an original "hometown" inherited from his or her parents. Communities were only obliged to give poor relief or other aid to those with local Heimat rights. Others could be forced to leave. After five years of continuous residence, males with independent households had a right to Heimat in a new community; those who were dependent, like servants and journeymen living with their employers, had to wait ten years. Marriage converted the "original" Heimat right to an "independent" one, with correspondingly greater rights in the community. These individuals were the equivalent of the old Insasse, or those who had received "settlement" in a community.[4]

Because the communities were allowed to charge fees for changing one's status, this system perpetuated many of the inequalities of the old system, despite the significant progress inherent in the removal of the communal veto over marriage and residence. In Nuremberg the fees charged for acquiring independent Heimat rights were actually increased for the poorest applicants—to a minimum of twenty-four Gulden, when ten Gulden per week was a good wage. This was greater than the cost of settlement before 1868. Other charges, for example for the acquisition of rights by individuals without an original Heimat in Nuremberg, were even steeper. These high fees presented a barrier to marriage, because application for a marriage license entailed obtaining independent Heimat rights. This could present significant financial obstacles for workers in bad times, as happened after 1873. Although the primary motivation of the city was not to restrict births or immigration, as had been the Malthusian intent of the old legislation, the state took over none of the poor-relief burden from the communities in 1868–1869. Nuremberg, therefore, like other municipalities, wished to maintain this source of revenue and limit its poor-relief expenditures. The net result was that those without means continued to face considerable discrimination when it came to residence and marriage.[5]

The second-class citizenship of lower-class males was only reinforced by the lack of any major political reforms. (Women, of course, had few rights independent of their husbands and fathers.) The new local government law of April 29, 1869, expanded the independence of the city government and eased the qualifications necessary to become a Bürger of the community. Yet this status—which alone carried with it the right to vote in local elections—was still conditional upon the maintenance of an independent household, the possession of local Heimat rights, and the payment of direct taxes to the state, something only those of lower-middle-class income or higher usually paid. Considerable fees were also charged, and the successful applicant had to outfit himself completely as a member of the reserves. In practice, workers were excluded from any influence over the city government, a situation reinforced by the city council's decision to retain the at-large, winner-take-all election of the outer council (*Gemeindebevollmächtigten*) after 1869. Not until the law was changed could the SPD gain seats on the council in the election of 1908. In the 1870s there were only some six thousand Nuremberg "citizens" in a city of over ninety thousand people.[6] Supported by this undemocratic franchise, the Nuremberg Progressives maintained their political hegemony over the city until the Weimar years, but at the cost of alienating the great majority of workers.

The significance of this legal and political discrimination, which was buttressed by the limited franchise for statewide elections and the weakness of parliamentary institutions in Bavaria and in the Empire after 1871, lies in the extent to which it reinforced the processes of politicization and class formation that had been under way for three decades or more. Though on the one hand the liberalization of Bavaria promoted both the development of industrial and putting-out capitalism and the politicization of all sectors of society, on the other hand the incompleteness of this liberalization increased class antagonisms and a feeling of social isolation among workers. The social formation of the working class in Nuremberg —a process reinforced by the relative homogeneity of the city's laboring population—proceeded all the faster because of the open discrimination felt by workers in their dealings with the city and the state. As elsewhere in Germany, the failure of the Bavarian liberals to achieve (or even to demand) manhood suffrage and parliamentary rule undermined the basis for a liberal-reformist labor movement and increased the class consciousness of workers. Inevitably this was to have effects, however slow and subtle, on trade-union organization too, for an increased consciousness of class could not but help to decrease the distance between skilled and unskilled workers and erode the barriers erected by craft consciousness among the skilled workers themselves.

The Founding of the First Metalworkers' Unions

The ambiguous liberalization of 1868–1869 also had an impact upon the ability of workers to organize. Although, as noted earlier, punishment for striking had already been abolished in 1861, the practical effects had been nil. The Association Law of 1850 proved to be a considerable obstacle to any organizational effort among workers, because any discussion of "public affairs" (*öffentliche Angelegenheiten*) made an association liable to be declared "political," after which it was closely watched and forbidden to have formal connections with other associations. Only after the opinion percolated through the Bavarian state bureaucracy in 1868–1869 that employee-employer relations were private and not public matters could unions be safely formed as nonpolitical associations.[7] This new freedom to organize was not unlimited, however. The Association Law could and would be used against socialist unions many times in the future, often in an arbitrary manner, as would sections of the Imperial Trades Ordinance that came into force in Bavaria on January 1, 1873. That ordinance put the freedom to organize and strike on a firmer legal foundation, while at the same time stipulating stiff penalties under section 153 for pressuring or threatening the unorganized or strikebreakers.[8] In practice the right to organize and strike was thereby limited, because the Nuremberg police and city government showed little more compunction than other authorities in the new Reich when it came to using these provisions to obstruct picketing in controversial strikes and to harass union organizers.

Despite these limitations, the greater freedom to organize that arose with the reforms of 1868–1869 was undoubtedly a factor in the appearance of the first unions in Nuremberg. This may have been bolstered by the general character of the ambiguous liberalization, which both impressed politically conscious workers with the possibilities for change and disappointed them with the limits of actual reform. As we saw in Chapter 2, the years before 1869 were ones of great political turmoil that led to an erosion of liberal support and the emergence of socialist ideas in the Workers' Educational Association. Disappointment with liberal performance in Bismarck's "revolution from above" and with liberal attitudes toward universal suffrage and the "social question" (that is, the social problems created by capitalism and industrialization) prompted a radical minority to accept the leadership of Bebel and the program of the First International. Out of this small group, almost all of whom were journeymen in the artisanal sector, came the first socialist union leaders in Nuremberg. In August 1869 Johann Faaz joined four other Nuremberg delegates at the Eisenach founding congress of Bebel and Liebknecht's new Social Democratic Workers' Party (SDAP).[9] At the same time, workers who remained sympathetic to the Progressive and People's parties also gradually became interested in unions because of the inadequacy of left-liberal remedies of "self-help" cooperatives financed without state aid. The catalyst to action for both groups was the launching of union-organizing campaigns by all factions of the German labor movement in late 1868.

Until that year the development of unionism in Germany had been limited to a few large north German cities, and unions had arisen largely independent of either the socialist or the liberal strands of the movement. Organization against employers did not correspond to the conception of the bourgeois liberals, who constantly asserted the harmony of the interests of labor and capital. For their part, the Lassalleans in ADAV were fettered by anti-union dogma inherited from Ferdinand Lassalle (who died in 1864). But spurred by the successes of the cigar makers and the printers—the first German national unions—the Lassalleans, the liberals, and those in the emerging Bebel-Liebknecht secession from the liberals all turned their attention toward union organization as a means of bettering the lot of workers or winning more adherents to their cause. Following the organization of Lassallean unions in August 1868, the left liberals Max Hirsch and Franz Duncker issued their "model statutes" for liberal unions in October, and similar statutes were published by Liebknecht's Leipzig newpaper, the *Demokratisches Wochenblatt,* in November. Reaction was slow but within a few months even south Germany was drawn into the new enthusiasm for trade unions.[10]

The first union in Nuremberg since the Revolution (discounting the ambiguous gold beaters' association mentioned in Chapter 2) was actually formed some months earlier—a printers' union in February 1868. But following the opening of the fall campaigns a number of unions were formed. The first and only Lassallean organization in Nuremberg, a carpenters' union, was founded in December, followed shortly thereafter by a liberal-inspired shoemakers' association. Bookbinders' and joiners' unions appeared in March 1869.[11]

On April 10, 1869, Faaz reported to the police the formation of the Union (Gewerksgenossenschaft) of German Metalworkers. As the name indicates, he wished to form not merely a local union but rather a national one—the second national metalworkers' union after the ADAV-controlled General German Metalworkers' Union, formed in August 1868. The statutes of Faaz's group were essentially the model statutes of the Eisenachers, specifying that all metalworkers could be members, including small masters with no more than one helper. Members were to be supported in case of firing or poverty, and an illness and burial fund, a wanderers' support fund, and an invalid and old age fund were all to be created. The statutes thus stressed mutual aid and a continuance of many of the functions of the old journeymen's associations. Strikes and higher wages were not named as the principal aims of the union—a realistic stance, given the weakness of the first organizations.[12]

Faaz and his two collaborators in founding the union were brass molders, but this may be more because of the personal influence of Faaz than because of any particular radicalism on the part of the brass molders. The trade itself did not play a large role in the labor movement during the seventies. Faaz had been born in Thuringia in 1838, and had settled and married in Nuremberg. He first appears in the records as one of the fifty-seven members of the Workers' Educational Association at its creation in 1866. In June 1868 he became the vice-chairman of that organization, and not long thereafter he must have joined the First International, as he was already listed a member in the spring of 1869.[13]

As the wedding incident of some months later shows, Faaz was an angry young man. The most revealing document is an advertisment written by him that called for an international metalworkers' congress in Nuremberg from August 14–16, 1869, to found an international union. The manifesto begins:

Colleagues! Brothers!

A profound movement has gripped the workers of all lands; everywhere we look we see that the working people, sighing under the yoke of the exploiting power of capital, have gathered up the courage to rescue themselves from the threat of ruin. Big capital, as the sole owner of our industry, as the possessor of all tools, like a vampire slowly but surely sucks the lifeblood out of the working people; it makes the sole possession of the worker, his labor power, into a commodity, which he must sell to the capitalist for the price of the most meager living. The result is that the most colossal riches are gathered in the hands of a few, while the worker, the creator of all wealth, must settle for a meager wage. It is exactly us—colleagues! brothers!—who suffer the fetters that the so-called modern means of production put on. In our branch this "modern means of production" is the most highly developed; we have those industry barons, who like princes in "the good old days" exercise unlimited control over the workers, who are like slaves. Without means or good fortune we are largely unable to make ourselves independent and become our own employers, we are therefore damned to live in eternal dependence, when we do not help ourselves.[14]

Two things are fascinating about this document. The first is the language, drawn presumably from Marx: labor power as a commodity, the polarization of wealth, and the worker as producer of all wealth. It is possible that Faaz had read some of the works of Marx through his membership in the International. The second is the conclusion. Here we see the lament of the skilled journeyman, the frustrated master artisan. Industrial capitalism is blamed for the inability of most to achieve independence, an ideal clearly still held in esteem. The distance between journeymen and small masters was still not very great; as the provisions of the union's statutes show, these masters were still accepted as quasi-workers. In the seventies the anticapitalist argument would be used again and again by skilled-worker socialists to attract small masters to the movement.

As a result of this call, delegations from north and central Germany, Bavaria, and Switzerland founded the now renamed International Metalworkers' Union in Nuremberg that August. The congress appears to have been a very small affair, with perhaps ten to twenty delegates. In one of the few events worthy of note, the Zurich delegation succeeded in having a strike fund reduced from first to fifth place in the list of goals for the union. Production cooperatives, legal protection for members, and funds for invalids, pensioners, and wanderers were considered to be more important. "A motion for the nonacceptance of small masters into the union, as well as another motion for the nonacceptance of women workers did not even find the necessary support."[15] Unfortunately, details of these last two discussions are unavailable.

The union did not remain international for very long; the Swiss members soon dropped out. In Nuremberg the local union did not achieve any notable successes. At the Eisenach congress in early August Faaz represented ninety-six members; a widely distributed poster attracted only fifty-four workers to a meeting on August 30. It is noteworthy that only skilled metal trades were listed on this poster as a further explanation of the term "metalworkers"—the unskilled were not excluded, simply forgotten. Of the three meeting organizers, two were brass molders and one was a locksmith.[16] Virtually no other information is available on the early composition of the membership. It is only known that two members of the First International, Johann Seischab (1843–1887), a tinsmith and son of a shoemaker, and Friedrich Hegewald, an iron molder, were prominently involved. Seischab later filled many minor posts in the local socialist movement, and Hegewald may have been related to Konrad Hegewald, the prominent bookbinders' leader and Social Democrat. A few other metalworkers, including a wire drawer and a pipemaker, are listed as members of the International in early 1869, but it is not known whether they were also union members.[17]

After August 1869 the union appears to have lapsed into relative inactivity. In November Nuremberg also lost its position as headquarters of the whole organization when a merger was effected with the dissident majority of the Lassallean metalworkers' union. Hanover now took the lead. The obscurity into which the local sank was further deepened with the coming of the Franco-Prussian War in July 1870. The nationalist upsurge among workers that followed severely, if only temporarily, damaged socialist activities all over Germany, and the antisocialist hysteria that ensued in the wake of the Paris Commune of 1871 further injured the party and the unions. It was the fall of 1871 before the socialist movement regained its momentum in Nuremberg.[18]

In the meantime the liberal unionists eventually formed a local of the Trade Union (Gewerkverein) of Machine-Building and Metal Workers in June 1870. Simon Trabert, variously described as a cutler *(Messerschmied)* and locksmith, was the leader and initiator. Of four other identified leaders in 1870, two were locksmiths and two were presumably unskilled (a "machine worker" and a "factory worker")—a very unusual situation for the early unions. Whether this so-called Hirsch-Duncker union attracted larger numbers of unskilled factory workers is unknown. (The liberal unions were watched less closely because their politics were more agreeable to the city fathers—though indeed by the early seventies the Hirsch-Duncker unions had an increasingly tense relationship with the Progressives in Nuremberg and nationally.) From the location of the local's pub and the residences of some of these leaders—all in Wöhrd—it appears likely that the union had a foothold in the main Klett factory in that suburb. Since the liberal unions advocated harmony between labor and capital and admitted employers as members, and since the paternalistic relationship between Cramer-Klett and his workers was quite good, the growth of moderate unionism in the plant would not be particularly surprising. But no great inroads into the factory are indicated by the sources; in fact the Nuremberg local appears to have remained very small and inactive throughout its existence, although no membership figures are available for the early period. In 1880 it had only sixty-one members.[19]

The Hirsch-Duncker union was thus, like its socialist counterpart, a conspicuous failure in attracting a wide measure of support in the Nuremberg metal trades. This must be attributed in part to both unions' industrial-union pretensions, which were a product of their political origins. The very concept "metalworker" was still foreign to metalworking journeymen, and it would take many years of campaigning combined with an accelerating class formation process to win skilled metalworkers to an industrial union. Since many trades had scarcely changed their self-understanding in decades, in the short run Nuremberg unionists would have been better off organizing craft unions. At the beginning of 1870 thirty-four braziers organized a fund to support wandering journeymen —a fund that was essentially identical to the old journeymen's association. Mandatory membership for all journeymen braziers was even included in the statutes—at least until the police told them it was illegal. A Gold and Silver Workers' Association was also founded in 1870, in part as a travel money fund, but appears to have lapsed soon after it began. Although there was no unbroken continuity between any journeymen's associations and craft unions, as appears to have been the case in Hamburg, the mentality of many journeymen was still contained within traditional boundaries.[20]

Craft unionism as a significant competing form of organization appeared first in August 1871, with the general revival of labor movement activity after the end of the war. Perhaps because of the temporary eclipse of the Social Democrats in the wake of the anti-Commune hysteria, and perhaps because of the dogmatic adherence of the small band of socialist unionists to the principle of industrial unionism, it fell to Hirsch-Duncker organizers to launch the new unions. In August and September the tinsmiths and the metal beaters launched local liberal craft unions.[21] Their founding initiated a new wave of union activity and strikes by artisan journeymen. But the most critical event of 1871 was a brief but massive protest by the machine-industry workers at Klett. The fate of this movement tells much about the problems of the early metalworkers' unions in organizing the machine industry. These problems were not to be solved for decades.

## The Klett Movement of 1871

Most mystifying, perhaps, of all the aspects of this movement for the ten-hour day is its sudden appearance, with little advance warning. On October 27 posters appeared calling for a public meeting the next day on shortened work hours at Klett, which had had an eleven-hour day since 1844. They were signed by the bookbinder Johann Hagenbauer, a prominent Social Democrat, "on behalf of the workers of the Cramer-Klett factory."[22] Somehow, in their agitation for the ten-hour day and support for a major strike in the Chemnitz machine industry, the socialists struck a responsive chord in the Klett work force. How long and by what means the workers had been agitated by the socialists is unknown, although a newspaper article on October 21 had already mentioned the possibility of a meeting. In any case the meeting drew 1,200–1,400, in the most conservative estimate: the largest labor movement assemblage so far in the history of Nuremberg.[23]

The socialists used diverse appeals and arguments to sway the Klett workers. The poster picked as its chief villain: "Big industry, the dispossessor of small crafts, which will degrade us to true wage slaves, if we do not confront it in time with closed ranks."[24] Like the popularity of state-supported cooperatives for small producers in the ideology of Lassalleans and Eisenachers, and like Faaz's manifesto, this claim again reveals the artisanal character of the early socialist movement—a situation with many parallels in France. At the meeting, the speakers gave the usual arguments for a shorter workday and higher wages as necessary to a human existence and also invoked the names of Lycurgus, Jesus, and Lassalle as fighters for human justice. To enthustiastic applause from the audience, demands were formulated for a ten-hour day, 25 percent extra for overtime, fixed piece rates, the elimination of fines, and a two-hour lunch break.[25]

Just before the meeting, however, von Cramer-Klett (now ennobled) had issued a proclamation that undercut the whole movement. He granted the first two demands and promised wage revisions in view of the recent and rapid inflation, efforts to reduce the increasingly serious housing shortage, and a workers' committee of men with over eight years' employment in the factory. He concluded with the statement that basic to the factory was the principle that relations between the company and the workers were an "internal matter [*häusliche Angelegenheit*]" and that no "external interference" would be tolerated. As one historian aptly described it, this declaration was written "in the style of a benevolent proclamation by a ruling prince to his subjects."[26] A further proclamation appeared on November 4, promising limitations on the amount of overtime and Sunday work, retroactive wage increases to October 30, and company payment of the one kreutzer per week deduction for the firm's benevolent fund.[27]

The intelligent tactic of granting almost all the demands of the workers, but as a personal favor, rather than as an agreement between equals, effectively destroyed the momentum the socialists had created. At the same time the stick was shown as well as the carrot. Four agitators in the factory were fired, and von Cramer-Klett used his considerable personal influence to harass the Social Democrats. Local printers refused to print the poster calling for a November 5 meeting, and it proved difficult to rent a hall. That meeting drew only two hundred persons, and the combative rhetoric was largely bravado. The Klett movement disappeared as suddenly as it had begun.[28]

Two aspects of this movement are striking: its spontaneity and its uniqueness. The sources being what they are, the events leading up to the October 28 meeting will be forever inaccessible. It appears, however, that it was the elementary justice of the demand for ten hours that most impressed the Klett work force. Demands for higher wages in view of the rapid inflation that had recently begun do not appear to have been much of a factor, in contrast to the artisanal protests and strikes that would occur in 1872. Klett's relatively high wages, which had been rising with the company's great boom in production since the mid-1860s,[29] may have contributed to the lack of protest on this score. Once the basic demand for shorter hours had been granted, the force went out of the movement.

The speed with which the workers abandoned the protest must also be related to the uniqueness of the event. There had been no comparable protests in decades. The Klett labor force was, on the whole, very docile before 1900, and it is quite surprising that the 1871 movement occurred at all. This docility was the product of many factors. We have already seen that the machine-industry workers were divided by locational segregation into separate workshops and by marked status and pay differences among skilled, semiskilled, and unskilled workers. These divisions obstructed the growth of factory solidarity and class consciousness. Docility was also a product of the particular characteristics of the Klett factory itself: employer paternalism, social welfare measures, and power springing from the large size of the firm.

Compared to other large firms in Germany, especially those of the iron and steel barons of the Ruhr, like Krupp, the social measures of von Cramer-Klett were modest and the control he exercised over his workers was relatively mild. But especially during the late sixties and early seventies, the dominance of the factory in the Nuremberg labor market (with a peak of over three thousand employees in 1872–1873), when combined with good wages, social measures, and the 1871 concessions, brought von Cramer-Klett considerable loyalty, or at least docility, from his workers. Beginning in 1855 he had founded and supplemented a benevolent fund for injured workers and the relatives of those killed in accidents. Later he added a school to help the children of employees increase their chances of entering trade schools, gave coke and waste wood for fuel at half price, and paid 5 percent interest on savings deposited in a savings plan. After the 1871 movement, he built twenty-nine houses with 154 apartments for loyal employees and paid grade-school fees for the children of workers.[30] Adequate protection for workers from sickness, old age, injury, and unemployment was still nonexistent, and all benefits were provided at the sufferance of the firm, which could fire malcontents at will. But still, by the standards of the time, these efforts were not trivial.

Von Cramer-Klett's charity seems to have won him some respect; even in the socialist newspaper his good intentions were sometimes defended by workers. An anonymous correspondent in 1873 wrote: "Herr v. Cramer is himself a far more humane man than all his pashas, mandarins, and other creatures put together."[31] As was so often the case in these letters, anger was vented against individual foremen or engineers as a result of the often arbitrary power they wielded over hiring, firing, wages, and piece rates. The "foreman system" so typical of late nineteenth-century industry thus also served to direct anger toward foremen and managers while protecting the reputation of the owners.[32] In the case of von Cramer-Klett, his reputation for humanity sometimes resembled the medieval myth of the good king deceived and deluded by his advisors.

Other than such complaints, nothing further was heard from the Klett workers for many years. The mayor, among others, believed in the mid-seventies that the Social Democrats had the loyalty of the majority of workers in the factory,[33] but this is doubtful, except perhaps at Reichtag election time when they could vote for Karl Grillenberger (1848–1897), the charismatic locksmith and socialist leader who began running for the seat in 1874. Otherwise the behavior of the Klett workers was completely passive, a situation reinforced by the drastic decline in the fortunes of the company after the overexpansion of its railcar capacity before the 1873 market crash. Total employment at the plant sank from over three thousand to under one thousand between 1873 and 1880 (see Figure 1.1). The incessant layoffs embittered many workers but left them absolutely powerless. Those who were not laid off—primarily the older, more experienced skilled workers with long service to the company—naturally wished to protect their jobs and their company benefits.[34] Thus, ironically, as the fortunes of the party among workers rose with unemployment, the activity of unionists in the plant fell as the result of it.

For similar reasons union and strike activity in other machine-industry factories was also minimal after 1874, but it is surprising how poorly the metalworkers' unions fared in that sector before 1874. Individual leaders worked in the industry; Grillenberger, for example, was employed at Klett from 1870 to 1873 and was probably at least marginally involved in the 1871 movement, although he did not emerge as a speaker until 1872.[35] Nonetheless there was not a single machine-industry strike in the 1870s. Only in the aftermath of the events at Klett in 1871 is it reported that the workers of the Häberlein foundry and machine factory demanded and got a raise and a ten-hour day.[36] No other movements for higher wages are recorded.

Berlin, in contrast, had not only had a machine-industry workers' union in 1848, but had also had another since 1866 that provided a basis for the organization of the Hirsch-Duncker national union. Because of a long-entrenched policy of cooperation between the skilled-worker elite and the machine-industry employers in Berlin, liberal unionism grew until a series of strikes from 1871 to 1874, primarily over wages, destroyed cooperation and thereby undermined the basis for the reformist union. The Lassalleans rapidly conquered the industry by 1874, but the depression that set in with the 1873 crash dealt a serious blow to all organizations. The socialist union thereafter was weak.[37]

Explaining why Nuremberg and Berlin developed so differently is not easy. Certainly the dominant role played by the Klett factory in Nuremberg obstructed the development of organization there. Berlin had a huge machine industry with many small and medium-sized firms, which were more conducive to organization because the owners possessed much less capital and power to use in conflicts. A second likely factor is the power of artisanal tradition or craft consciousness. In Bavaria the retention of guilds in many trades until 1868 must have helped to keep journeymen/skilled workers closer to their original craft identities; in Prussia, by contrast, partial trade freedom had existed since Napoleonic times. Third, the social formation of the working class had already proceeded much farther before the Revolution in Berlin than in Nuremberg,[38] and thus skilled workers in the Prussian capital must have had a stronger class identity, however weak, than skilled workers in the Nuremberg machine industry. In the dialectic of craft and class, the contradictions between craft and class consciousness in Nuremberg seem still to have far outweighed any mutual reinforcement. Only when craft consciousness led to union organization and strike activity in the eighties and nineties did it tend to stimulate increased allegiance to class.

The Klett movement was an energetic but short-lived upsurge that helped revitalize the Social Democrats but failed to bring them lasting support among the Klett workers. What little interest in unionism that did exist, whether socialist or nonsocialist, was found among craft workers.

## The Rise of Craft Unionism and Strikes

Rather than in the machine industry or in other large factories, the upsurge in union and strike activity in the metal trades was concentrated almost entirely within the artisanal sector. Craft unionism, although never more than modest in size, grew quickly after the formation of the Hirsch-Duncker tinsmiths' and metal beaters' organizations in the summer of 1871, and a small strike wave ensued in 1872. The tinsmiths perhaps excepted, these strikes occurred in crafts or sections of crafts that were largely artisanal: the construction locksmiths, the metal beaters, the tinsmiths, and the blacksmiths. Four other primarily artisanal trades did not strike but did form craft unions by 1873: the mathematical instrument makers, the brass molders, the wire drawers, and the gold beaters.

This journeymen activism may be attributed primarily to three factors: (1) the rapid inflation of 1871–1873, which brought with it demands for higher wages; (2) the simultaneous severe shortage of skilled workers because of the boom, which gave craftsmen considerable leverage in the labor market; and (3) the greater solidarity within these trades, which derived from their relative cohesion in spite of the intrusion of capitalist relations between journeymen and masters. When open differences between masters and men erupted, journeymen could still draw on traditional craft identities and personal knowledge of other members of their craft because the transformation of production had not proceeded very far. They were not paralyzed by the heterogeneity of the work force that confronted their compatriots in the machine industry.

The inflationary boom also meant that journeymen concentrated on improvements in wages and hours. With the slow but inexorable death of living-in, most journeymen became dependent solely on wages, and thus more sensitive to the market. But this is not surprising. What is surprising from the standpoint of British, French, or North American labor history is the absence of strikes or union organizations devoted to the maintenance of control over apprenticeship rules, work rules, or authority on the shopfloor. The policies of Nuremberg and Bavaria, like those of all German governments, had long favored the privileges and authority of guild masters and by extension industrial employers as well, because the authority of masters and employers was seen as necessary to an authoritarian social and political structure. Thus German journeymen did not have many craft controls and privileges to defend, a situation that weakened their power but made them less likely to hold on to corporate traditions and craft exclusivity and more likely to be open to radical ideas and multicraft and industrial unionism.[39]

All union and strike activity between 1869 and 1905 are summarized in Appendixes A and B. It is clear that the liberal (Hirsch-Duncker) unionists dominated the founding of new unions between 1871 and 1873 (see section 1, Appendix A). The Social Democrats held to their one organization, and initially no craft unions were even sympathetic to them, although the organizational meeting for the Trade Union of Tinsmiths on August 5, 1871, featured a controversy between the numerous socialists present and the journeyman tinsmith J. M. Nüssel, soon to be the leader of the local Hirsch-Dunckerites. The socialist tinsmith Johann Seischab and his compatriots did not succeed in capturing the meeting, but their presence foreshadowed later power struggles that would eventually result in the defection of the union to the socialist camp.[40]

Most craftsmen who organized, in contrast, were still unwilling to break fundamentally with their masters and the Progressive Party. Compared to Britain, German liberalism lost its working-class base remarkably quickly because of the events of the late sixties and the strength of the class formation process,[41] yet it clearly still held the allegiance of many Nuremberg journeymen before 1873. The recent war and anti-Commune hysteria must have had lingering effects upon the popularity of officially condemned Social Democratic ideas, and the Progressives (and remnants of the People's Party) could draw upon a strong ideological commitment to economic and political liberalism built up in the 1860s among many artisans. Traditional deference to the highly educated liberal notables did not disappear instantly, and adherence to moderate ideas had an economic foundation as well in the better relations of employees to employers in some industries, as with the Berlin machine-industry craftsmen before 1871. In Nuremberg the most faithful adherents of liberal unionism were the metal and gold beaters, who still had a large measure of independence and a relatively high standard of living under the prevailing piece-rate system. The willingness of the beaters to accept cooperation with their masters was reinforced by the unique structure of these trades resulting from putting-out capitalism. The small masters were almost completely dependent on the merchants who advanced them capital and materials and sold their products in foreign markets. In addition, it was still relatively easy for journeymen to borrow money from the putters-out to become small masters. Journeymen and masters were thus inevitably not as sharply divided as they became in most trades, and the two groups even cooperated occasionally in the three-cornered struggles among workers, employers, and putters-out in the seventies and later. The metal beaters, perhaps as a result of their financially weaker situation, organized first in early fall 1871, but only about one-quarter of the approximately one hundred journeymen in the trade were members. Eighty gold beaters launched their own liberal union in early 1873, but it was not active and lasted only three years. It was controlled by the older journeymen, who excluded from membership those with less than three years' experience. This elitism may explain the inactive and short-lived nature of the union.[42]

A few neutral or formally apolitical craft unions and quasi-journeymen's associations also appeared in the seventies. Disregarding the ephemeral braziers' and gold and silver workers' associations of 1870, the first was created by the mathematical instrument makers *(Reißzeugmacher)*. On November 11, 1871, forty-three of the approximately one hundred journeymen in the trade met "regarding a wage raise." The chairman stated that "the mathematical instrument makers were not any less hurt by the increased rents, etc., than journeymen of other trades and therefore could not any longer hold back with their demands for wage hikes."[43] The actions of other workers, including those at Klett, were clearly a motivating factor. After a disorganized debate lacking political content, demands for a 25 percent raise and a lowering of the current eleven-hour day were decided on. A few weeks later an agreement was made with the employers granting the first demand only. In February 1872 an "Association of Mathematical Instrument Makers in Nuremberg" was constituted by fifty-nine members of the trade, including small masters, who were also allowed to join. In fact two master compass makers *(Zirkelschmiede)*—an outdated name for the craft—held the first two offices in the union. It appears to have been very inactive and completely apolitical, but it survived until 1879.[44]

The activity of the mathematical instrument makers foreshadowed the small wave of strikes over inflation in 1872, as did a movement among the tinsmiths. The Hirsch-Duncker union had circulated ambitious wage demands, but because of the "stubborn resistance" of the "greater part of the employers" the tinsmiths were forced to back down when they met on November 25. Lack of support may explain the timidity: only thirty-four men appeared at the meeting. The approaching winter may have caused some second thoughts too. At this meeting the acceptance of women workers was also discussed, but owing to lack of interest the matter was not pursued further. In none of the crafts where large numbers of women were employed, such as toymaking and the beating trades, did skilled workers show much interest in the seventies in organizing their female helpers. Even in the socialist party a decidedly unemancipated doctrine was still the rule. Women were to be organized, but in a socialist society they were to be returned to their "natural" occupations: wives and mothers.[45]

The spring of 1872 brought renewed activity for higher wages in view of the worsening inflation. According to the index constructed by Rainer Gömmel, the cost of living rose in Nuremberg (on a scale in which 1910–1913 equals 100) from 63.7 in 1870 to 84.1 in 1873, before leveling off with the depression in the late seventies.[46] The index jumped 9.4 points or 13.5 percent from 1871 to 1872 alone, because of the overheated boom fueled by reparation money extracted from France. Under this inflationary pressure wage movements began in two of the largest trades: the locksmiths and brass molders. The locksmiths eventually progressed to a strike in cooperation with the socialists, but the wage movement (a campaign for higher wages) of the brass molders immediately bogged down in infighting over craft versus industrial unionism. At the first meeting on March 17, which attracted fifty journeymen plus a few unskilled laborers and Social Democrats from other trades, a debate immediately ensued over the presence of the outsiders, and any involvement with the socialist metalworkers' union was rejected. A committee of antisocialists was picked to draft statutes for a union, but a week later Faaz intervened and almost succeeded in capturing a meeting with the argument that the local craft union would be isolated and lacking in strike funds, which the International Metalworkers could provide. He was elected to another committee, which eventually came back in April with a compromise draft for a local craft union with ties to both the socialist and the Hirsch-Duncker unions. Faaz, forced to retreat, made the argument that the union would seek no ties to the International Metalworkers immediately, but might have to do so in a strike. Even this local craft union, however, did not come to fruition. Without explanation, nothing happened for months, and then at the beginning of 1873 a neutral craft organization was founded. In perhaps the strictest language of any statutes, this union admitted only "those who have been fully trained in the brass molding trade, and can present a proper apprenticeship certificate." Traditional craft consciousness had triumphed, but this did not suffice either to achieve a wage increase or to create a stable organization. The union dissolved in 1874.[47]

The locksmiths in the artisanal sector of the trade—ornamental ironwork and construction—were open to cooperating with the socialists, although they ultimately proved as indifferent to industrial unionism as the brass molders had. The locksmiths' movement, led by the socialist Albrecht Wolf, had by March 10 already led to the circulation of demands for a 25 percent raise and a ten-hour day. An independent union was ruled out and locksmiths were encouraged to join the International Metalworkers, to which twenty of their compatriots already belonged (whether from artisanry or industry is unknown). One meeting drew eighty, and the next drew sixty, of the approximately one hundred journeymen in the artisanal sector, and on April 2 a strike was begun. Unfortunately its resolution is unknown, although some strikers were still out almost two months later, and some did win their demands. But the socialist union, which provided strike support, did not ultimately benefit. A year and a half later Grillenberger complained that his fellow locksmiths had profited from socialist support and then turned around and ignored the union. Few, if any, had joined the International Metalworkers. Without an organization the achievements of 1872 were soon lost, a pattern that would often be repeated.[48]

The locksmiths' strike was shortly followed by a successful six-day strike in late April by the Hirsch-Duncker metal beaters, who also wanted a wage increase. Because many of the masters had already acceded to the demands, only two larger firms with fifty metal beaters were struck. Perhaps the most interesting aspect is not the strike itself, about which we know little, but rather the rationale for striking offered by the Hirsch-Duncker leader, Nüssel, in a meeting. He condemned strikes in principle, in line with policies of the liberal unions, but defended this strike in practice because of the "rising living costs and the constant oppression of workers." The strike was necessary to achieve just demands, he claimed. The only difference between the Hirsch-Dunckerites and the Social Democrats was that the liberal unionists did not try to politicize the "worker question." In another 1872 speech he attacked the capitalists and speculators for the severe housing shortage, and in 1873 was even quoted as saying that the Progressive Party was useless and that he would rather vote for the Social Democrats.[49] His alienation reflected the growing gulf between the Hirsch-Duncker unions and the liberals, who were hostile to any unions at all in a political situation increasingly polarized, nationally and locally, along class lines. Nüssel's rhetorical radicalism may also have reflected pressure on the liberal unionists to act in defense of workers' rights when the doctrine of harmony between employers and employees was betrayed by the stubbornness of the employers.

Such stubbornness prompted Nüssel to lead his own union—the tinsmiths—into the second Hirsch-Duncker strike of the year. A wage movement begun in June managed to attract 114 of some 300–400 journeymen tinsmiths to a meeting at which the leadership formulated demands for a 15 percent raise for those on time wages, and 25 percent more for those on piece rates. The rank and file said little. This quiescence may account for the ultimate results of the strike. The continued refusal of the employers to cooperate led to a strike on July 22, but it appears to have petered out by the end of August.[50] The number of strikers is unknown, but it is probable that the relatively large size and heterogeneity of the craft, with its multiple bases in the toy industry, light metalworking, and construction, made the task of organizing and maintaining an effective strike much more difficult than had been the case with the metal beaters or the construction locksmiths—or, for that matter, with the blacksmiths, whose strike was yet to come.

This failure may ultimately have eroded the liberals' position in the tinsmiths' union, but it is clear that liberal unionism was still thriving in 1872 and 1873. Only with the depression that began in late 1873 did the fortunes of the Hirsch-Duncker movement start to diminish. Although the socialist unions were also hit very hard, the depression helped to turn many workers to the left, a development accelerated by the enormous popularity of Grillenberger as party leader. Ultimately the rise of the Social Democrats to dominance in Nuremberg working-class politics set the stage for the recovery of socialist unionism in the eighties and nineties. The Hirsch-Duncker unionists, meanwhile, were saddled with their anti–class conscious doctrine in the face of a class formation process that continually reinforced the dominance of socialism in Nuremberg. Liberal unionism was never again to be as significant as it had been in 1871–1873.

The last metal-trades strike of 1872—indeed the last before 1874—came from the highly traditional blacksmiths. In this case it appears that the Social Democrats were responsible for rousing the journeymen to action. A two-day strike in September of all fifty journeymen (employed by twenty-two masters) achieved a 10 percent raise and decreases in hours.

Also abolished was the familiar "Du" form of address for journeymen by masters, which in this context was condescending, paternalistic, and a striking indication of how little conditions in this trade had changed. Forcing the masters to use the polite "Sie" indicated a desire to be treated as equals and adults. This victory did not, however, herald the coming of a new rebelliousness and self-assertiveness to the journeymen black-smiths. Little was heard from this craft for many years, perhaps because of the continuous influx of new, ill-educated blacksmiths from rural areas, as suggested in Chapter 1. The socialists certainly drew little profit from the strike. Some months later Grillenberger denounced the black-smiths as a "miserable" lot for leaving the socialists in the lurch.[51]

The failure of their industrial union to make any significant progress in the metal crafts—a fate shared by the Hirsch-Duncker metalworkers' union—left the Social Democrats quite frustrated. An appeal issued at the end of November 1872 was still relatively polite. It attempted to bring workers to the union by attacking the "arrogant big masters, who let themselves be cursed as industrialists [*Fabrikanten*]." The cause of the so-cialists' outrage was a new master locksmiths' association that sought to use a system of release certificates to control unionists and organizers.[52] An article written by Grillenberger some ten months later, however, heaped scorn on the metal trades for being the most poorly organized:

> It is . . . the metalworkers who are best suited to make a weighty contribution to trade-union action, yet it is exactly among the metalworkers that we find the greatest indifference . . . to the social movement in general. Knowing . . . that they should be the first to understand the union idea because of their constant contact in large factories, one wonders why the organization of the metalwork-ers is so inadequate, and why in comparison with other labor organizations it has accomplished so little. If we ask the reasons for this depressing situation, we are met with the most varied answers. Some believe that the splitting of the workers into different political camps is at fault, others say that the majority of metalworkers still make too much money, they have it too good, etc. Both of these answers are partially correct but are not adequate to solve the problem. On the contrary, there are branches that earn much more than the locksmiths and machine builders but do not have to slave as much as they for that wage, and are well organized to boot, even very well organized. . . . I will only men-tion the printers here. Among the metalworkers the main problem is the anti-quated guild spirit still characteristic of many, which is expressed in the phrase to uphold the honor of the "craft," while looking over one's shoulder at mem-bers of other trades. "I'm a locksmith, I'm a brass molder, I'm a mathematical instrument maker, what do the International Metalworkers have to do with

me?"—one hears such expressions often. On top of that the so-called "artisan journeymen [*Meistergesellen*]" have a partial antipathy toward the "factory types [*Fabriker*]" and vice versa.

He concluded with an unflattering comparison between the powerful journeymen's associations of the old metal trades (the "sooty ones," "these courageous sons of Vulcan") and the current "pitiful cowardly race" of metalworkers.[53]

Although clearly perplexed by the divisions that beset the metalworkers, Grillenberger pinpointed the most important reasons why skilled workers both in metalworking and the machine industry were so badly organized. They were both relatively well off and almost completely fragmented by craft pride and heterogeneous working environments. The printers, in contrast, were a small and homogeneous craft faced with a clear threat of deskilling through mechanization of the printing press. It would have been more accurate to compare them to individual elite metal trades like the iron molders or gold beaters than to the as yet artificial ideological construct "metalworkers." But if one turns to these trades, the same question arises: Why were these elite trades so quiet in contrast to the printers? In all probability the lack of a clear economic or technological threat to either craft was the main reason. The gold beaters did have quiescent unions in the mid-seventies and the eighties, but only as the economic crisis of the beating trades worsened because of the decline of gilding in ornamentation did they become more active. From the iron molders nothing was heard until 1886—at about the time that piece rates and rationalization began to erode their position. It should also be mentioned, of course, that neither trade possessed the remarkable literacy typical of the printers.

Grillenberger himself, based on his extensive experience at Klett, rated technological change as the one force that would wipe out the differences between the crafts. "For example at Klett and Co. do not shoemakers work as locksmiths, former master locksmiths on the other hand as machinists, and other honorable masters from every sort of guild as day laborers, etc.?"[54] But in his prediction of the imminent demise of skilled labor, Grillenberger, like other socialists in the seventies, was far ahead of the facts. Socialist ideological conviction, when combined with strong artisanal values that stressed the importance of good work, led him to see the gradual erosion of the skilled worker's independence, all-round ability, and job control as a very rapid and threatening process.[55] He was correct that there were increasing numbers of poorly trained journeymen in industry like the *Maschinenschlosser* ("machine locksmiths"), as described in another article undoubtedly written by him:

> The locksmiths, the matadors of the "sooty ones [*Russigen*]" have always had a higher reputation than the tailors, for example, although unjustly. And now even the Maschinenschlosser do! . . . [Yet] almost all of them are one-sided. . . . Each makes one part to one instrument, week after week one and the same job. No wonder when they become intellectually crippled and stupid; no wonder, when an otherwise competent and useful all-round worker in his trade constantly goes backward instead of forward in his competence due to monotonous, mechanical and mentally deadening labor.[56]

Many of the craftsmen in the machine industry, however, did not have such uninspiring work, and the artisanal sector was not about to disappear despite the predictions of the socialists. As the failure of industrial unionism and the modest accomplishments of craft unionism in the seventies suggest, the great majority of skilled workers did not feel as endangered by deskilling as did the radical minority. When they took any sort of strike or union action at all, it was only to defend their living standard or to moderate the insecurity of their lives by creating substitutes for the lost benefits of the journeymen's associations.

The results of the modest strike wave of 1872 were thus quite frustrating for the socialist metalworkers, and this was to be doubly confirmed in 1873 when, somewhat mystifyingly, no strikes took place and no significant inroads in new trades were made. In about the only event worthy of note, the Hirsch-Duncker tinsmiths' union, under the influence of its growing socialist minority, participated in the founding of a national tinsmiths' union that would become more and more explicitly Social Democratic by 1875. The Hirsch-Duncker leader Nüssel was eventually removed as chairman in 1874, and from that time on the Nuremberg local may be counted as a socialist union. But the effect upon the size of the organization was probably nil. In 1878 the Nuremberg police estimated that it had only thirty to forty members.[57]

The Failure of the Unions and
the Growth of the Socialist Party

The end of 1873 brought the beginning of the so-called Great Depression of 1873–1896. The name itself is something of a misnomer; the period was not a single depression but rather a prolonged period of slow growth interspersed with sharp recessions, particularly from 1873 to 1879 and 1890 to 1895–1896. In the 1880s the cycle was somewhat milder, with upturns from 1879 to 1882 and from 1886 to 1890. Capital accumulation therefore did not stop, but worsened economic conditions tended to drive out and impoverish more small masters, while other masters profited.[58] Both processes aided the continuing economic and social formation of the working class in Germany by enlarging the size of working class at the expense of independent proprietors and other social classes. Working-class consciousness grew as a result, but its expression came almost entirely within the political sector. In spite of the short-run damage done by the Socialist Law of 1878, the strength of the Social Democratic Party grew from election to election, above all in large Protestant cities like Nuremberg with considerable numbers of skilled workers. As suggested in the Introduction, this was in no small part due to the role of the state in Germany, which through its hostility to socialism ironically contributed to the rise of a class-conscious movement ultimately more united and powerful than those in other Western countries. Not faring so well in the Great Depression era, however, were the unions aligned with Social Democracy. Prolonged periods of high unemployment made stable organizational gains difficult. As long as the labor market remained weak, workers, even in the most privileged trades, did not have much leverage to use in strikes and wage movements. Unions were therefore crippled because they often could not deliver the kinds of concrete benefits necessary to attract the indifferent majority. It was only after 1896 that the socialist unions succeeded in becoming mass organizations.

For the Nuremberg metalworkers' unions the situation was no different. The frustration that ensued from the failure to translate the 1872 upsurge into lasting organizational accomplishments was only deepened by the worsening economic situation in the middle and late seventies. The unemployment rate in the city, as calculated by Rainer Gömmel, rose from 0.8 percent in 1872 to 5.8 percent in 1876 and, at its worst, to 8.0 percent in 1879.[59] Klett's massive layoffs can only have exacerbated the situation for metalworkers in particular. Strikes became exceedingly rare and the unions stagnated or even declined, a not unwelcome development for the employers. The Chamber of Commerce commented in 1876: "In regards to the relations between employers and employees, this period of weak trade has altered it to the benefit of the former, because there is no absolute shortage of workers as there was in the first years after the war, when discipline and obedience were almost impossible to achieve." [60] Discipline and obedience did indeed reign supreme. Workers were left to express their anger at the ballot box, in anonymous letters to the socialist newspaper, or in occasional on-the-job disturbances like a locksmith's physical assault on an arrogant engineer at the Häberlein machine factory in 1876. That incident resulted in the mass firing of the locksmiths and metal turners when they applauded the actions of the culprit rather than throwing him out, as demanded by the owner. [61]

On the organizational front, only three more crafts founded unions before 1878. The filemakers created a very short-lived fund to support traveling journeymen in 1875, and in 1874 and 1876 the metal pressers twice founded unstable organizations to defend their interests as well as to provide benefits similar to the old journeymen's associations. The only new union of consequence was the Locksmith Journeymen's Union of 1877, a product of the long-standing antipathy between artisanal and factory locksmiths already alluded to by Grillenberger. The first statutes of the union stipulated that only journeymen locksmiths working for a master or in factories with fewer than twenty workers would be accepted. In spite of this requirement, the union was loosely affiliated with the socialists. The restriction itself was removed in May 1878. Other than social activities, the union appears to have done nothing. [62] It at least survived until the Socialist Law, unlike many of the other craft unions (e.g., those of the brass molders, expired 1874; the filemakers perhaps in 1875; the metal pressers in 1875 and 1878; the gold beaters in 1876; and the wire drawers in 1877).

Strike activity in this period was also minimal (see Appendix B). Of the four job actions, the only craftwide movement in the style of 1872 was the two-part struggle of the metal beaters in 1874. In response to the chronic overproduction crisis that was just beginning to plague metal beating, the putters-out imposed price cuts that forced the dependent masters to make wage cuts, in violation of the 1872 settlement. A one-month strike supported by the Hirsch-Duncker Berlin headquarters forced the masters to give in. But the crisis was not alleviated in the slightest, and the masters and putters-out were soon talking of wage cuts again. Toward the end of June a near-total strike by Middle Franconian metal beaters—encompassing virtually the entire national production of metal leaf—spread from Schwabach to Nuremberg and then finally to the center of the trade, Fürth. Some one hundred journeymen along with an equal number of female helpers struck in Nuremberg, demanding a 50 percent cut in work time as a solution to overproduction rather than wage cuts to lower prices. In Fürth the strike included some six hundred male and female workers, who characteristically enough for this peculiar craft were encouraged and supported by many of the masters, and even a few putters-out, in the hope that a pause in production would help stop prices for metal leaf from plummeting. The strike ended finally in Fürth in mid-August with wage increases for most workers. The results in Nuremberg are not recorded. But the accomplishments, if any, did not last long. Prices continued to decline over the next few years and the position of the metal beaters was slowly undermined. In 1880 the union had only twenty members.[63]

Judged by the meager number of strikes alone, the militance of workers would seem to have declined drastically in these years before the Socialist Law. Yet the membership of the SDAP (or, as it was called after unification with the Lassalleans in 1875, the SAPD or Socialist Workers' Party of Germany) in the city and its suburbs grew from 123 in 1871 to 536 in 1873, and then to 698 in 1874 and 985 in 1875, when it was the second-largest socialist party organization in Germany. This growth took place despite legal harassment from the city and the state, especially after 1874, when many socialist party organizations were dissolved in Bavaria, including Nuremberg's in April. Substitute organizations were set up, although they too sometimes met the same fate. Repression was no more successful in the electoral realm, where universal suffrage for German men over twenty-five in Reichstag elections gave the Social Democrats their only opportunity to win. In the first election in 1871 Faaz got only 340 votes, but in 1874 Grillenberger garnered 5,355, and in 1877 he received 10,025 in the first round and 12,090 in the runoff. Only the united efforts of all the bourgeois parties staved off victory in that second round, and only by a few hundred votes.

The next summer a new election was called by Bismarck after two assassination attempts on the Kaiser, in order to create a sufficient Reichstag majority to outlaw the Social Democrats. In spite of a hysterical, government-instigated press campaign to equate the socialists with anarchists and assassins, Grillenberger actually gained a hundred votes over his first-round performance in 1877. (Because of the unity of the opposition, there was no runoff.) In 1881, aided by disagreements between the Progressives and the more conservative National Liberals, he finally conquered the seat, which was then held continuously by Social Democrats into the Weimar Republic.[64]

Grillenberger himself had much to do with these victories. By all accounts a brilliant popular orator, able to speak very clearly while at the same time using dialect and popular expressions to appeal to ordinary workers, he built a solid base of support by exploiting the alienation from the city's Progressive Party felt by so many workers and even by many small masters. His charismatic personality and appeal to craftsmen were visible to the socialist journalist Wilhelm Blos at their first meeting in 1872, when Grillenberger was still a skilled worker at Klett:

> His external appearance was still that of a traditional journeyman artisan. . . . He strode in impressively in a black Sunday coat with a not quite modern top hat . . . ; in his hand he carried a walking stick with a large billiard ball. One would take him sooner for a well-off Kleinbürger than a factory worker. But one saw immediately that he was an extraordinary man. In his fresh, regular, friendly face, framed by short blond hair, shone blue eyes of spirit and fire. A sunny hilarity infected his surroundings when told with his sonorous voice anecdotes and jokes, of which he had an endless supply. He could imitate the various dialects with great ability.[65]

Grillenberger's strong streak of reformist populism, which had its roots in his apprenticeship as a guild journeyman in the early 1860s, and in his marriage and personal success after 1874, led him to deemphasize class consciousness and radical rhetoric. He thereby attracted many lower-middle-class voters in addition to his working-class base, and he apparently was even successful in reaching some peasants in the rural parts of the Nuremberg electoral district. He did not garner most of this support through agitation for the party program, which in the 1870s was not Marxist but was still quite radical in advocating a democratic republic with state-supported producer cooperatives as stepping stones to socialism. Rather he emphasized the unfairness of the tax system, the contempt of Bismarck's Reich and the Progressive Party for the interests of the workers and the "little man," and the alleged do-nothing policy of the laissez-faire liberals in the city and elsewhere in the face of mounting unemployment and economic distress. He was aided in his campaign by an energetic, though necessarily often informal and secret, party organization, by his fellow union and party leaders, almost all of whom were journeymen in origin, and by the party newspaper, which he edited after 1873. His tactical genius in combatting city and state harassment and repression also stood him in good stead.[66]

But whatever his talent, organization, and populist appeal, a sense of class identity among workers—however nonrevolutionary—provided his essential base of support. Grillenberger was fortunate to operate within a very favorable environment, marked as it was by the regional homogeneity of the city's population, its Protestant majority, and its large numbers of skilled workers. In this connection it is again useful to compare the example of Augsburg, where after stormy beginnings in 1869–1871, the Social Democratic movement failed to develop into a significant political force. The explanation lies in the character of the local working class, dominated as it was by unskilled Catholic textile workers laboring in large factories. As a result the Augsburg workers were utterly dependent upon the factory owners.[67]

What the victories of the Nuremberg party tell us about the relative strengths of craft and class consciousness among skilled metalworkers is of course difficult to determine. No occupational breakdowns of party membership are available for this period so it is not even possible to determine whether metalworkers were overrepresented or underrepresented in the political wing of the socialist labor movement. A number of prominent leaders were metalworkers—Grillenberger, Faaz, Seischab, and Grillenberger's friend and fellow locksmith Johann Scherm[68]—but the weakness of the unions and persistence of craft snobbery in the metal trades would lead one to suspect that underrepresentation was more likely than the opposite. We simply do not know. It is easy, however, to imagine a skilled metalworker in the late seventies who was simultaneously clannish and proud of his craft while thinking of himself as a worker and a Social Democrat. The two identities were far from mutually exclusive, even if craft consciousness still helped to obstruct industrial unionism from making any progress. But pride in craft was not always to play this role. After the Socialist Law destroyed the unions in October 1878, new local craft organizations were gradually set up. These organizations ultimately unified into an industrial metalwokers' union, albeit one whose power was based on the power of skill and craft. Craft and class consciousness were thus linked in a dialectical process—sometimes weakening, sometimes strengthening each other. How they developed under the conditions of political oppression in Germany from 1878 to 1890 is the subject of the next chapter.

# 4

# REPRESSION, REVIVAL, UNIFICATION

The Socialist Law period was both an interruption and a transition for the socialist movement in Germany. For the first five years after 1878 the repression was so heavy that virtually all activities had to be conducted illegally; this poses problems for the historian, of course, because so many activities went unrecorded. The repression also disrupted and limited the development of the unions throughout the eighties; thus our knowledge is once again limited because of the limitations on public activity. Ironically, the Socialist Law ultimately benefited both the unions and the party: class consciousness received a boost from the open hostility of the authorities to all signs of political independence and dissent among the working class, and the unions benefited in the long run from the enforced limitation to craft organization, mostly at the local level. Beginning in the mid-eighties with the foundation of a number of local craft unions, many of which were politically neutral, a lively if still relatively small movement arose that brought many new skilled workers and trades into organizations. This did not prevent, however, a growing orientation toward the socialist movement and a rising trend toward the acceptance of the unskilled and federation with other crafts, especially in the strike-prone period of 1889–1890. When the Socialist Law expired in 1890, the great majority of socialist craft unions joined a new national industrial metalworkers' union—albeit one with local craft sections.

## The Socialist Law and the Nuremberg Metalworkers' Unions

After Bismarck's orchestrated campaign of antisocialist hysteria, the "Law against the Publicly Dangerous Endeavors of the Social Democracy" came into effect on October 21, 1878, and immediately destroyed the organizational basis of the movement in Nuremberg. In the weeks before final passage of the law, the party's electoral association and most of its affiliated unions voluntarily dissolved. Of the three socialist metalworkers' unions still in existence, the tinsmiths disbanded on September 28, the locksmiths on October 4, and the metalworkers on October 18.[1] Only three unions in the metal trades survived, and of these, the inactive and more or less neutral mathematical instrument makers' organization expired sometime before late February 1879. That left only the two Hirsch-Duncker organizations in existence, but they profited not at all from the disappearance of their Social Democratic rivals. In 1880 the machine-building and metal workers had only sixty-one members; the metal beaters only twenty. Even the metal beaters' union expired in 1882, leaving only one Hirsch-Duncker metalworkers' organization until the equally insignificant Nuremberg local of the Trade Union of German Tinsmiths and Metalworkers (Gewerkverein der deutschen Klempner und Metallarbeiter) was founded in 1888.[2]

As is suggested by the failure of liberal unionism to revive, the greatly increased repression did not succeed in undermining or destroying the continued hold of socialism—however reformist—over politically conscious Nuremberg workers. In the short run the Socialist Law may have hampered the organizational consolidation of the movement in the city, but in the long run it reinforced the feelings of political and social discrimination among Nuremberg workers and the class consciousness that grew out of those feelings. While party activities carried on through informal or secret meetings, singing and educational societies, and open or covert electoral activity, the leadership and the rank and file had to deal constantly with police supervision of all suspicious meeting places and the possibility of spies and informers. But thanks to Grillenberger's clever editing and leadership, and to a lesser extent to the relative liberalism of the Nuremberg authorities after 1883, Grillenberger managed to publish the local party newspaper (which from October 1, 1878, became privately owned under the innocuous name *Fränkische Tagespost*) without interruption through the entire Socialist Law period, a feat unique in Germany. The price, however, was that the *Tagespost* was almost entirely colorless, particularly before 1883. During the eighties the printing plant also sometimes secretly produced part of the run of the illegal party paper, the *Sozialdemokrat*, which was edited in Zurich. Nothing substantial was ever found by the police, although it was not for want of trying. In 1889 the staff brought in a large keg of beer to celebrate the one hundredth police search of the premises![3]

The law had many contradictions—the greatest of which was the ability of socialists to run for and sit in the Reichstag when their party was banned as a dangerous threat. Grillenberger's electoral victory in 1881 occurred in a campaign in which not a single socialist meeting or pamphlet was legally permitted, but this did not stop secret meetings, the distribution of handbills, and the efficient functioning of an informal organization. The campaign and victory energized the local party militants. In 1882 Bismarck and his advisors, spurred by the failure of heavy-handed repression to destroy Social Democracy, and by the hope that social insurance legislation would lure workers away from socialism, introduced what was termed the "mild practice." Meetings and organizations were tolerated within limits. In Nuremberg a local party campaign organization, the Association for the Securing of Popular *(volkstümlicher)* Elections, was founded in late 1883. As in other parts of the country, this period produced serious internal strains in the party over the limits of social reform in Bismarck's Germany. Even the charismatic but rather autocratic Grillenberger was challenged by a rare local party revolt in 1884 over a Reichstag vote; the Nuremberg party activists seem to have been consistently to the left of their leader. But these internal troubles did not affect the SAPD's constantly growing electoral strength. The social legislation was manifestly inadequate, and the continuing petty harassment increased working-class consciousness. In Nuremberg Grillenberger almost gained an absolute majority on the first ballot in 1884, and he did accomplish this in 1887 and in every election thereafter. Similar electoral successes throughout Germany resulted in the reintroduction of heavier repression in early 1886, but this was moderated in Nuremberg by relatively lighter administration of the law by the city council than was typical elsewhere.[4]

After the catastrophe of 1878, the union movement was somewhat slower to revive than the party. In the metal trades there was not much of a movement to revive; the unions of the seventies had failed to build significant organizations because of the economic depression and the apathy of metalworkers. The repression of the late seventies and early eighties then worsened matters by dispersing much of the old union leadership, while the founders of Nuremberg socialism—men like Grillenberger, Scherm, Seischab, and Faaz—had moved into other roles, whether minor or significant, in the party newspaper or ancillary organizations and had left their old trades behind. The metalworkers' union movement was thus virtually forced to start over again in the mid-eighties. But this was not entirely disadvantageous. The conditions of the Socialist Law made, for the most part, only local craft unions *(Fachvereine)* or small national craft unions feasible. Anything more ambitious was harassed or dissolved as a socialist organization. This prevented the premature formation of a national industrial metalworkers' union, as had been attempted previously in the sixties and seventies. Craft organization as yet corresponded more closely to the needs and mentalities of metalworking journeymen, whether they voted socialist or not.

Section 2 of Appendix A summarizes all metalworkers' unions created between 1879 and mid-1891, when the Deutsche Metallarbeiterverband (DMV) was founded. Most unions were started either between late 1882 and late 1884 or between late 1887 and mid-1890. This pattern was the product of the interaction of the economic situation with the climate of repression under the Socialist Law. In the first wave the predominant factor was the "mild practice," which allowed much more room for local craft unionism to flourish.[5] The economic cycle was less important, because though the mild upturn of 1880–1882 was over, the recession of the mid-eighties was also relatively mild, within the overall conditions of high unemployment between 1874 and 1895. The second wave of union formation was probably more strongly influenced by the faster economic upswing of the late eighties. Increased repression beginning in 1886 may be a factor in the interlude of foundings in 1885–1887, but this was moderated by the city administration's lighter hand. This relative liberalism did not, of course, spare the most important socialist unions from close police supervision.

Most of the unions founded before or during the first wave were small craft organizations, often with weak or nonexistent ties to the Social Democratic movement. This was entirely natural, given that too open an identification with the movement would tempt the police to harass or close an organization. These new unions were also founded and led by an entirely new generation of activists, most of whom were probably in their early twenties. In the Fine Mechanics' Union of 1883, the one case where we have evidence, virtually all of the leaders were between the age of twenty and twenty-five in the mid-eighties.[6] The new activists wished to create unions matching the perceived needs of their trades; only gradually did many of these leaders and organizations identify themselves more and more closely with the Social Democrats.

To examine the motivations behind the formation of these new craft unions, the factors that shaped organizational behavior of metalworking craftsmen, and the nature of the craft-class dialectic under the Socialist Law, it will again be useful to investigate a few trades in detail. First, three trades with officially neutral organizations will be discussed: two highly traditional crafts with organizations resembling journeymen's associations (the tin molders and filemakers), and a newer craft with organizational behavior strongly shaped by elitism (the fine mechanics). I will then focus on three trades that were more or less explicitly aligned with the socialists from the outset: a small homogeneous craft and a large heterogenous one, both showing openness to craft federation or industrial unionism (the metal pressers and the locksmiths and machinists), and a factory trade with a history of elitism and unusual shopfloor power (the iron molders).

Of the neutral craft unions that appeared with the "mild practice," among the most traditional were the associations of the tin molders (December 1882) and filemakers (January 1884), each of which was initially created to help colleagues on the tramp or those out of work because of unemployment or illness. In essence they were much closer to being journeymen's associations than unions. The vocabulary employed by their members clearly demonstrates the slowness of technological and organizational change and the strength of artisanal customs in these two tiny crafts.[7] The preamble to the Filemakers' Association statutes emphasized the need to enhance the "feeling of honor" (*Ehrgefühl*) of journeymen (the increasingly archaic word Gesellen was used, rather than Gehilfen) through "respectable support" to prevent begging by the unemployed. The Tin Molders' Association at first called its leader the "journeyman superior" (Altgeselle), and both groups sometimes used the traditional word Geschenk ("gift") for travel money given to wanderers. The filemakers also possessed the craft signs and flags stemming from the guild era.[8] As the eighties wore on, however, subtle changes took place in the orientation of these two bodies. A statutes revision by the tin molders in 1886 at least opened the possibility that it would accept workers who were not apprenticed, and the union increasingly associated itself

*Repression, Revival, Unification*

with the Social Democrats. But it refused to join the DMV in 1891. The filemakers joined a loose national network of associations in their trade in 1886, a network of socialist orientation, and in 1890 defended their admission of a filemaker who had never finished his apprenticeship. That individual had already been rejected by a number of other Bavarian unions in the trade. The filemakers joined the DMV, but formed their own section rather than merge with the locksmiths and machinists.[9] Although craft consciousness was still important, even the most traditional trades were clearly under the growing influence of socialism and class consciousness. Like so many skilled workers, these craftsmen saw no contradiction in declaring allegiance simultaneously to both craft and class.

If the tin molders' and filemakers' unions had started as neutral groups out of caution and traditionalism, other explanations must be sought for the behavior of the fine mechanics, a formerly free trade devoted to the construction of complex mechanisms. This craft acquired a new importance and a stronger factory base with the rise of electrical engineering; fine mechanics in the small but rapidly growing firm of Schuckert were predominant in the first, neutral craft union of 1883.[10] The elitism of this craft sprang from its quasi–white collar status, reinforced by an unusual amount of recruitment from the lower middle class. In 1890 the fine mechanics were attacked by the leader of the locksmiths and machinists, Johann Großberger, as "the aristocracy of the workers . . . , who suffer greatly from delusions, because as a rule they are the sons of better families, and go to work in collars and cuffs." [11] Großberger's remark is confirmed by an earlier letter from a fine mechanic himself, who warned of the exploitation of apprentices in the trade because of excessive demand for positions:

> Chiefly I would like to direct my warning to the social groups *[Stände]* who consider themselves superior, because it often happens that sons, who were supposed to receive a higher education but failed to reach their goal, are left with no choice but to learn a trade. Out of false shame they do not want to become so-called ordinary workers, but rather come to the unhappy idea of becoming fine mechanics, because it is a *refined* business. . . . [After their inadequate apprenticeship] they work for quite low wages, only in order to be treated daintily, *undermine our wages,* and are the carriers and spreaders of that wretched caste spirit which is so noticeable in our trade.[12]

This letter is eloquent testimony not only to the peculiarities of the fine mechanics but also to the class snobbery that often divided the lower middle class from the working class in German society. The result was an organizational behavior marked by factionalism, weak organizations, ambivalence toward the socialists, and a narrow craft exclusivity. When the local of the Union of German Fine Mechanics (Verband der deutschen Mechaniker) was formed in 1887, it only decided to open membership to mathematical instrument makers under pressure from national headquarters.[13] This reluctance was mutual—the instrument makers kept their independent organization. The case of the fine mechanics demonstrates that craft consciousness could be basically obstructive in some cases.

In the case of craft unions formed by socialists, the relationship between craft organization and class consciousness was more complex. From the very beginning, German socialist leaders seem to have assumed that industrial unionism was the form of organization most suited to their principles. But we have seen the fate of that idea in the 1870s, although it must be said that German workers also seem from the beginning to have been more open to ideas of federated crafts or industrial organization than their compatriots in Britain and the United States.[14] Under the Socialist Law this idea lived on, but craft unions with socialist orientation arose as they had in the seventies. Many of these organizations were not formed by prominent socialist activists but rather by journeymen/skilled workers sympathetic to the cause. A good example is the Metal Pressers' Union formed in late 1881. Although it was an explicitly closed craft union, accepting only skilled practitioners of the trade, the Union had an openly socialist political orientation. It managed nonetheless to attract a significant fraction of the metal pressers: a February 1885 membership of 60 may be compared to a police estimate of 110–120 metal pressers in the city in April 1884. This organization was only one of two Nuremberg unions to associate with the abortive attempt to form a national metalworkers' union in 1885 (the Vereinigung der Metallarbeiter Deutschlands, or VMD), and it eventually affiliated with the DMV without hesitation in 1891.[15]

Why should this small craft be well organized, left-wing, and willing to combine with other crafts so early in the Socialist Law era? The best explanation is that the metal pressers constituted a fairly homogenous group whose labor market position was good, though they simultaneously faced a slow erosion of their skill and their control over their work because of technological change and increasing specialization of production. Although most still worked in small shops under master metal pressers, many probably had at least some experience in small and medium-sized toymaking factories, and they earned the lower wages typical of the Nuremberg toy and light-metal industries—in one survey 15.50–

16.50 M per week in 1888.[16] A simple stamping machine also threatened to take away some of the easier jobs, beginning in the mid-eighties,[17] but of more importance was the rapid expansion of the Nuremberg metal toy industry, which allowed some masters to mass produce for the toy factories.

Especially illuminating in this regard are the comments of an apprentice who ran away from his master's shop in August 1891 because his only work was to "repetitively *[schablonenhaft]* make 1,200 dozen mouthpieces for children's trumpets weekly" for a wage of three marks. He complained that he was learning little and that his work was making him "bad tempered." One journeyman in the shop thought this was "completely justified" and that "it was for other workers also highly unpleasant, boring and detrimental to one's ability to perform other jobs, when one has to make one and the same object in mass quantities." However, the one other journeyman in the shop sympathized with the master's position. He thought mass production unavoidable and recognized that the work was nothing but "factory work." He thought it the journeyman's responsibility to change jobs after his apprenticeship to gain the skill and knowledge he lacked from his apprenticeship.[18] Other accounts substantiate the existence of mass production and the inadequate training of excessive numbers of apprentices,[19] which together tended to depress the overall wage level. Faced with this slow erosion of their position, as well as decreasing variety and skill requirements at work, but strengthened by the solidarity and homogeneity of the craft, the metal pressers became organized and radicalized. This, in conjunction with the isolation of the trade to only a handful of places (only one other metal pressers' union existed in 1891),[20] may also explain their desire to associate with other workers in an overarching metalworkers' union. In this case craft and class consciousness reinforced more than they obstructed each other.

The situation is more ambiguous in the case of the locksmiths and machinists. Because this group was so large and heterogeneous and embodied much of the machine industry work force, it became the focus of attempts by socialists to form unions on an industrial basis. Consequently, the locksmiths' and machinists' organization was originally founded as the "Metalworkers' Union" toward the end of 1884 by editor, former locksmith, and local socialist leader Johann Scherm and by locksmith Georg Groschupp. Since the spring of 1882 they had participated in the Nuremberg local of the national metalworkers' illness insurance fund, which provided a substitute for their organizational ambitions.[21] In September 1883 Scherm also became the editor of the *Deutsche*

*Metallarbeiter-Zeitung*, a weekly newspaper begun and printed by Grillenberger in order to reinvigorate and hold together unionism in the metal
trades in the absence of a national union.[22] The paper quickly became a
success, and after 1891 it was the central organ of the DMV, again thrust-
ing Nuremberg to the forefront as one of the most important German
cities in the metalworkers' movement. Despite these advances no general
local union was formed immediately, although the intention had been expressed as early as August 1883. The reason is unknown; presumably
Scherm and the others thought it inadvisable, either because of the Socialist Law or because of justified skepticism about the reaction of skilled
craftsmen to multicraft or industrial unionism.[23]

Proximate cause for the founding of the new union was the national
metalworkers' congress called for the small Thuringian city of Gera at
Christmastime in 1884. That congress ambitiously decided to set up a national union, the VMD, headquartered in the supposedly liberal state of
Baden. But the union did not survive eight months; it was dissolved in
August 1885 as a socialist organization. Months prior to that event the
newly founded Nuremberg local was forced out of the VMD by the city
council, who declared the local a political association and threatened to
dissolve it in two weeks if it did not withdraw.[24]

Its status reconverted to that of a nonpolitical association, the union
continued to exist, but it did not at first thrive. Impeding its growth was
the as yet insurmountable craft consciousness of most skilled metalworkers. Although it defined its jurisdiction at the outset as only those
apprenticed metalworkers whose trades did not already have a craft
union[25]—a considerable retreat from the industrial union principles, if
not the reality, of the old International Metalworkers—the union was
compelled in January 1886 to change its name to the Trade Union of
Locksmiths and Machinists. In addition to the competition of the craft
unions, the locksmith Anton Siebert explained:

> The sentiment of the local metalworkers, who are almost without exception for
> craft organization, made the achievement of a respectable number of members
> unthinkable. In fact lately only locksmiths, etc., were members of the associa-
> tion, so that the change of name was largely *formal*, and a concession to the lo-
> cal locksmiths working with masters, who, when asked to join the union,
> countered that they would only join if it corresponded in external form to their
> trade.[26]

Locksmiths and metal turners dominated the leadership from the beginning,[27] but as this evidence indicates, they came largely from the

machine industry. The old division between artisanal and industrial lock-smiths continued to rankle.

The change of name—which did not include any change in the def-inition of membership—may have stopped a decline in the number of members, but it did not spur any increase. Through early 1887 it stag-nated at a level of 130 members and then rose slightly.[28] An explosion in interest only occurred in 1888–1890 (see Appendix A). The obstacles to organization were familiar: the difficulty of penetrating the large machine-industry firms, especially Klett, the rivalry between the two branches of locksmiths, and the problems of convincing the majority of workers, whose only commitment to Social Democracy may have been their Reichs-tag vote, of the usefulness of unionism. To the complaint of a member in September 1887 that it was "very difficult" to convince "most workers" that the union accomplished anything, one leader, the fine mechanic Max Haugenstein, stressed the propaganda value of the burial and be-nevolent fund run by the union, and indeed those functions were quite important for the first few years.[29] The innate weakness of the union and generally negative experiences with strikes all over Germany in the eighties made the leaders of the Trade Union of Locksmiths and Machin-ists, and Social Democrats generally, very skeptical about striking.[30] Until the membership breakthroughs after 1895, prominent socialist unionists viewed unions not as vehicles for improving working conditions but rather as party auxiliaries devoted to mutual aid and political "conscious-ness raising." But this view may not have been shared by the many local craft unions that arose independently of, but in broad sympathy with, the socialist movement.

One such organization was that of the iron molders. Unlike that of the locksmiths and machinists, this union did not have an explicitly political origin or an industrial union agenda, however watered down. But like that craft, the iron molders showed a strong craft consciousness that com-plicated attempts to break down the barriers between trades. In Chapter 1 I described the work process and elite position of the iron molders in the machine industry and noted their complete detachment from the early labor movement, in all probability because of their position. A handful of individuals excepted, no support for Social Democratic organi-zations was visible in the ranks of the iron molders before 1886. Thus the sudden appearance in that year of a vaguely socialist Iron Molders' Asso-ciation Glückauf (the last word is a traditional greeting among miners and iron workers) is difficult to explain. Travel money for wandering iron molders was the first justification offered for the union,[31] but this was hardly a new problem. Consciously or unconsciously, the iron molders were probably motivated by the gradual erosion of their privileged position and by the struggles of molders elsewhere. Just weeks before the union was formed, a commentator in the *Metallarbeiter-Zeitung* noted the appearance of new iron molders' organizations all over Germany in the wake of a Leipzig molders' strike. That struggle stemmed in part from the introduction of the molding machine and semiskilled labor.[32] Resistance to mechanization was not a feature of molders' struggles in Nuremberg in coming years, but opposition to piece-rate payment was important—a sure indication that the molders' control over the pace and character of their work was threatened.

In spite of this threat, job control was definitely not broken in the early years of the union. Befitting their elite position, the molders built a strong organization that earned respect from the employers equaled by no other metalworkers' union. Membership initially was about 150, and later rose to 300 by early 1890; this was close to complete enrollment of the skilled.[33] The employment bureau set up by the union temporarily dominated hiring of iron molders in Nuremberg. Allegedly all foundries except Klett's had recognized the bureau by February 1889, and apparently even Klett had used it intermittently before 1891, because a Klett engineer appeared at a meeting between molders and foundry masters in April 1891. He complained of problems with the bureau, but recognized its worth.[34] Considering the paternalistic anti-union stance upheld by that firm, this was a rare event indeed. Also quite rare for Germany was the existence of formal workers' control over the hiring process—as I noted in the last chapter, German skilled workers had few guildlike controls to defend in contrast to France, Britain, and North America.

In keeping with the relatively privileged situation of the iron molders, their union in its early years had a decidedly elitist, conservative, and masculine tone. The yearly celebrations of the founding of the union inevitably included presentations by the molders's wives and daughters of ceremonial trophies, ribbons, or pictures, and speeches were given praising "the work, the loyalty, and the feeling of duty of the men of labor."[35] Another celebratory poem went: "Where men are found / Who for honor and right / Courageously come together / There dwells a free race."[36] Such masculine overtones were not uncommon. Running through working-class culture and the mentality of skilled workers in particular were assumptions about sex roles that reinforced their self-image and self-worth as craftsmen. Even the rising young and radical leader of the locksmiths and machinists, the metal turner Carl Breder, patronizingly instructed his members' wives to press their husbands to attend meetings instead of obstructing them (an old complaint in the movement) by saying "for just as the wife is obliged to fulfill her duty in the house, so is it no less the duty of each man to try to better his knowledge and situation." [37] Nevertheless the pointedly masculine emphasis of the molders' rhetoric stands out. It probably derived from the combination of high skill and heavy physical labor typical of the craft.

Exploiting their position of power, the iron molders by 1890 had almost succeeded in eliminating piece-rate labor for skilled molders.[38] By 1891, however, there were signs of erosion in the union's position. Complaints about the introduction of molding machines and the concomitant expansion of the numbers of semiskilled workers appeared for the first time, which may explain the opening of membership, at least informally, to those without apprenticeships in 1890–1891. At the same time the Klett company increasingly threatened to expand piece-rate payment greatly and to eliminate paying time and a quarter for overtime in view of the worsening economic depression since late 1890.[39] These threats were not immediately carried out, but within three years this conflict would escalate into an epic struggle between the iron molders and the machine-industry employers, spearheaded by Klett, over piece rates—a struggle that would herald the beginning of the end for the unique power of the molders.

As the six crafts examined here reveal, whatever the inexorable rise of socialism in the electoral arena, craft consciousness was the overriding factor in the character of the unions formed under the Socialist Law. This craft consciousness had diverse origins and diverse results. The strong sense of craft among the iron molders arose almost entirely out of skill and shopfloor power—they had no guild tradition to draw on. For the fine mechanics, skill was compounded by an unusually high social status and origins for skilled workers. But this did not translate into effective organizations. Of course skill, with the labor market power that arose from it, was always crucial, yet it is clear that craft consciousness was also founded in many other cases on significant continuity with the past. It is striking to what extent the traditions of the old journeymen's associations lived on into the eighties in spite of the generational break. The vocabulary of the tin molders and filemakers is not the sole indication of this; it is also visible in the artisanal parades, complete with flags, that were held in the mid-eighties.[40] Virtually all of the unions also maintained hostels and job bureaus and distributed travel money, which demonstrated once again the continuance of long-distance wandering as a distinctive institution among journeymen. The benevolent, sickness, and burial funds sustained by some organizations also paralleled the activities of the pre-1868 associations. As in the case of help for wanderers, these services were not anachronistic survivals but actually met the needs of journeymen and skilled workers in coping with the insecurity of their lives.

Although continuity with the past strongly marked the vocabulary, form, and actions of most craft unions under the Socialist Law, there was also significant change. Even in 1888—before the strike wave and organizational growth of the following two years, which are treated in the next section—metalworking unions had grown far beyond their size in the 1870s. The relatively mild economic climate of the eighties, with its growth in real wages, was influential, as was the relaxation of the climate of repression after 1883. Politically the decade saw the further strengthening of electoral socialism under Grillenberger's leadership, which reflected an underlying class formation process that had its impact in the union realm as well. By the late 1880s almost all of the neutral craft unions, like those of the tin molders, filemakers, and even the fine mechanics, had drifted into the socialist orbit. The dominance of Grillenberger and the party in the Nuremberg working class was simply unchallenged. The liberals had squandered whatever influence over workers they once had, and the minority Catholic subculture was still small and inactive. Under these circumstances previously ambivalent union leaders had little choice other than to accept the leadership of the only working-class party. A growth in working-class consciousness was thus both the cause and effect of Social Democratic dominance.

But, as we have seen, this by no means eliminated the power of craft consciousness at the trade-union level. The organized metalworker—still a distinct minority, to be sure—had dual loyalties. Beyond the vote and the rhetoric of party meetings, solidarity with the unskilled, with female workers, and with other trades was observed more in the breach than in everyday practice. But signs of change were present. By 1891 most unions were at least theoretically willing to admit unskilled helpers, even if they did not have much success in attracting them, and almost all accepted unification into a national metalworkers' union—the theme of the last section. But to understand these events we must examine the period from 1888 to 1890, which provided an important stimulus to the growth of unionism and the idea of joint action with other trades and the unskilled. These years also mark a major change in the social and organizational behavior of skilled metalworkers: strikes, heretofore rare, acquired a new importance in the struggle for better working conditions.

Years of Unrest: 1888–1890

The year 1889 was a major turning point for workers' movements throughout Europe. The giant and spontaneous Ruhr miners' strike of May and London dockworkers' strike of August were outbursts of labor unrest that attracted international attention and had an impact even in Nuremberg. But though these incidents may have increased enthusiasm for strikes among workers in the city, they do not explain the onset of the strike wave or the growth in the size and number of union organizations since late 1888. In this period union organization spread to previously unorganized sectors, like the blacksmiths and the stokers and machinists (who tended steam engines), and the penetration of the locksmiths' and machinists' union into the machine industry increased considerably in this period as well. Even women, as we will see, were brought into unions in light metalworking and the beating trades.

A crucial factor in this upsurge was the very favorable business situation at the end of decade, with its attendant effects on unemployment and the cost of living. According to Rainer Gömmel, the unemployment rate in Nuremberg sank from 5.0 percent in 1885 to 1.9 percent in 1889, while the previous price deflation was reversed with a rise in the index of living costs from 78.2 in 1888 to 82.6 in 1889 and 84.0 in 1890 (1910–1913 = 100).[41] Workers were thus in a better position in the labor market than they had been at any time since the beginning of the so-called Great Depression, though they simultaneously experienced an unaccustomed period of inflation in the prices of necessities. To these economic stimuli were added the influence of growing socialist activity and labor unrest in Germany and elsewhere since the mid-eighties, as well as the long-term process of the social and political formation of the city's working class. Considerable as the internal divisions in the working class were, a decline in the social distance between skilled and unskilled and growing differences between employers and workers can only have had positive effects on the propensity to organize and strike.

The results for strike behavior are summarized in Table 4.1. In contrast to the small strike wave that occurred in the metal trades in the early seventies, there were virtually no strikes between 1876 and 1885, but there were fifteen in the second half of the decade. All of these took place

Table 4.1. NUREMBERG METALWORKERS' STRIKES, 1871–1890

| Period | No. of strikes | Average size | Defensive/ offensive | Failure rate |
|---|---|---|---|---|
| 1871–1875 | 7 | 90.0 | 4/3 | 16.7% |
| 1876–1880 | 1 | 26.0 | unknown | unknown |
| 1881–1885 | 3 | 17.0 | 2/0 | 50.0% |
| 1886–1890 | 15 | 81.6 | 6/9 | 20.0% |

SOURCE: See Appendix B.
NOTE: The "average size" is calculated from the lowest figure in the "maximum size" column in Appendix B. The "failure rate" is determined by the number of failed strikes divided by the total number. Both in this case and in the case of the division between defensive and offensive strikes, these numbers are determined by the information available. Thus there are sometimes discrepancies with the total number of strikes when there is missing information. The numbers of strikes are also so small before 1886–1890 that the calculations based upon them have little statistical significance. "Defensive" and "offensive" are defined in Appendix B.

between late 1888 and late 1890. The average number of strikers in the late eighties (81.6) rose once again to the approximate level of the early seventies (90.0—a figure that is probably too high because of missing information). This increase in size reflected the reappearance of large craftwide strikes first seen in 1872, as well the first large machine-industry strike at Schuckert in 1889. The low failure rate and dominance of offensive actions (where workers took the initiative to better their conditions) also reflect the characteristic features of these early strike waves: workers were striking for improved wages and hours in inflationary economic booms, while employers were still too poorly organized to respond very effectively. Major strikes also took place in the building trades and other nonmetal industries in this period, and there were wage movements without strikes in the metal trades too. The iron molders received 7 percent wage increases at the Klett and Earnshaw machine factories in late 1889, although not as direct responses to the demands of the workers, and 5 to 6 percent in other factories.[42] More impressively, the mathematical instrument makers actually achieved a formal agreement with the employers in August 1889 equalizing piece rates, raising wages, and lowering the workday to ten hours.[43]

The impact of this period of labor unrest on strike behavior, organization, and openness to cooperation with other trades and women can best be understood through an examination of three groups of workers: the tinsmiths and the light metalworking trades, the beating trades, and the machine-industry workers. The first two groups were responsible for almost all of the strikes in 1889 and 1890, as well as the first introduction of women to metalworking unions. In the machine industry there was significant union membership growth, but there was also a disastrous strike, which illustrated the formidable organizational problems that remained.

The small and scattered strikes in brass and iron molding during the fall of 1888 became a strike wave in the spring of 1889 in the toy factories. Beginning as a successful defensive action in the Plank factory to fend off the firing of four workers who asked for shorter hours, the movement quickly spread spontaneously to other firms with the demand for the ten-hour day and wage improvements. These actions were quickly successful; many factories gave in without a strike.[44] The owners of these medium-sized toy factories had no organization and were quite vulnerable because of the tight labor market. A strike or movement encompassing only half the workers in a firm sufficed to make the employers grant concessions, especially since those who struck were skilled workers.

These successes seem to have galvanized the socialist Tinsmiths' Union, which in late 1888 and early 1889 had been denounced by the more energetic Social Democrats as degenerating into an entertainment society.[45] In early June a general movement was launched to draw in tinsmiths in both the manufacturing and the construction branches of the trade. By this time the nationwide upsurge in worker protest was having an effect; leading speakers at meetings invariably mentioned the many strikes. Negotiations were launched with the Tinsmith's Guild, a voluntary employers' organization formed under the new (and ineffective) guild law of 1881. Some twenty masters and small firms subsequently accepted the demands, which included a ten-hour workday, a minimum wage, the abolition of piece rates, and other wage improvements. Most of the remaining masters were then defeated in a strike.[46]

For the victorious majority it was another easy but illusory victory, achieved in large measure because of the disunity and lack of preparedness on the part of the employers. At the same time there were evident signs of disunity among the tinsmiths. Less than one quarter of the six hundred to seven hundred journeymen in this craft struck, and the construction tinsmiths were especially noteworthy by their absence in meetings and during the strike. Many were apparently pacified with an offer of one mark per week extra for construction work. The strike wave in the spring and summer of 1889 did boost the membership of the union to some three hundred members, but even this did not suffice to sustain the accomplishments of the summer. A number of leaders were fired in the fall, and many concessions were soon revoked by the employers.[47]

The weakness of the tinsmiths' organization—a product of heterogeneous working environments, a split between the construction and factory sectors similar to that plaguing the locksmiths, relatively low skill, and increasing replacement by women in factory work—undoubtedly helps to explain the union's sudden interest in late 1889 in organizing women workers. In contrast to the gold beaters, during the strike wave neither the union leadership nor the rank and file had made any attempt to involve women in the movement, and in view of their easy victories they did not need to involve them. But the ephemeral nature of the accomplishments of the summer and the ease with which skilled labor could sometimes be replaced with unskilled prompted a new interest in the problem. This interest was reinforced by a growth in the discussion of women's issues throughout the Social Democratic movement in 1889 as a result of an influential pamphlet and speech by Clara Zetkin. Other Nuremberg union leaders raised the idea of organizing women at this time too.[48]

To avoid another dissolution by the authorities, as had befallen the short-lived Association for the Representation of the Interests of Working Women in 1885, a number of separate women's unions were created in the spring of 1890. One of these was the Trade Union of All Women Workers in the Sheet Metal and Metal Wares Industry. The guiding spirits from the beginning were the leaders of the tinsmiths' union, and the meetings were dominated by them in the absence of active participation by many women. The problems were formidable. Unskilled workers as a rule were extremely difficult to organize because of lack of education, craft pride, commitment to industrial work, and bargaining power, and this situation was compounded by the double burden of work and housework borne by most female workers, by the passive socialization of women, and by the paternalism of male workers themselves. The union, which had signed up seventy-four women in the beginning, gradually failed because of lack of interest. In March 1891 its remaining members were absorbed by the tinsmiths.[49]

At least on paper, the acceptance of women by the tinsmiths' union was an important breakthrough. In reality, however, the union and its successor section in the DMV showed less and less interest in female workers over the next few years. Nonetheless, the results of the strike wave in the light metal trades, whether in working conditions or in the organization of women, do signal important long-term changes in this sector. The level of unionization rose, more workers saw the power of strikes to change conditions, and the first tentative opening to unskilled workers was made. Craft consciousness was the foundation of action among the tinsmiths and related craftsmen, but class consciousness and socialism were apparently also having an impact.

The pattern of strike behavior in the beating trades was somewhat different. Women played a significant role in the strikes, the strike wave carried through 1890, and spontaneous strikes were rare. The overall economic situations faced by gold beaters and metal beaters were also dissimilar. The light metal trades did not face the long-term dilemma of the beating trades: how to salvage what was left of their relatively privileged situation in view of the chronic economic crisis in their industries. The metal beaters' decline had started as early as 1873, with the onset of the Great Depression, and had worsened since then as the shift away from pseudo-gilding was compounded by the rise of bronze paint as a substitute for metal leaf. The gold beaters, by contrast, did very well until 1883, because of Nuremberg's domination of the British market for gold leaf. A change in taste in the 1880s then reversed the upward trend, and overproduction and sharply reduced prices became the norm. The downward pressure on wages for both trades, when combined with the consolidation of socialist politics in the Nuremberg working class, sufficiently radicalized the two originally neutral unions so that they aligned themselves with the Social Democratic camp by 1889.

The similarity of the economic problems afflicting the two crafts notwithstanding, the strikes and meetings of 1889–1890 reveal significant differences between the gold and metal beaters in the realm of organizational behavior and craft consciousness. In April of 1889 the First German Beaters' Congress was held in Nuremberg, prompted by the economic crisis and by calls for support from striking Dresden gold beaters. By the end of the congress their Nuremberg counterparts had walked out because they refused to accept the criticism of others, particularly the metal beaters, who accused them of exploiting younger journeymen and apprentices through a subcontracting system.[50]

At the root of the disagreements were differences in the work process and division of labor in the two crafts. Metal beating did not require especially high skill, and the metal alloy was normally only beaten in the "form" once. Gold leaf could be made much thinner, and this could require three or more successive sequences of hammering. In the later stages of beating the leaves were extremely thin and considerable skill was needed to achieve maximum thinness, thus saving gold while preserving high quality. With the expansion of gold beating after 1840, a more complex division of labor arose in which growing numbers of women were trained for the specialized jobs of inserting and removing the leaves from the forms, preparing the forms for use, and trimming the finished product. Men were sometimes drawn into this specialization process too. Older and more experienced beaters employed young journeymen as "setters" *(Setzer)* to do the preliminary beating for a fixed weekly wage—a form of subcontracting. Apprentices, who were required to sign up for a perhaps excessively long period of four years, were also often paid out of the pocket of the senior journeyman.[51] The division of labor in metal beating, in contrast, never proceeded much beyond the introduction of female labor. Each journeyman normally had only one female "layer-in" *(Einlegerin)* as a helper and nothing more. Masters probably paid apprentices directly.

Supported by the labor of the setters and apprentices, the senior gold beaters earned high wages by working-class standards: 25 to 40 marks per week and occasionally even more. As is clear from the outraged reaction of the gold beater's union to the charges of exploitation, they also used their position to control the organization, and they displayed an elitist craft consciousness not unlike that of the iron molders.[52] It is therefore a little surprising that women were actually members of the union in 1890, although at what point after the formation of the union in 1883 they were accepted as such is unknown.[53] The explanation for the acceptance of women lies in the strategic position of female helpers in the beating trades. The tasks assigned to them were complex enough to require short apprenticeships of six months to a year; they were semiskilled, not unskilled, workers. A journeyman also needed a competent female helper to make maximum wages under the complicated piece-rate and incentive system that reigned in the industry. Marriages within the trade were quite common, perhaps because of this situation.[54] Finally, once women acquired a permanent place in the beating crafts after about 1840, they were no longer viewed as a threat by journeymen. The failure of mechanization and the heavy physical demands imposed by the beating process effectively ruled out the displacement of men by women that was occurring in light metalworking. Following the reorientation toward socialism that took place in the two trades in the late 1880's, apparently a closer than normal cooperation between the two sexes developed in this industry.

The prominent role of women is shown by the near-total strike by the gold beaters' union in August 1889, in which 226 of the 422 strikers were female. This strike and another in 1890 attempted to defend the piece rates of the workers in the face of the chronic oversupply of gold leaf. Although successful in the short run, in the long run the economic situation only deteriorated, which forced marginal small masters to violate the agreement of 1889. By the spring of 1891 it was necessary to call a second beaters' congress to decide on appropriate measures. At this congress the gold beaters had to admit the inadvisability of training excessive numbers of apprentices. A limit of one apprentice per five journeymen was set— another rare case of worker control, something we have only encountered among the iron molders. Later in 1891 the union launched a new campaign for a ten-hour day to limit production, but it was only partially successful in convincing the masters to agree. The crisis could not so easily be overcome.[55]

In metal beating, too, women became important in the union and in strikes, although they were certainly not treated as equals. But the lower skill and poorer economic condition of the craft led to weaker organizations and fewer lasting accomplishments. The disillusionment was such that the membership of the union plummeted from about two hundred to sixty-six from 1890 to 1891.[56] The results of the strike wave in the beating trades were thus, as in the toy and light metal industries, not completely positive. Concrete achievements in terms of wages and hours proved to be difficult to sustain because the unions were as yet too weak, and the economic crisis too severe. Nonetheless the years 1889–1890 did produce a significant change in the level of organization (if only for the gold beaters), in the degree of class consciousness, and in the acceptance of women as union members.

The third group of workers to be decisively affected by the events of 1888 to 1890 were the locksmiths and machine-industry workers. In their case strikes did not play a major role, with one ill-fated exception. The Schuckert strike of September–October 1889 demonstrated once again the difficulties presented by the task of mobilizing the heterogeneous work force in the machine industry, especially when the considerable power of a large firm was arrayed against the union. Accomplishments during the period were not lacking, however. The locksmiths' and machinists' union underwent a massive expansion that made it much larger than any other metal trades' organization had ever been. Most of that expansion occurred in only a few months. At the end of 1888 a membership of 300 was claimed, and in July 1889 it reached 800. Thereafter it fluctuated upward, reaching a maximum of 904 at the end of 1890. Of these, 57.6 percent were locksmiths, and 23.0 percent were metal turners.[57] The union also launched a ten-hour-workday movement among the construction locksmiths in the summer of 1889, which may have eased some of the tension that existed between the factory and construction branches. That the old rivalry was not dead is shown by the desire of one construction locksmith, expressed in a meeting, for a separate organization.[58]

Whatever the proportion of locksmiths that were attracted from the artisanal sector, the size of the union and the occupations of nonlocksmith members indicate that new members were largely recruited from the machine industry. Some members must have worked at Klett, but the problems of organizing the workers there remained as formidable as ever. It was only in 1889 that the firm pulled out of its long slump and climbed permanently over its minimum size of about one thousand employees in Nuremberg (see Figure 1.1). Throughout the eighties the skilled work force there consisted mostly of older workers with considerable experience and loyalty to the firm. For the union organization they were immovable. One prominent militant, Konrad Brendel, commented in June 1889: "The workers at . . . [Klett] should also take part in the movement; they should not believe that they have already reached Eldorado."[59] The iron molders' union may have had more luck in organizing there, but for the locksmiths and machinists the many small and medium-sized machine plants, which employed from tens to hundreds of workers, likely formed the most fertile ground for organization. Apparently many were also organized at the electrical engineering firm of Schuckert.

The iron molders excepted, the workers at Schuckert were the only ones in the machine industry to campaign for and win concessions during the 1889 strike wave. The concessions themselves, a ten-hour day and time-and-a-quarter pay for overtime (conceded in May), and a 10 percent wage increase (given in July), naturally did not come from negotiations; direct concessions to worker demands were unimaginable in the labor relations of large firms at the time. Owner and electrical inventor Johann Schuckert (1846–1895), trained as a fine mechanic and son of a Nuremberg master cooper, had the mentality of a paternalistic master artisan.[60] Treatment of the workers as equals was for him impossible. Like

Cramer-Klett's concessions in 1871, these improvements in wages and hours were designed to undercut the movement and preserve the owner's reputation as a benefactor.

Apparently these measures worked, as even the *Tagespost* commentators declared them satisfactory. It was therefore a complete surprise when in September the strike came "like lightning out of a blue sky," as the socialist paper put it. The sole cause was the firing of Carl Breder, who had just resigned as chairman of the locksmiths' and machinists' union some two weeks earlier. It appears that he had resigned to appease the company, and then was fired anyway for delivering a speech on the eight-hour-day campaign to be launched with the first May Day in 1890. The strike quickly expanded to about half of the six hundred workers in the factory, and huge public meetings attracted over a thousand participants. But failure came quickly; Schuckert found the action incomprehensible, and most women workers and fine mechanics reportedly did not support it. Many strikers returned after a company ultimatum to return or be fired, and the rest were indeed dismissed. Leaders Breder and Brendel were blacklisted and forced to leave town for a short period.[61]

It is indeed an irony that this strike was fought over Breder, who seems to have done little to prevent it. His frequently expressed reservations about work stoppages proved in this instance to be prescient. Spontaneous defensive strikes to prevent the dismissal of individual leaders or agitators had as a rule little hope of success and were in any case hardly worth the cost involved. Before an effective strike policy could be developed by the unions, the rank and file would have to be well organized enough to forego such actions when they appeared hopeless.

The need for an effective central organization to formulate strike policy as well as to coordinate strike support from around the country when important work stoppages did take place was thus evident in the Schuckert strike, just as it was throughout the strike wave of 1889–1890. These years of unrest also seem to have fostered class consciousness at the trade-union level, among leaders as well as followers. A greater acceptance of unskilled helpers seems to have occurred generally in the socialist metalworkers' unions of Nuremberg, and the factory strikes of this period must have demonstrated the need to cooperate across craft lines. Two years of mobilization boosted the popularity of unionism among skilled metalworkers too, although the failure of most strikes to deliver long-lasting results probably reinforced previous skepticism about strike action. With the end of the Socialist Law approaching on October 1, 1890, thoughts again turned to the creation of central organizations in the metal trades. One question remained: Was craft or industrial unionism to be the determining principle?

## The Ambiguous Victory of Industrial Unionism

Since the destruction of the VMD by the authorities in 1885, the problem of the best form for national organizations of metalworkers had been repeatedly discussed in the *Metallarbeiter-Zeitung*, in local meetings, and in national congresses. The first national meeting since 1884, the Weimar congress at the end of 1888, wisely decided to avoid starting a new industrial union. As a substitute, five national coordinators (*Vertrauensmänner*) were appointed to coordinate strike support and where possible to prevent unnecessary strikes. The Fürth metalworkers' leader, Martin Segitz, was coordinator for all metalworkers who did not fall under the jurisdictions of the coordinators for the tinsmiths, blacksmiths, iron molders, and locksmiths and machinists. This system was not every effective, but at the next congress in May 1890, also at Weimar, uncertainty over the reaction of the authorities to a general union led the congress majority to vote for the continuation of this system for another year. Carl Breder became the national coordinator for the locksmiths and machinists, although not without resistance from Hamburg, which had been the seat of all the other coordinators. Behind this conflict also stood an argument about the best form of unionism. Breder had since 1888 pushed for the formation of an industrial union, whereas the previous coordinator from Hamburg wanted a craft union and in fact did found an abortive national union of locksmiths and machinists shortly thereafter. The decision to found a national metalworkers' union, the DMV, only came at the Frankfurt congress in June 1891. In the meantime a number of other national craft organizations has been founded since the mid-1880s, including ones for blacksmiths, fine mechanics, and gold workers. The only Nuremberg metalworkers' union to join one of these craft unions was the fine mechanics local founded in 1887.[62]

As violent and as personal as some of the debates over craft versus industrial and local versus national unionism were, it is nonetheless striking how quickly the principle (if perhaps not the reality) of industrial unionism triumphed in the German metal trades. In the Introduction I mentioned the contrasting examples of Britain and the United States, where industrial unions in this sector did not exist before the 1920s or 1930s. In the German case at least three interlocking factors were crucial. First was the political origin of the German union movement, particularly the dominance of socialism. From the first metalworkers' unions formed in 1868–1869, prominent socialist leaders tried to form industrial unions on ideological principle, regardless of whether the great majority of skilled metalworkers were ready for this or not. (Eric Hobsbawm has spoken of "the foresight of the continental pioneers of industrial unionism, based upon a combination of feeble unions and radical ideology.")[63] As we have seen, the campaign for industrial unionism did not prevent the numerous foundings of local and national craft unions by socialist sympathizers in the 1870s and under the Socialist Law. Second was the open hostility and repression exercised by the German governments, which reinforced the class formation process among German workers and thereby buttressed the paramount position of socialism. Third, and last, was the organization of employers in the German metal industries, particularly during the period 1888–1890, when the national metal industrialists' association was created and a series of lockouts in north Germany were staged in an attempt to break the unions of the iron molders and of the locksmiths and machinists. These developments gave final impetus to the idea of solidarity across craft boundaries, at a time when national craft unionism was only beginning to flourish. Competing craft organizations of iron molders, blacksmiths, gold workers, and others did continue to exist after 1891, but once the DMV was successfully launched, its large size and financial power tended to reinforce its dominance. Almost all of the craft unions were eventually absorbed by it.[64]

The irony, and perhaps the genius, of the early organizational structure of the DMV was that it allowed craft and industrial unionism to exist in an uneasy symbiosis. When the idea of a union became current in early 1891, the coordinators, including Segitz and Breder, proposed that the national organization allow the existence of individual craft sections on the local level where this was preferred. (Smaller locales tended to have unitary metalworkers' unions; big cities had more craft unions.) This became the basis for the agreement to found the union at the Frankfurt congress, and it eased the final stage of unification.[65] The backbone of the metalworkers' union movement under the Socialist Law—the local craft unions—could thus maintain their existence while accepting the principle and advantages of industrial organization. The resulting organizational form might be called a federation of crafts rather than a true industrial organization. This interpretation is supported by the composition of the early membership, which was almost entirely skilled. Yet the acceptance of the principle of industrial unionism was still a crucial symbolic step. The DMV's aim, in line with its socialist ideology, was to become a union for all metalworkers. In contrast the Amalgamated Society of Engineers in Britain before the First World War had a restrictive membership system based upon skill and experience.[66]

The original organizational form of the DMV was somewhat contradictory, and Nuremberg may have embodied the contradictions and the strengths of this arrangement more than any other city. Influenced no doubt by the ideological predominance of socialism and class consciousness in the city, almost all of the Nuremberg craft unions in the metal trades entered the DMV in 1891 without the slightest hesitation. They changed their labels and carried on as craft sections of the DMV, with virtually no formal institutions linking them together at the local level. Nuremberg far exceeded any other German locality in the number of sections. There were twelve formed between July and September 1891: those of the locksmiths and machinists, tinsmiths, iron molders, fine mechanics, blacksmiths, brass and bell molders, mathematical instrument workers, metal beaters, tin molders, stokers and machinists, metal pressers, and filemakers. Since all sections accepted, at least in theory, unskilled and semiskilled workers in their areas, collectively the sections formed an industrial union. Yet in reality craft consciousness lived on in the isolation of the sections from each other, even while it contributed to the success and growth of the union as a whole. In Chapter 5 the development and gradual integration of the DMV up to 1905 will be examined in more detail.

Of the socialist metalworkers' unions in Nuremberg only three split over joining the DMV, and only one did not join. The occupations involved are both instructive and predictable: the gold beaters, the iron molders, the tin molders, and the stokers and machinists.

The gold beaters' union was the sole socialist organization not to join. In March 1891 the great majority of its members were incorporated into the German Gold and Silver Workers' Union (Deutscher Gold- und Silberarbeiter-Verband, or DGSV), a small organization based upon the jewelry workers of Pforzheim (Baden). The financial advantages of a national union may have been the motivating factor, and both the Nuremberg local and DGSV leaders claimed that they would bring this organization into the DMV after it was formed, but craft consciousness was definitely an issue as well. Throughout 1890 the leaders of the gold beaters, including their most prominent young orator, Daniel Stücklen, had tried to start a national beaters' union, but the idea had foundered in part because of the indifference of other cities and in part because of the hostility of the metal beaters' union, which was more strongly influenced by socialism and industrial unionism. Once the gold beaters' union joined the DGSV they proved in no hurry to go over to the DMV and the majority of the organized gold beaters remained with the DGSV until 1899.[67]

Less is known about the divisions in the ranks of the tin molders and stokers, and in any case they were much less significant. A minority seceded to form a section in both cases, while the majority carried on—the tin molders out of traditionalism, the stokers out of a lack of commitment to modern unionism. The one major controversy was among the iron molders, where the reverse occurred: the majority of active members pushed through the unification plan and the minority seceded, eventually to form in November 1891 a local of the new Central Association of German Iron Molders. Resistance to the DMV centered in the old leadership and especially in the chairman of the union, Konrad Sebald, who embodied its cautious elitism. He praised the local craft union as an organization "that never came forth with impossible demands, and provoked nothing." An iron molders' organization could accomplish more, "especially since it then would only have a tiny little group to support" in strikes, he said. The struggle became so bitter that the union leadership refused to give expense money to the elected delegate to the Frankfurt congress, who was bound by the meeting to support unification. In July another meeting approved going over to the DMV by a vote of eighty-six to twenty-two. Apparently a majority of the activists had by 1891 left behind some of their elitism. But since there were only 181 members in the DMV section at the end of the year, as opposed to 280 in the local union in April, they clearly did not bring all of the rank and file with them. A number of inactive members were probably lost to the labor movement, at least temporarily, because of the split and dissolution of the old union.[68]

Despite this setback, the net gain in the strength of the union movement since the destruction of the unions in 1878 was clearly large. The Socialist Law was indeed oppressive, but by eventually allowing the growth of local craft unionism, it helped to put the unions on the right track: first attempt to organize skilled workers on the basis of their well-entrenched craft identities, and only later attempt to bring them together into larger cooperative units. The repression also ironically reinforced the feelings of political and social second-class citizenship among German workers and thus had ultimately contributed to the victory of the principle of industrial unionism. This victory was ambiguous, in that the organized structure of the DMV in Nuremberg was still stamped by the craft consciousness of skilled metalworkers, but it nevertheless provided

125

the ultimate basis for the integration of the skilled trades, and later their unskilled helpers, in one dominant organization. The contradictions of this organizational form also allowed the union to tap the power of skill and craft for wider ends—and skill and craft remained the ultimate power upon which the labor movement was founded. In the dialectic of craft and class, the period 1878–1891 had seen craft consciousness and class consciousness often conflict in the organizational development of the metalworkers' unions. Now, however, the two could sometimes act together. In their mentality, self-expression, and organizational behavior, metalworking artisans had come far in their transformation into skilled metalworkers.

But that transformation was certainly not complete. By 1891 the Nuremberg skilled metalworkers had built a union movement that in its richness and size was exceeded only by those in Hamburg and Berlin. The city's union leaders had played a prominent part in the national metalworkers' movement of 1883–1891. And by April 1891 some twenty-five hundred metalworkers were members of socialist unions, and perhaps two or three hundred were members of other organizations.[69] Yet this was only approximately one-sixth of the metalworkers of Nuremberg. Many skilled trades were only weakly organized, and the unskilled, with few exceptions, were completely outside the unions. The largest machine-industry plants remained extremely difficult to organize. Strikes were still uncommon, and skilled metalworkers could exert little collective influence over their wages, hours, or working conditions. The divisions between the crafts, as embodied in the DMV's organizational structure and in rivalries with competing craft unions, continued to hamper cooperative efforts in strikes and wage movements. None of these problems was ever completely soluble. Nevertheless, in each of these areas the next fourteen years would see important strides forward.

# 5

## THE MATURATION
## OF INDUSTRIAL UNIONISM

As we examine the transformation of consciousness and organizational behavior among Nuremberg skilled metalworkers, it is useful once again to look at the processes of industrialization and population growth that lay at the root of social conflict and class formation in the city. The national occupational censuses of 1882, 1895, and 1907 provide data much superior to anything available for earlier decades. From this base it is possible to assess the nature of the rapid changes that took place in the character of the city and its industrial population around 1900.

### Population Growth, Economic Development, and Nuremberg's Metalworkers

The total population of Nuremberg gives some idea of the stormy economic development of the city, especially after the ending of the so-called Great Depression in 1895–1896. From a population of 102,874 in June 1882, the city grew to 155,014 in June 1895 and 301,258 in June 1907. The doubling in twelve years from 1895 to 1907 somewhat exaggerates the true growth rate, because it includes the 1898–1899 annexations of a ring of suburbs with some 30,000 inhabitants. Reflected in these incorporations was a pattern of increasing suburbanization as population growth in the expensive, run-down, and often unsanitary old city ground to a halt. Workers dominated the population of the semicircle of older and newer suburbs in the south of the city, where industrial and residential areas were often mixed together. The expansion of working-class housing southward was further increased by the relocation in the 1890s of both Klett (after 1898, M.A.N.) and Schuckert to new factories at what was then the southern edge of the city.[1]

The 1895 and 1907 censuses also allow us insight into the working-class character of the city and the importance of metalworkers in it. In 1895 nearly two-thirds (63.9 percent) of the labor force were listed as "workers" or "servants," even when servants who lived with their employers are excluded. With their dependents, these workers and servants formed half (49.8 percent) of the city's population. By 1907 these figures had increased to 69.1 percent and 58.0 percent respectively. In both cases industrial workers (a category that includes artisan journeymen) formed about 78 percent of these workers and servants; the rest were primarily employed in trade and transport. Of Nuremberg's industrial workers, 32.9 percent in 1895 and 42.3 percent in 1907 were employed in census categories V (metalworking) and VI (machines and instruments), which together approximate the number of metalworkers in the city. By 1907 there were over 30,000 metalworkers in Nuremberg: the census counted 17,126 workers in metalworking and 14,169 in machines and instruments. With their dependents, these metalworkers constituted one-fifth of the entire city population in that year.[2]

A birthplace survey carried out during this census also provides information about the composition of the working class. Table 5.1 summarizes the birthplaces of Nurembergers according to whether they were born in the city or outside, in communities of more or less than two thousand people (here called "urban" and "rural"), and according to geographical location. The data confirm the ethnic or regional homogeneity of Nuremberg's population, a factor that contributed to class formation at least negatively, by eliminating one potential source of internal division in the working class. Five-sixths of all workers came from northern Bavaria, and metalworkers differed little in this respect from the other parts of the city population.

More interesting variations are visible when the type of community is considered. Industrial workers were much more likely to be born outside

Table 5.1. BIRTHPLACES OF NUREMBERG RESIDENTS, 1907
(PERCENTAGES)

| | Type of community | | | | |
|---|---|---|---|---|---|
| | *Urban* | *Rural* | | *Nuremberg* | *Other* |
| City population | 53.3 | 46.7 | | 48.0 | 52.0 |
| Industrial workers | 52.0 | 48.0 | | 33.9 | 66.1 |
| Workers–mtw. | 57.2 | 42.8 | | 40.0 | 60.0 |
| Workers–mach. | 53.7 | 46.3 | | 35.1 | 64.9 |

| | Geographical location | | | | |
|---|---|---|---|---|---|
| | *N Bav.* | *S Bav.* | *SW Ger.* | *N Ger.* | *For.* |
| City population | 82.3 | 5.8 | 3.0 | 5.6 | 3.2 |
| Industrial workers | 83.5 | 5.9 | 2.6 | 4.3 | 3.7 |
| Workers–mtw. | 85.0 | 5.3 | 2.4 | 4.2 | 3.2 |
| Workers–mach. | 83.3 | 5.6 | 2.8 | 4.9 | 3.5 |

SOURCE: Kaiserliches Statistisches Amt, *Statistik des Deutschen Reiches*, N.F., 210.2:310–315.

NOTE: Mtw. – Metalworking; Mach. – Machines and Instruments; N Bav. – Northern Bavaria; S Bav. – Southern Bavaria; SW Ger. – Southwest Germany (including the Bavarian Palatinate); N Ger. – Northern Germany; For. – Foreign. Because of rounding, not all rows add to 100%.

the city than were members of other occupational groups, which reflects the influx of poor small-town and rural northern Bavarians into the city. Workers in metalworking, in contrast, were more likely than either industrial workers as a group or machine-industry workers in particular to come from the city and from urban locations generally. Since this sector encompassed the toy and light metalwares industry and most of the traditional artisanal trades, this difference may arise from the greater need for skilled workers in that sector as well as the tendency for female workers to come more frequently from Nuremberg or other towns (in metalworking, 42.5 percent of women workers were born in the city, and 60.6 percent were from "urban" areas).[3] Conversely the machine industry was probably attracting a greater share of rural male unskilled workers by 1907.

Other interesting differences between the two major sectors of Nuremberg's metal industries are brought to light by census figures on female employment and firm size. The employment of women in Nuremberg was continually increasing (see Table 5.2). Employment of women as workers in the metal industries was increasing even faster than the average increase in the labor force, but there were radical differences between the two sectors. In metalworking large numbers of women were employed—primarily in the toy industry, light metalwares, and gold and metal beating. In 1907 41.3 percent of all women workers in this sector labored in the toy industry alone. The machines and instruments sector, in contrast, employed relatively few women. Of the 1,441 female workers in this sector in 1907 (compared to 5,995 in metalworking), three-quarters (72.0 percent) were concentrated in the electrotechnical industry and mathematical instrument making. Before the First World War, traditional machine industry enterprises like M.A.N. and its smaller competitors remained an almost exclusively male preserve.[4]

Table 5.2. WOMEN EMPLOYED IN NUREMBERG, 1882–1907 (PERCENTAGES)

|  | 1882 | 1895 | 1907 |
|---|---|---|---|
| City labor force | 22.4 | 24.8 | 29.0 |
| Industrial workers | 22.1 | 25.2 | 28.5 |
| Workers-mtw. | 20.4 | 23.5 | 35.0 |
| Workers-mach. | 2.5 | 6.7 | 10.2 |

SOURCES: Kaiserliches Statistisches Amt, *Statistik des Deutschen Reiches*, N.F., 107:284–289, 207:257–258; Schwab, *Verschiebungen*, 25.

NOTE: 1882 figures are female percentages of all employees, including owners and white-collar workers. Actual female percentages of *workers* would be slightly higher. Mtw. – Metalworking; Mach. – Machines and Instruments.

Differences in the structure and nature of the two sectors are also revealed by the census surveys of individual firms or shops *(Betriebe)*. The data in Table 5.3 relate the number of employees (i.e., including owners and white-collar workers) to the number of firms. Because very large firms engaged in different product lines might be split into more than one Betrieb for census purposes, these numbers may be slightly low. Nonetheless we may note the rapid concentration and growth process that was occurring in the machine and electrotechnical industries, spearheaded by M.A.N. and Schuckert. Change was much more gradual in the metalworking sector, with its large numbers of small factories, artisan masters, and domestic workers. The continuing predominance of small producers in this sector is demonstrated by the fact that in both 1895 and 1907 over two-thirds of all firms had only one to five employees. But even in the area of machines and instruments the number of firms with five employees or less only declined from 70.7 percent to 59.5 percent over the twelve-year interim.[5] These figures may be misleading, however. The actual percentages of employees working in each firm size class are available only for 1895 (see Table 5.4). Close to three-quarters of all employees in machines and instruments worked in Betriebe of 201 employees or more as early as 1895, and even in metalworking little more than a quarter were employed in artisanal shops of ten employees or less. Factory work was becoming the dominant form of employment for all metalworkers.

Despite their limitations, these census figures give us an impression of the rapid changes that were taking place in the size and character of the

Table 5.3. EMPLOYEES PER FIRM, NUREMBERG, 1882–1907

|  | 1882 | 1895 | 1907 |
|---|---|---|---|
| Industry and artisanry | 4.8 | 6.2 | 8.2 |
| Metalworking | 5.8 | 10.0 | 13.7 |
| Machines and instruments | 11.8 | 24.2 | 43.2 |

SOURCES: Kaiserliches Statistisches Amt, *Statistik des Deutschen Reiches*, N.F., 116:71–75, 217:277–281; Bavaria, Königliches Statistisches Bureau, *Die Ergebnisse der Berufszählung im Königreich Bayern vom 5. Juni 1882*, III. Theil: *Die bayerische Bevölkerung nach ihrer gewerblichen Thätigkeit*, 384–415.

Table 5.4. DISTRIBUTION OF EMPLOYEES IN FIRM SIZE CLASSES, NUREMBERG, 1895 (PERCENTAGES)

| | Number of employees per firm | | | | |
|---|---|---|---|---|---|
| | 1–5 | 6–10 | 11–50 | 50–200 | 201+ |
| Industry and artisanry | 26.6 | 9.8 | 22.8 | 19.9 | 20.9 |
| Metalworking | 16.6 | 10.7 | 32.3 | 29.5 | 10.9 |
| Machines and instruments | 6.7 | 4.4 | 8.9 | 8.9 | 71.1 |

SOURCE: Kaiserliches Statistisches Amt, *Statistik des Deutschen Reiches*, N.F., 116:71–75.

metalworking and machine-industry labor forces in Nuremberg, especially after 1895. The rapid growth in the number of women employed and in the size of workplaces implied significant alterations in the position of skilled workers in the production process and in their relation to their employers. Often that implied an erosion of the power of the skilled. Rationalization—whether in the form of piece rates, the greater employment of semiskilled and unskilled labor, or mechanization—began to have a noticeable effect on the nature of the work carried on by apprenticed craftsmen in the factories. This is reflected in the struggles and strike behavior of the iron molders, bicycle workers, and machine-industry workers, to be examined below. Although rationalization and industrialization threatened—and sometimes undermined—the power of the skilled, these developments also often presented new opportunities to the trade unions to mobilize both the inactive majority of skilled workers and the essentially unorganized unskilled. The growth of factory labor, the decline in the relative significance of the artisanal sector, and the threat to the power of the skilled, when combined with the favorable environment for the socialist movement that Nuremberg presented, all tended to strengthen class consciousness and the need for organization and to weaken craft consciousness. How did the party and unions fare? How did the DMV in particular cope with the difficulties created by massive growth?

The Maturation of the DMV

The fourteen years following the formation of the DMV saw its rise in Nuremberg to the position of a large, well-organized, centralized, and increasingly bureaucratized industrial union. But before we examine this process it is important to look briefly at the further development of the Nuremberg SPD (the official party name since 1891) as evidence for the broader context of working-class formation at the political level.

Electorally, Social Democracy continued its inexorable rise in the city. In 1893 the local party finally broke through the restraints of the limited franchise, winner-take-all, indirect election system for the Bavarian Landtag and took all four Nuremberg seats. Grillenberger and Scherm were two of those new deputies. Since the Reichstag seat remained completely safe, with first-ballot majorities climbing to 60 percent, the complete exclusion of the SPD from municipal government became a glaring discrepancy. The undemocratic system of a very restricted franchise and winner-take-all elections sustained the control of the liberals until a municipal reform was pushed through the Bavarian parliament in 1908. Before that time a confrontational relationship between a bourgeois city government and a predominantly socialist working class (together with an allied section of the lower middle class) remained the overriding political reality in Nuremberg. The very restrictive conditions of the Association Law gave the police ample opportunities to harass and dissolve socialist meetings and organizations even after 1890, and these measures were often reinforced by Reich and Bavarian state authorities. Only in 1898–1899 were the laws loosened enough to create a regular Social Democratic local party organization out of the electoral association formed in 1883. Total membership grew from 1,900 in 1891 to about 7,400 in 1905 and over 21,000 on the eve of the First World War. Also flourishing were the great variety of voluntary organizations so typical of the Imperial German socialist subculture. Dozens of singing, gymnastic, educational and other societies grew out of the rich soil of the intensely working-class neighborhoods in the old city and southern suburbs.[6]

The Nuremberg metalworkers took part in this process of deepening working-class formation. In 1894 36 percent of local party members were skilled metalworkers, and some of the 9 percent of members who were unskilled must have worked in metal industries too. These numbers slightly exceeded the proportion of metalworkers among industrial workers in 1895 cited above. What the small number of activists and the large number of passive voters among metalworkers actually thought about socialism is much harder to determine, but it is interesting that Nuremberg was consistently to the left of the very reformist Bavarian party. Grillenberger faced another party revolt over the SPD delegation's vote for the Bavarian budget in 1894, and three years after his sudden death in 1897 the building resentment of the activist rank and file against their authoritarian leader erupted in an internal party crisis. Thereafter local control prevailed, and the Nuremberg party majority supported the orthodox Marxist position of Bebel and Kautsky in national party conflicts. The heavily working-class character of the Nuremberg party and its confrontational relationship with employers, bourgeois liberalism, and the state lay at the root of this distrust of reformism and emphasis on class consciousness in ideology. Tactically, of course, reformism still ruled. Electoral politics and daily organization building, not revolution, were the lifeblood of the party.[7]

The great expansion of industrial unionism in the metal trades took place in this political context. Officially the DMV was politically neutral, but this did not conceal its close relationship to the socialist movement. The promotion of class consciousness by the SPD and its organizations can only have fortified industrial unionism and hindered competing craft and nonsocialist organizations. With the growth of the DMV's membership came the bureaucratization of the local DMV and the slow unification of the craft sections into a single local. As craft consciousness declined, class consciousness and organizational commitment generally rose, but the form of the bureaucratic industrial union created its own difficulties. The success of the Nuremberg DMV could not hide some of the limitations that were sooner or later to plague the German Social Democratic movement.

THE GROWTH OF THE DMV AND ITS COMPETING ORGANIZATIONS

An incredible diversity of craft sections and locals existed within the local DMV before 1905 (see Appendix A, section 3). In that year the last five sections merged with the so-called General Local (Allgemeine Zahlstelle), which had been formed in 1895–1896 by the locksmiths' and machinists' section to push through the idea of industrial organization. Of the craft or multicraft sections only the locksmiths and machinists, the iron molders, the metal pressers, the mathematical instrument industry section, the brass molders, the tinsmiths, the blacksmiths, and the gold beaters (not created until 1897) were important. The remainder were always quite small and either folded or joined the General Local at an earlier date. Two suburban locals also existed even after the city's incorporation of their towns in 1899: the Schniegling-Doos local (absorbed in 1902), with its base in the bicycle factories to the west of the city; and the Mögeldorf local, on the far east end of the city, which, because of its distance, maintained its independence until 1907.

Sixteen unions, seven of which had been formed earlier, competed with the DMV. Most of these may also be disregarded as insignificant, either because they were local craft unions of minuscule size or, as in the case of the Hirsch-Duncker (liberal) unions, because they never achieved much influence in Nuremberg despite long-lived and stable national organizations. Significant competition came from just four unions: the local gold beaters organized in the DGSV, the Central Association of Iron Molders and Foundry Workers, the Central Union of Blacksmiths (all socialist in orientation), and the Christian Metalworkers' Union (CMV). The three major competing socialist unions were all eventually absorbed by the DMV, though not without vigorous controversy as well as ruthless tactics on the part of the DMV national leadership, who possessed much larger financial resources.[8]

Eclipsing the Hirsch-Duncker unions as the main competitors of the Free (socialist) unions were the Christian organizations formed about 1900. In Nuremberg a Christian metalworkers' union appeared in 1898, and by 1900 it had joined the new national Christian union. Unfortunately no membership figures are available before 1910. In that year local membership exceeded a thousand, while DMV membership had reached nearly eighteen thousand in Nuremberg. But when we consider that by 1907 Catholics already formed 30.4 percent of the city population, 33.8 percent of workers in metalworking, and 36.4 percent of workers in machines and instruments, it is clear that this essentially Catholic organization did not succeed in capturing a segment of organized metalworkers equivalent to the Catholic portion of the labor force.[9] Although an increasingly well organized Catholic subculture existed in Nuremberg toward the end of the century—Mayors Stromer and von Schuh commented on the fact in 1889 and 1896, respectively—Catholic institutions must not have been entirely successful at integrating migrants to the city. Politically this was certainly the case; the Catholic Center Party remained insignificant in local politics. As suggested in the Introduction, this pattern may parallel that in Düsseldorf, where migrant Catholics were much more susceptible to the appeals of the socialist movement than those born and raised locally.[10] In general it appears that the class formation process in Nuremberg was not greatly obstructed by confessional divisions.

The absence of adequate membership figures for the CMV and other unions makes it difficult to gauge the relative strengths of the DMV and its competitors or to assess accurately the overall organization rate (defined as the percentage of workers in a particular sector organized into unions). From the standpoint of sheer numbers only two competitors appear to have had significance: the DGSV local before 1899 and the CMV by 1905. Judging by the jump in the DMV gold beaters' section membership from 257 in June to 741 in December 1899, the DGSV local may have had 500 members, and in earlier years perhaps more. The CMV may have reached 500 members in 1905.[11] Altogether all competing unions in Nuremberg before 1905 probably had a thousand members and sometimes less. In relative terms these numbers were decreasingly significant, because the DMV's growth far outstripped that of its remaining competitors.

For the DMV there is much more data because of the availability of the *Deutsche Metallarbeiter-Zeitung (DMZ)*, which became the official union organ upon the DMV's foundation in 1891. Until 1903 the paper remained in the city (union headquarters were in Stuttgart), with Grillenberger's old friend, Johann Scherm, staying on as editor. Regular membership reports in the *DMZ*, combined with the yearbooks and publications put out by the expanding union bureaucracy after 1903, permit a fairly exact reconstruction of local membership. This information is summarized in Figure 5.1, which charts total membership in the city (including the two suburban locals), and membership in the largest subsection, the General Local and its predecessor, the locksmiths' and machinists' section. In overall membership the city's DMV grew rapidly in two distinct phases, from 1894 to 1898 and from 1903 to 1905 (and beyond). This periodization corresponds roughly to the economic situation: the rapid growth from 1895 to 1899 and 1903 to 1907 was punctuated by sharp recessions from 1891 to 1895 and 1900 to 1902. Membership growth diverged from the business cycle most noticeably in 1899, but much of the drop in that year's figures stemmed from the sharp fall in the General Local's size from 2,663 on December 31, 1898, to 2,145 at the end of 1899. This decrease occurred because of the hiring of a paid official, who tightened controls on payment of dues and thereby eliminated many lapsed members from the rolls. Figures prior to this time were actually somewhat inflated because of the laxness of administration.

This 1899 incident hints at a serious problem that lay behind the seemingly inexorable growth in total membership: a sometimes astounding turnover in the rank and file. For example, in the course of 1904 the

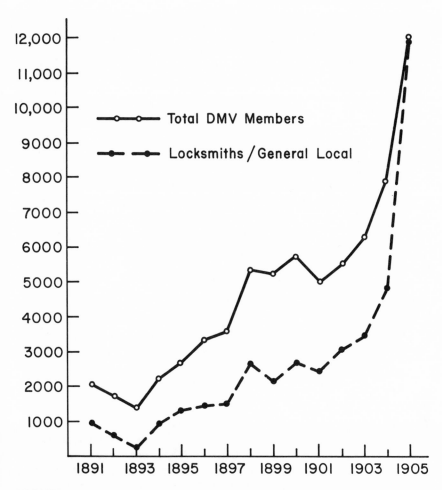

FIGURE 5.1. Nuremberg DMV Membership, 1891–1905

SOURCE: *Deutsche Metallarbeiter-Zeitung; Metallarbeiter-Zeitung.*
NOTE: Figures represent membership at year's end. Suburban locals are included in the data for total DMV members.

Skilled Metalworkers of Nuremberg

Table 5.5. FLUCTUATION IN DMV GENERAL LOCAL
MEMBERSHIP, 1904

|  | Men | Women |
| --- | --- | --- |
| Gains | | |
| New members | 2,241 | 472 |
| Members from other places | 523 | 0 |
| Members from Nuremberg sections | 14 | 0 |
| Members from foreign unions | 58 | 0 |
| Returned from military | 30 | 0 |
| Losses | | |
| Left town | 740 | 0 |
| Quit | 679 | 285 |
| Struck for back dues | 120 | 45 |
| Expelled | 3 | 0 |
| Died | 14 | 0 |
| Called up to military | 90 | 0 |
| Net Increase | 1,220 | 142 |

Source: "Allgem. Zahlstelle Jahresbericht 1904," StadtAN, Vereinsarchiv Nr. 190.

General Local grew from 3,475 members including 150 women, to 4,817, including 292 women (see Table 5.5). The net result was a fluctuation rate (losses divided by final membership) of 41 percent for the local as a whole, and 113 percent for women! The leadership attributed this turnover, especially among the women, to the successful toy industry campaign of that year, since major wage movements and strikes always attracted a certain proportion of new members who only wanted union strike pay, and lacked long-term commitment to the union. Whatever the reason, these numbers were typical for the DMV nationally during this period. The turnover problem had been the cause of much discussion and consternation in the union since the mid-1890s and was directly responsible for the growth in its benefit structure and bureaucracy, to be discussed below.[12]

What did this fluctuation imply for the nature of the union and its sections and locals? Essentially the membership at any time was made up of

138

a core of leaders, older members, and activists, and an inactive majority of highly unstable character. A large number of workers were members for at most a year or two, and then quit; or they left town in the great migrations of the industrialization period; or they fell behind in their dues because of unemployment, low wages, or lack of commitment. This does not mean that these workers did not possess a modicum of class consciousness—they probably had at least a sense of working-class identity in a society beset by upper and middle-class snobbery and open economic, political, and administrative discrimination against workers. Nor does it mean that the skilled among them (who still formed the great majority of the organized) did not possess some craft consciousness born of their training and traditions. As I have stressed, these loyalties could be and were held simultaneously by the same people—along with other loyalties and identities. The peculiar environment of Nuremberg in fact fostered both working-class formation and strong craft traditions—and they sometimes reinforced each other. Nonetheless loyalties to class and craft could not guarantee that workers would join or remain committed to membership in a union. The vagaries and hazards of working-class life—unemployment, old age, illness, the need or desire to move on, lack of education, working environments hostile to organization or communication among workers, barriers of craft, of skill, or of sex among workers—all contributed to a low commitment to trade-union organization among the rank and file. In the face of these difficulties it is actually remarkable that the Social Democratic movement—not only the unions, but also the SPD and its penumbra of voluntary associations—built such large organizations by 1914 and struck such deep roots in the working class.

Fluctuation of membership was a problem for the Nuremberg DMV in this period, however, as it was for other unions. This instability, along with the related problems of skill, sex, and age barriers in the work force, presented one of the main obstacles to achieving a high organization rate. The lack of a skill meant for many workers a lack of bargaining power as well as a lack of identity and pride, and the DMV, organized and structured on the basis of the power and craft consciousness of the skilled, had a difficult time attracting or integrating the unskilled. Gender barriers were inextricably bound up with this problem, because women workers (the cutters and helpers in gold beating perhaps excepted) lacked formal skills and also suffered all the disadvantages of a discriminatory, patriarchal society. Finally, age was a factor because of the so-called life earnings curve typical of workers in this period.[13] During their twenties and early thirties skilled workers earned relatively high wages as their experience grew and their physical strength reached its peak. Usually unencumbered by heavy family responsibilities at that time, they were more willing to take risks. But once they had children to feed, their margin of extra income disappeared and their ability to risk their jobs through union activities or strikes declined. After the age of forty workers' physical powers began to decline as well, and at fifty they were old men, often unable to hold skilled jobs any longer—if they lived that long. Those without older children at home to help support them would then have serious money problems. Thus the union, even more than the work force, was predominantly made up of skilled men between eighteen and forty years of age. Data are lacking for Nuremberg, but for the DMV as a whole almost three-quarters of its membership in 1907 were aged eighteen to thirty-five. Nearly half of all members were in their twenties.[14]

In spite of all these barriers, and in spite of the reservations about growing membership figures that high fluctuation rates imply, the DMV in Nuremberg was able to achieve a good organization rate by 1905—a sign of its maturity as an industrial organization. In 1895 the union had organized less than 20 percent of the metalworkers in Nuremberg and its suburbs,[15] but by the end of 1905, which saw a massive growth in membership due in part, as we shall see, to the great strike/lockout of that year, the organization rate reached about 40 percent. Of some thirty thousand metalworkers in the city, twelve thousand were members of the DMV. (If competing unions had one thousand members, the overall organization rate was 43.3 percent.) By 1912 the DMV had half of all Nuremberg metalworkers as members.[16] These numbers were very respectable for any union organization at any time. Thereafter the organization rate did not improve, an indication of the stagnation of the union and the Social Democratic movement as a whole in the Weimar period.

Part of the reason for the spectacular growth of the Nuremberg DMV after 1903 was its breakthrough into the ranks of women and the unskilled. Specific figures for the unskilled are generally unavailable, although we do know that there were sixty-three male "helpers" (*Hilfsarbeiter*) and twenty-five women out of 1,102 members in the General Local in the first quarter of 1896.[17] The percentage of women is not as inaccessible, but the data are scattered. In general there do not appear to have been more than a few dozen female members prior to the organization of the gold beaters' section in 1897. After the absorption of the DGSV local there were 546 female members in that section in mid-1900 (63.7 percent of section membership) and 660 female members in all, or 11.4

percent of the Nuremberg DMV. By the end of 1905 female membership rose to 1,451, but because of the fast growth of male membership, this was still only 12.1 percent of the total. The real breakthrough came later. With the arrival of Helene Grünberg in the city in 1905 as one of the chief employees of the Workers' Secretariat, a campaign to organize women began. In 1912–1913 DMV female membership in the city reached about 6,200—some 30 percent of the membership.[18] This marked a fundamental transformation, indicating once again the maturity of the local DMV as an industrial union.

BUREAUCRATIZATION AND UNIFICATION

Rapid membership growth, a high fluctuation rate, a changing membership composition—all put considerable strain on the structure of the Nuremberg DMV. In its original form there was no unitary organization in the city or any professional union bureaucracy. Fragmented in the nineties into about ten sections (Nuremberg consistently held the record within the union for craft organization), the local membership was linked by few central institutions. Regular but poorly attended joint meetings were held for the first few years, but later they seem to have lapsed. The distribution of travel money to departing members—a late version of the old artisanal custom—was given over in 1891 to the office of the *Metallarbeiter-Zeitung* and in 1892 to a Central Hostel for Metalworkers set up by the sections. There were also regular northern Bavarian metalworkers' conferences, and they elected an agitation commission for the region. Both conferences and commissions were inevitably dominated by Nuremberg. The commissions notwithstanding, coordination among the sections was very weak, and there were no paid union officials of any kind. All section officers and commission members were volunteers working in their spare time with little or no remuneration for their efforts. Greater professionalization or centralization was thwarted by the small size and weak financial position of the DMV nationally and locally and by divisions along craft lines in the city. Squabbling between the sections and debates over unification were never ending in the nineties.[19]

Leading the drive for unitary industrial unionism was the locksmiths' and machinists' section, which already had a multicraft or quasi-industrial union character because of its representation of most groups of skilled workers in the machine industry. The tactics of this section's leadership were not always appropriate, however. Disparaging remarks about "caste spirit" and a "labor aristocracy" accomplished little. The culmination of this campaign came when the prominent orator of the late eighties, Carl

*141*

Breder, returned from Augsburg in the summer of 1895. He had spent four years there as editor of the SPD newspaper and nominal party leader, but the failure of the socialist movement to make significant gains in Augsburg caused factional infighting that was exacerbated by Breder's abrasive personality. Eventually he was forced to leave. Under his leadership the locksmiths launched the General Local at the end of 1895, even when all the other sections (except the insignificant harmonica makers) decided not to cooperate. In 1896 the General Local, apparently supported by the national executive, seized control of travel money distribution without consulting the sections. Breder further alienated the tinsmiths' section and the strikers at the Carrette toy factory that same year by attempting to force the strikers to give in early. The last straw was his attempt to bias the election of delegates to the 1897 DMV General Assembly in favor of the General Local. A meeting called in March 1897 by the section leaders but boycotted by the General Local resulted in an outpouring of hostility to Breder personally and the tactics of the local generally. Breder was forced to step down as chairman, but not before he had done considerable damage to the possibility of uniting the sections.[20]

Breder is virtually the only prominent metalworkers' leader after the 1870s for whom we have biographical information. Born in March 1864 into a family of silk weavers in Bielefeld (which made him a rare north German in the Nuremberg movement), he was variously described as a locksmith and as an "iron turner" *(Eisendreher)*. Conceivably he was both, as many turners were not formally apprenticed in that occupation. He first appeared in the executive of the locksmiths' and machinists' union in January 1886, and from 1888 to 1891 he played a prominent and not always happy role, especially in the Schuckert strike and as national coordinator for the locksmiths and machinists (see Chapter 4). He was described by the police in 1888 as having a rather intellectual appearance: a small dark mustache, glasses, and small face, with a "relatively elegant" bearing. Like so many talented agitators, he used the labor movement to rise out of the working class. In 1890 he became the owner of a cigar store before he left for the editor's job in Augsburg the next year. After returning he became a reporter for the *Fränkische Tagespost* as well as a union leader. In 1898, records show him to be the owner of the most important SPD pub and meeting hall, the Café Merk. He held a few minor local SPD posts thereafter and eventually died in March 1918.[21]

Breder's personality undoubtedly prevented his ascent from daily manual labor in another direction: upward through the DMV bureaucracy, which began to expand around 1900. As far as is known, the first full-time Nuremberg employee of the union was the General Local's "business manager," Wilhelm Kümmerle, who assumed the post in 1899.[22] Not coincidentally, this was also the same year in which the DMV finally adopted unemployment insurance for members after a long and acrimonious national debate. This massive benefits program aimed at stabilizing the perturbing fluctuation rate among the rank and file by motivating them to remain members long enough to receive weekly benefits in case of unemployment. In this the program does not seem to have been very successful, although union membership did rise nationally. At the same time unemployment insurance imposed higher dues and a more extensive system of administration. Bureaucratization and centralization of authority were further strengthened by the evolving strike policy of the union leadership, which imposed ever more extensive conditions upon the initiation of strikes in order to prevent the wastage of funds. Eventually offensive actions had to be proposed to Stuttgart headquarters months in advance.[23] This process added further burdens to the already extensive duties of the voluntary local leaders and may have contributed to the General Local's hiring of Kümmerle in 1899.

Further bureaucratization at the local level was slow, before the unification of the sections in 1905. The one major step was the creation of a "district leader" (*Bezirksleiter*) for District X (Bavaria east of the Rhine) in 1903. Given Nuremberg's predominance over Munich within the DMV, it was inevitable that the seat of the district leader be in the city. Chosen for the position was the locksmith Karl Enßner (1858–?), a Protestant from Middle Franconia and a longtime member of the leadership of the locksmiths' and machinists' section and the General Local. Enßner was also prominent in the local SPD around 1900. The national DMV congress in Nuremberg in 1901 had created the district system, but the election of a district leader for Bavaria was resisted at first by the southern Bavarians especially, on grounds of expense and lack of need.[24] Why they gave in two years later is unknown, but the expanding administrative burden of unemployment insurance and the complex strike policy of the DMV were probably factors. Pressure from national headquarters undoubtedly also existed.

The resistance to the election of a district leader was the last stand of the fight against bureaucratization of the Nuremberg DMV. During the nineties many members had objected to both paid officials and unemployment insurance on the grounds that the expense would be high, requiring higher dues, which would drive away new members. Missing from the fight over the position of a district leader, however, were many arguments brought forth in the early and mid-nineties. Mirroring the opinion of many members of the socialist movement, Andreas Hassel, a metal turner and prominent member of the locksmiths' and machinists' section, described the union in 1893 as a "training school for socialism," that is, an appendage of the SPD. He opposed as financially impossible any effort to institute unemployment insurance, and by implication he dismissed any hope that the amelioration of the workers' position under capitalism was possible.[25] But the swift growth in the number of members and the frequency of strikes in the late nineties brought credibility to the idea that improvements in working conditions could be achieved in capitalist society through trade-union action. Reformism became—consciously or unconsciously—the attitude of the union leadership. The gradual appearance of a reformist and increasingly bureaucratic union elite did not provoke much resistance from the membership. The one exception was the protest of the metal pressers' section against the creation of unemployment insurance in 1899. In this context the members of the section angrily denounced the high pay of the union bureaucracy relative to workers' wages.[26] But such protests were rare. The remarkable success of the local DMV, especially in later years, was the greatest shield the Nuremberg leadership had against rank-and-file dissatisfaction.[27]

From the point of view of the industrial union advocates in the General Local and at national headquarters, the last remaining obstacle to the reorganization of the DMV structure in Nuremberg was its fragmentation into sections. Before 1900 the big local absorbed only two minor sections, that of the metal beaters in 1896 and of the fine mechanics in 1897. In the latter case it may be relevant that the chairman of the section had embezzled its treasury.[28] Major gains came only in 1900–1902, with the disappearance of the sections of brass molders (1900); grinders and polishers, metal pressers, and the Schniegling-Doos local (1902); and the tin molders (1903). That left only five major sections: the iron molders, the tinsmiths, the blacksmiths, the gold beaters, and the mathematical instrument industry. Under increasing pressure from Stuttgart these sections, which were among the last of their kind in the national union, finally agreed to merge with the General Local at the beginning of March 1905. Elected were four paid officials—a significant expansion—as well as a board of craft representatives to defend the interests and promote the organization of the various skilled groups. Craft consciousness was not about to disappear.[29]

Although the disappearance of the sections is symbolically very important, two questions remain to be asked: (1) To what extent was the unification actually a victory of class over craft consciousness? And (2), how effective was the new unitary organization?

An answer to the first question is difficult because the sources do not allow us to look behind the scenes to see what motivations existed when the sections decided to give up their independence. It would certainly be naive to think that some abstract commitment to class was a prime reason for any of the mergers. Practical considerations, such as the difficulties and burdens of maintaining a small section, the existence of pressure from national headquarters, or the growing irrelevance of organizational divisions along the old craft boundaries, must have been paramount. By the same token resistance to unification was not based merely on an insular craft consciousness. A leading member of the brass molders' section, Ludwig Zeiträg, defended the craft sections in 1897 with the arguments that they were less impersonal and thus could retain more members, their meeting attendance was better, and it was easier for newer and more inarticulate members to speak. Above all, they were cheaper because they did not need paid officials, as a unitary local would.[30] Ironically, Zeiträg's section became in 1900 the first major one to merge with the General Local. We do not know why, but it is reasonable to speculate that the increasing size and diversity of the section—it attracted all varieties of skilled and unskilled workers in the brass and bronze industries—made an organizational definition based upon traditional artisanal lines increasingly inappropriate. Strike coordination may have been a factor as well, because only weeks after the merger a bitter and broad-based strike broke out at the J. C. Braun fire-fighting equipment factory. That strike included many locksmiths and others usually organized in the General Local.[31]

The disappearance of the other major sections in 1905 did not eliminate the dialectic of craft and class. The craft representative system in the unified local functioned to defend the interests of the extremely heterogeneous groups of workers represented by DMV. Certain groups had even more autonomy. The metal beaters and the ever-troublesome construction locksmiths were each granted a measure of independence within the General Local as early as 1901.[32] Through these arrangements the leadership attempted to appease journeymen in the artisanal sector who still had a strong craft identity. Skilled worker pride and bargaining power remained the foundation of the union. If the DMV was to maintain and strengthen its position it was essential that the needs of the various crafts be satisfied so that craft consciousness could continue to be channeled into industrial organization and reformist class consciousness.

The second question remains: How effective was this organizational form, that is, the centralized industrial union organized into citywide locals? Judging by the high organization rate, growth in membership, and gains in wages and working conditions achieved by the Nuremberg DMV after 1900, it was very successful. However, the effectiveness of the DMV nationally has been criticized from a left-wing perspective by Elisabeth Domansky-Davidsohn.[33] She points out that the unitary big city locals that evolved from artisanal origins (that is, citywide craft organizations along the lines of the old guilds and journeymen's associations) were often unsuited to organizing large firms. Factory locals would have been more appropriate. It is true that a huge unified local, such as existed in Nuremberg after 1905, tended to be bureaucratic and that the leadership was not easily accessible to the rank and file. But even in the sections and their predecessors, the pre-1891 local craft unions, the leadership tended to run union affairs without the active participation from the majority of members, since so many were inarticulate or unwilling to devote much time to meetings. Perhaps in response to the problem of organizing the large firms, "workshop meetings" of workers in individual factories became more and more common from the nineties on, and around 1900 "shop stewards" *(Werkstattvertrauensmänner)* elected in the workshop meetings appeared as links between the General Local and members in the big factories.[34] Around 1904–1905 crucial breakthroughs were made at M.A.N. and other large firms, so the union's organizational form does not appear to have been a fundamental obstacle. The difficulties of organizing the machine industry stemmed, as detailed in the previous two chapters, mostly from the heterogeneous nature of the work force and the power of the employers.

In fairness to Domansky-Davidsohn, it bears repeating that Nuremberg presented a highly favorable environment for the DMV: large numbers of skilled workers, a prominent light metalworking and artisanal sector, and a largely homogeneous and Protestant working class. Virtually absent was the steel industry, which proved almost impossible for unionists to penetrate before 1918. But it is questionable whether even there the DMV must bear the blame. Whatever the flaws of the union's organizational form stemming from its artisanal origins and its base among skilled workers in small and medium-sized factories, it is questionable whether any union could have organized the Rhine-Ruhr steel industry before 1918 given the unskilled work force, the extreme power of the employers of that region, and their undying hostility to unionism. It is equally questionable whether that should lead one to question industrial unionism itself, as Domansky-Davidsohn does.[35] The DMV may have been ahead of its time, but ultimately craft unionism would have been found wanting as the appropriate form for organizing metalworkers in most metal industries, which employed increasingly heterogeneous groups of skilled workers as well as more and more semiskilled and unskilled workers. The DMV was hardly a failure in any case, even if it, like the other socialist unions, did not retain its massive influx of new members during 1918–1920. Its flaws were those of the German socialist movement as a whole: excessive bureaucratism and caution that led almost to a fetishism of organization—a problem that had its roots in the siege mentality fostered by endless state harassment.[36] Industrial unionism as such was not the root of the problem.

The Growth of Strikes and Wage Movements

Parallel to and intimately connected with the growth and development of the DMV and its competitors was the rise in the number of strikes, lockouts, and other labor conflicts after 1894. This change was just as critical and transformative in its implications for Nuremberg metalworkers as was the simultaneous rise in the organization rate. Previously conflicts between workers and owners had been essentially confined to two strike waves: 1872 and 1889–1890. Neither of these waves initiated a sustained period of strike activity (in large part because of severe economic depressions that followed them), and improved working conditions, hours, and wages proved ephemeral in most cases. After 1894 strikes, lockouts and wage movements became a normal part of employee-employer relations in the Nuremberg metal trades, and real gains in remuneration, work time, and working conditions could be sustained. Beginning in 1903 the DMV was also able to obtain formal labor contracts. At the same time the major labor conflicts of the period reveal processes of rationalization and the erosion of the position of the skilled worker in the factories. In some cases, most notably the iron molders, defeat and decline emerged from these conflicts.

All strikes and lockouts between 1891 and 1905 are summarized in Table 5.6, which may be compared to Table 4.1 for the period 1871 to 1890. A steady increase in the number of strikes and lockouts, after a lull in the deep depression of the early 1890s, is apparent. The average size of job actions also increased sharply in the last period, but this number is greatly inflated by the huge lockout of 1905. Without it the average size would be 130.9. The figures from the whole period covered by this table

Table 5.6. NUREMBERG METALWORKERS' STRIKES AND
LOCKOUTS, 1891–1905

| Period | No. of actions | Average size | Defensive/ offensive | Failure rate |
|---|---|---|---|---|
| 1891–1895 | 7 | 110.0 | 5/2 | 28.6% |
| 1896–1900 | 21 | 92.1 | 3/18 | 33.3% |
| 1901–1905 | 31 | 367.1 | 15/15 | 34.5% |

SOURCE: See Appendix B.
NOTE: The "average size" is calculated from the lowest figure in the "maximum size" column in Appendix B. The "failure rate" is determined by the number of failed strikes divided by the total number. The Bavarian lockout of 1905 is not counted in the "defensive/offensive" column for that period. "Defensive" and "offensive" are defined in Appendix B.

are comparable to a German average strike size of 109 from 1899–1914, a figure only half that for France and one-quarter that for Britain.[37] This was the case, at least in Nuremberg, because of the continuing importance of a large number of strikes by skilled workers in the artisanal / small factory sector (see Appendix B). The "defensive / offensive" data are more mixed. The high number of offensive strikes between 1896 and 1900 reflects a broad but less intense strike wave from 1898 to 1900, at a time when unemployment was low (less than 2 percent) and inflation was climbing.[38] The onset of a new recession from 1900 to 1902 produced a lull before a new wave of strikes culminated in the spectacular conflicts of 1905, which will be discussed in a separate section. The much higher number of defensive strikes showed, however, a new aggressiveness on the part of employers, who began to respond in a more organized way to the rise of unions.

Unionization also had a significant impact on the strike behavior of workers. Prior to the massive growth in the DMV's membership, long-range planning in strike actions was virtually absent. Before the end of the nineties, most strikes were spontaneous actions that sprang from the need to fend off wage reductions, the imposition of piece rates, or the tyranny of a particularly obnoxious foreman, or they erupted as offensive strikes in periods of low unemployment and rising prices in order to remedy poor wages and long hours. Only in the strike wave of 1898–1900 does one find a significant number of union-launched actions based upon calculation of the labor market situation: for example, the strikes of the gold beaters, blacksmiths, and mathematical instrument makers in 1899, and the 1900 iron molders' strike. Thereafter tightened controls by the DMV bureaucracy ensured that most strikes were not spontaneous, and the ones that were launched without permission did not always receive union financial support.[39] Unfortunately the sources reveal virtually nothing about the role of the local and national executives in making strike decisions. It is noteworthy, however, that between 1891 and 1905 there were no major protests by the Nuremberg rank and file against the bureaucratic regulation of their spontaneity in labor conflicts.

To go beyond broad generalizations it is necessary to discuss the experiences of skilled workers in particular trades or industries. Two important changes in the character of labor conflicts and employee-employer relations occurred between 1891 and 1905. In the first case, rationalization and deskilling in the work process, although not entirely absent before, now emerged as open issues of conflict in the mid-1890s, specifically among the iron molders and the bicycle workers. These conflicts signaled a decline in the power of some skilled workers, but a second change, the rise of formal labor contracts after 1900 in two sectors—the beating trades and the toy and light metal industry—showed the growing power of the DMV to improve the working conditions of skilled and unskilled metalworkers.

RATIONALIZATION IN IRON MOLDING AND BICYCLE PRODUCTION

In the course of two major battles—in 1894 and 1900—the iron molders lost their privileged position in the machine industry. They still remained crucial skilled workers with a central place in the work process, to be sure, but the unique power possessed by the old local union between 1888 and 1890 was gone, and with it went most of the remaining craft-conscious exclusiveness of the iron molders. The crucial struggle came in January–February 1894. The molders were not defeated, but they were forced to accept a compromise on the principle of piece-rate wages. Widespread payment by the piece, and the acceleration of the work pace that grew out of it, could no longer be fended off.

As noted in Chapter 4, signs of erosion in the molders' position began to appear as early as 1890 with the beginnings of the depression. Disagreements between the molders and the employers increased in 1892 and 1893 as the crisis forced the latter to consider ways of reducing the relatively high wages of the molders and of enforcing efforts to speed up production. The strength of the molders, although divided into two organizations (the DMV section and the Central Association local), still proved sufficient, however, to force three firms to retract mandatory piece rates in 1892–1893. Worsening unemployment nonetheless destroyed whatever power was left over hiring and firing through the now divided employment bureau. In August 1893 the Klett company moved to force mandatory piece rates on its molders. Company documents show that the directors discussed the eventuality of a strike, but the molders did not act. The older molders with long company service, who often had worked by the piece on a voluntary basis, refused to protest. Wages were also somewhat better at Klett, in any case, and the firm was obviously not one to be challenged lightly.[40]

The strike therefore did not erupt in August 1893 but rather in January 1894, at a time of the capitalists' choosing. In December 1893 the director, and from 1892 to 1918 the dominant personality at Klett, Anton Rieppel (1852–1926), organized the Association of Metal Industrialists of Nuremberg, Fürth and Vicinity. Mutual support during strikes was a major goal of the association. The founding of this group ushered in a new phase in the conflict between capital and labor in the Nuremberg machine industry: a struggle of organized blocs. On January 2, 1894, in the midst of the depression and winter unemployment, the Berg and Keck foundries announced that piece rates would henceforth be mandatory. On January 15 about eighty molders struck for abolition of this form of wage payment.[41]

Why were the organized molders so militant about this issue? They certainly feared that piece rates would be used to reduce earnings. This fear was justified by the normal practice of nineteenth-century employers, which was to reduce rates arbitrarily and without warning if earnings were considered too high. They also feared that piece rates would foster competition and disunity among workers, thus damaging union solidarity. But a January 26 statement by the joint strike committee expressed the heart of the matter: the anxiety of the threatened craftsman. Iron molding was a tricky business based on experience and intuition rather than exactitude, and failures were common. From this situation came endless conflicts between molders and their foremen or masters over responsibility for castings that had to be discarded for defects. Under a piece-rate system, deductions could be made for every failure, regardless of whether the molder, the equipment, or the materials were to blame.

The strike committee feared that this, combined with a speedup in work pace enforced by lower rates, would result in both a loss of wages and a decline in quality of work. The concern of the craftsman speaks through its announcement: "The local iron molders have constantly striven to raise their craft, and through conscientious education of apprentices, and restriction of their numbers, to produce good competent workers. That would by general introduction of piece-rate labor become impossible; 'cheap and shoddy' would also become the by-word in our trade."[42]

The strike rapidly expanded as the employers' association farmed out work to other firms, provoking further walkouts. This included twenty-eight of seventy-eight molders at Klett, the first strike that had ever occurred there. But the threat of escalation by the employers and a lockout at Klett forced the union leadership to appeal for mediation by the labor arbitration court. On February 8 the unions and the employers accepted the agreement proposed by the mediators: the molders would accept piece rates, but a minimum day wage was to be paid if piece-rate earnings fell below the minimum or if there were numerous failed castings without evidence of ill will on the part of the molder. Additionally, employers were not to fire molders for striking, they were to pay time and a quarter for overtime over sixty hours, and they were to cooperate with a standing grievance commission of union members in setting day wages and in settling future complaints.[43] All in all, it was a very respectable agreement despite the concession of the principle at stake. It was precisely this concession, however, that signified the slow erosion of the power of the iron molders.

It is noteworthy that conflicts over mechanization and semiskilled labor did not play a significant part in this conflict or in the struggles to come. Installation of molding machines at Klett at the beginning of the nineties, and at Schuckert at the end of the decade, shows that this technological innovation did not go untried.[44] But it was as yet unsuccessful in supplanting the essential skills of the hand molder. The decline in the elite position of the molders sprang mostly from the concerted attempts of the employers to undermine that position. On the one hand, conflicts for the first four years after 1894 were minor, and on the other, the molders' organizations were not able to move the Metal Industrialists' Association to lower hours and raise wages. In 1898 and 1899, however, strikes broke out at Schuckert over piece rates and demands for a speedup. But the 1899 strike was to prove a complete failure, because many remained in the foundry and the employers shared Schuckert's strike work. Even more unfortunately for the workers, the spontaneous outbreak of this strike prevented the launching of a coordinated movement by the Nuremberg molders in 1899. That had to be put off a year.[45]

The decisive battle came in 1900. The goals were strict adherence to the provisions of the 1894 agreement, plus a nine-hour day, minimum hourly wages, a wage raise, better ventilation, and creation of open books showing piece rates (to help clarify the endless controversies in the shops). The strike began in April with not much more than half of the six hundred foundry workers cooperating, and the unexpected onset of a recession and the well-organized efforts of the employers to farm out strike work throughout Germany spelled further trouble. Where German unions faced aggressive and organized adversaries, success was difficult. After three months the strike was abandoned as a total failure.[46]

In the aftermath of the 1900 defeat the iron molders were quiet in Nuremberg and did not participate very actively in the movements and strikes before and during 1905. Their powerful position and their ability to act alone had for the most part disappeared. In the process they also lost a good portion of their elitism. The same process was occurring nationally and internationally; studies of Augsburg and Schaffhausen (Switzerland) mention the erosion of both the molders' dominance and their craft consciousness in the nineties as a result of the rise of piece work, speedups, machine molding, and other rationalization measures.[47] In part because of these changes, independent craft unionism was no longer viable in Germany, and the Central Association gave up its independence to the DMV in 1901. The craft-conscious molder was by no means an extinct species by the beginning of the twentieth century, but he was now more likely to accept cooperation with other metalworkers as a necessity.

Rationalization also provoked a reaction in the bicycle industry, which, except for electrical engineering, was the fastest-growing new sector of the Nuremberg machine industry in the 1890s. The invention of the bicycle in its modern form at the end of the 1880s created a new mass consumption item in all industrialized countries. As early as 1890 the mayor of Nuremberg noted that bicycles were encouraging surburbanization by allowing workers to commute large distances.[48] The city became a center of German bicycle production, no doubt because of its rich endowment of skilled metalworkers. The extent and character of the bicycle industry in Nuremberg between 1886 and 1910 is summarized in Table 5.7. A revolution in productivity occurred between 1890 and 1905: the number of bicycles produced per man-year increased by nearly a factor of 8.

This productivity revolution was fostered by piece rates, speedups,

Table 5.7. NUREMBERG BICYCLE PRODUCTION AND WORK FORCE, 1886–1910

| Year | No. of workers | No. of mach. tools | Bicycles produced | Bicycles per man-year | Machine tools per worker |
|------|------|------|------|------|------|
| 1886 | 30 | 15 | 240 | 8.0 | 0.50 |
| 1890 | 415 | 230 | 3,550 | 8.6 | 0.55 |
| 1895 | 1,260 | 690 | 23,200 | 18.4 | 0.55 |
| 1900 | 1,505 | 1,025 | 43,800 | 29.1 | 0.68 |
| 1905 | 1,715 | 1,285 | 112,100 | 65.4 | 0.75 |
| 1910 | 1,685 | 1,415 | 127,000 | 75.4 | 0.84 |

SOURCE: Seubert, "Entstehung der Nürnberger Fahrzeugindustrie," 66–67.

specialization of tasks, and greater mechanization. However, the number of machine tools per worker did not grow drastically, especially before 1895 (see Table 5.7, col. 5). The earliest phases of the growth in productivity were probably due mostly to the introduction of piece rates. At one major firm, Frankenburger and Ottenstein, piece rates were introduced for almost all workers at the end of 1893. This move doubtless sparked resistance. Rarely are we allowed to see events as they happened on the shop floor, but a revealing incident at this plant occurred a few months later. A fine mechanic named Schiller became the target of intense hostility among the workers because he acted, in the parlance of American workers at this time, as a "rate buster." By violating informal restrictions on output imposed by the skilled workers, he provoked major piece-rate cuts by management. He was labeled a "lackey of capital," among other things, essentially for working too hard. The organized workers in the factory sent a delegation to the owners and pressured them into firing him. David Montgomery has already shown how common this sort of output restriction was in the United States at the time, both as a defense against rate reductions and as a form of control over the shop floor. It seems likely that these sorts of informal controls were widespread in Germany as well.[49]

Frustration among the workers over the productivity drive boiled over at two plants in early 1895. The first strike, over new penalties for lateness, was quickly settled on a compromise, but the second, provoked by piece-rate cuts at the pioneer firm of Marschütz, developed into a public confrontation that was unusual for the Nuremberg working class. With the help of other bicycle manufacturers, the owner began to recruit strikebreakers. Violent clashes then broke out between the strikers and the strikebreakers, with crowds of workers from neighboring bicycle plants supporting the strikers. Massive numbers of police protected "those willing to work." A number of strikers were locked up for insulting and pressuring strikebreakers, and the city government's abuse of the law was carried to the point that a prominent Nuremberg SPD leader, Karl Oertel, was eventually sentenced to two months in jail for "blackmail" *(Erpressung)* for attempting to intervene on behalf of the strikers in negotiations with Marschütz.[50]

This disaster undoubtedly discouraged further strikes. The productivity revolution accelerated in the next decade (see Table 5.7), but it provoked no public response. For the period after 1898 the lack of strike activity may be attributed in large part to the widespread unemployment in the industry. In that year an overproduction crisis hit the industry as expansion outstripped demand. Emerging from this crisis was the reorientation of the industry toward the mass production of cheap but solid bicycles in the early twentieth century. New specialized machinery was introduced to allow greater productivity, which eroded the control and variety in work to which skilled workers were accustomed and permitted the hiring of many semiskilled machinists. But unemployment, the difficulties of organizing the heterogeneous work force, and the potentially high piece-rate earnings for some skilled workers probably helped dampen the enthusiasm of the bicycle workers for further job actions. The local DMV made various attempts to rouse them, but with limited success. Other than one strike at a bicycle parts firm in 1905, there were no further walkouts until a new series of strikes broke out in 1908. By that time, however, the DMV had allegedly organized 95 percent of the bicycle workers in the city.[51]

THE RISE OF LABOR CONTRACTS

Confrontations between unions and new aggressive employers' organizations was only one of two contradictory trends in Wilhelmine labor-capital relations. The other was the rise of formal labor contracts. Outside the highly organized printing trades, a legally binding contract between a trade union and an employer was a radical idea in turn-of-the-century Germany. Most artisan masters and industrial capitalists held to the view that trade unions were subversive organizations whose only purposes were to create disharmony between workers and employers and to recruit new members for the socialist party. Around 1900 some masters and small employers, who generally were confronted by the best-organized skilled workers, began to concede the usefulness and even necessity of regulating wages and competition in cooperation with the unions. This cooperation was promoted by the existence of the new, if rather ineffectual, guilds *(Innungen)* created after the guild law of 1881. In Nuremberg especially they united the masters of many trades into single organizations that made negotiations easier, provided the masters were ready to negotiate.

The first contracts in Nuremberg metalworking were achieved by the gold and metal beaters in 1902 and 1903. The background was the continuing overproduction crisis in gold and metal leaf, which provoked a constant battle over the form of wage payment. For the iron molders, piece rates were a threat to their job control, craft pride, and standard of living; for the gold and metal beaters they were a means of sustaining what was left of their once elite position. During the period 1891–1905, there was simply not enough demand to sustain prices and employment at previous levels, and all attempts to limit production were frustrated by the existence of many small masters dependent on the credit of the putters-out. In gold beating these masters were the first to introduce payment by the week, which was accompanied by a greater division of labor among gold beaters and therefore higher productivity with no increase in wages.[52] Thus, ironically, the struggle to retain piece rates was also a struggle to limit rationalization in gold beating, but the issue was not so much stopping the speedup or the decline in the quality of work as it was a defense against overproduction and lower earnings.

Prior to the late nineties, economic conditions for the beating trades were so bad that the journeymen could undertake virtually no offensive actions. With the improvement in the demand for gold leaf at the end of the decade, the determination of the gold beaters to recoup their position began to revive. The two organizations—the DGSV local and the DMV gold beaters' section—together initiated a movement in 1899 to achieve the abolition of payment by the week and an eight-hour day with compensatory piece-rate increases. About one thousand workers struck or were locked out in Middle Franconia, and as in 1889, women once again played a prominent role. They formed more than half the strikers and also took an active part in meetings and debates—a unique situation in this period. Strike discipline was maintained superbly, but the financial drain of the two-and-a-half month struggle brought the DGSV close to collapse. The DMV had to take over its strike pay obligations, and the gold beaters' section eventually absorbed the Nuremberg local. The financial crisis also forced the unions to compromise on a nine-hour day and piece-rate increases.[53]

The metal beaters, meanwhile, had sunk into disorganization and apathy even before the dissolution of their section in 1896. "Only a short time ago the metal beaters counted themselves among the so-called 'free workers'," a *Fränkische Tagespost* article claimed in 1892. Now they were close to sinking to the level of the "lowest factory proletariat," a fear expressed by the gold beaters' leader Heinrich Dohm for his own trade that same year.[54] The metal beaters' organizational revival came only in late 1899, after the gold beaters' movement, a metal beaters' strike in Fürth, and numerous other wage movements in the artisanal trades during 1899. Regular meetings by the organized metal beaters soon developed into a semi-autonomous section within the General Local. Strikes in 1900 and 1902 achieved limited wage increases and a fifty-six hour week in some shops.[55] The 1902 strike was not able to force the masters to accept a contract like that already agreed to in gold beating, however. That would wait until 1903.

The gold beaters' agreement of 1899 did not succeed in limiting production significantly in the long run, and the recession of 1900–1902 soon greatly exacerbated the economic crisis of the trade. Temporary improvement arrived in 1902 with the orders for the coronation of King Edward VII of Britain. To secure the rising prices at their higher level, a contract was concluded on March 18, 1902, between the DMV and the employers' organization for Nuremberg and Schwabach. It stipulated piece rates and set up procedures for governing the amount of work time, that is, the overall level of production. The effort to control overproduction proved futile, because demand soon slackened once again and it was difficult in any case to eliminate "wild" shops, which were operated by small masters outside the contract. These shops frequently survived only through the exploitation of large numbers of apprentices, who were used as cheap labor and then fired when their time was up. The chaotic conditions in gold beating eventually led to the collapse of the contract in 1904, but it was resurrected in 1907. Something had to be done to stabilize production. The metal beaters' contract followed in 1903 after a major strike / lockout that paralyzed all Bavarian production. This agreement was maintained until at least 1906.[56]

Many other contracts were also signed in the artisanal sector before the war. The greatest achievement of the Nuremberg DMV was not, however, primarily in this sector. In 1904 the union succeeded in winning a contract that covered most toy-industry firms, both large and small.

Except for a weak movement in 1896, the tinsmiths and other workers in the sheet-metal trades remined largely quiescent until 1903. The tinsmiths' section also showed no further interest in organizing unskilled women. The long-run result of the absorption of the women workers' union in 1891 (see Chapter 4) was negligible; in early 1895 there were only three female members in the section. The section displayed more interest in the construction tinsmiths, but they proved a problem to organize. An attempt to extend the movement to that sector in 1896 and again in 1897 was a complete failure, because of worker apathy.[57] The only craft among the sheet-metal trades that was well organized was metal pressing, but this was a small and insular trade whose organized members tended to act alone in wage movements.

There were at least three important preconditions for the breakthrough in 1904: (1) an improved economic situation after the recession of 1900–1902; (2) growing union membership; and (3) better cooperation among the DMV craft sections and the General Local. In May 1904 the local DMV, coordinated by the new district leader, Enßner, started a joint movement of all the relevant sections, whereas an abortive movement in 1903 had been initiated by the tinsmiths' section alone.[58] The union demanded a contractually fixed workweek of fifty-four hours, with minimum wages for various grades of skilled workers, helpers, and women workers. Other stipulations included wage and piece-rate increases, overtime premiums, and layoffs according to seniority. Surprisingly, Anton Rieppel, the director of M.A.N. in Nuremberg and chairman of the Metal Industrialists' Association, then offered to negotiate on behalf of the toy industry and light metalwares firms, which were members of the organization.[59] This action is all the more surprising because the association and its successor, the Association of Bavarian Metal Industrialists (VBM), fought against contracts and the formal recognition of the DMV in the struggle of 1905 and in the events that led up to it in the fall of 1904. In the case of the toy industry movement, the crucial factor was probably the lack of involvement of the large machine-building firms who most firmly held to a policy of anti-unionism. The industrialists in light metalworking clearly must have felt more vulnerable, both because of the higher organization rate among their workers and because of the business cycle upswing then under way. Enßner and the DMV leaders, buoyed by massive meetings that attracted two thousand and more workers, were able to convince the employers to accept a compromise contract on June 10. The two-year agreement specified a fifty-seven-hour week from June 15, fifty-six hours from January 1, 1905, a 5 percent raise, and guaranteed minimum wages for all male workers. The factory owners refused to guarantee a day wage for women, claiming that new untrained women who could not initially earn their minimum wage were arriving daily from the countryside. The union leadership reluctantly accepted this concession. Shortly thereafter a strike by the newly roused construction tinsmiths produced a similar contract.[60]

Many provisions of the contract, especially those governing minimum wages and the setting of piece rates, proved difficult to enforce. One brief strike in the fall of 1904, and one more in 1905, forced recalcitrant employers, unused to the strictures of a contract, to comply.[61] The achievement of this agreement was nonetheless a great triumph for the union in its struggle for power and recognition—and it was ultimately a victory won by the union as an organization, and not so much one gained by the workers themselves. The decisive factor was not the power on the shop floor of proud and craft-conscious skilled workers. Although the skills of the tinsmiths, fine mechanics, metal pressers, and other craftsmen in the toy and sheet-metal industries were still important, they had never been particularly well off, powerful or well organized, and their place within the factories was slowly being eroded by the influx of unskilled women.[62] This may have motivated more skilled workers to accept the union, but what was decisive in the last analysis was the maturity, financial resources, and good organization of the DMV nationally and locally. The days when the skilled metalworkers of Nuremberg could create union organizations according to local needs and inclinations were passing; the DMV had become a large bureaucratic organization with a measure of independence from the rank and file that had helped to build it. This brought disadvantages, notably a growing gap between the union leadership and the average metalworker. But this must be weighed against the much greater power that was gained to better the lives and working conditions of workers. Despite the frustrations and disappointments of the subsequent events of 1905, which we will consider next, the great strike and lockout of that year once again demonstrated the new power position of the DMV in Nuremberg and its maturity as an industrial organization: the union was informally recognized by the employers, and the barriers to organization of the machine industry were finally broken down.

The Breakthrough in the Machine Industry

Until the turn of the century the workers of the largest machine-industry firms (the iron molders excepted) remained immovable for the unions. The reasons were not new: the heterogeneity of the work forces of M.A.N. and Schuckert obstructed communication and cooperation among workers, and the power possessed by those firms both to threaten and to entice the average worker into loyalty discouraged the great majority from organizing. Perhaps three-quarters of the workers at the two firms were not union members. Concerted campaigns in 1896 and 1897 for shorter hours and wage improvements yielded very little. Most of a series of meetings for the various workshops of Klett / M.A.N. held in the summer of 1897 by the metalworkers' and woodworkers' unions were poorly attended because of fear and apathy among the workers.[63] The next year negotiation with the Metal Industrialists' Association was tried, but it refused to grant even small wage raises or minor reductions in the sixty-hour week. The employers understood the balance of power; "the organized are in the minority," they told the union representatives.[64] Only in a campaign of resistance to new identification cards at Schuckert in December 1897 did workers there noticeably rouse themselves against the firm. The cards were thrown into boxes and returned to management in large numbers, but nothing further came of the movement.[65]

Like the issuance of identification cards to control the movements of workers within the plant, it was rationalization measures in the broadest sense, that is, including measures to strengthen time and work discipline, which eventually motivated many skilled workers to join the DMV or to participate in the movements of 1904–1905. At Klett / M.A.N. a campaign to force greater adherence to the rules concerning work time and shop discipline began when Rieppel assumed full control in 1892. The shop rules of 1893 and 1900–1901 placed more extensive controls on and fines for lateness and absence from the workplace. The language of these rules was typically authoritarian: workers were expected to show "strict adherence to the work time set down," "obedience to their superiors," "loyal fulfillment of duties," and "respectable behavior at all times in the shop," among other things. Similar work intensification measures were reported at Schuckert in this period.[66]

The workpace was further intensified through more and more refined methods of piece-rate calculation and through gradual technological change. Improvements in machine tools and measuring instruments permitted the mass production of some machine parts, although a thorough rationalization along these lines was largely confined to the production of consumer items like bicycles and sewing machines. Even so, at M.A.N. specialized positions were created in the machine shops to translate blueprints into detailed instructions for the use of machine tools and to control the exactitude of machine parts produced. In other words, most machine-industry craftsmen were slowly losing their grip on the planning and control functions left in their work. Specific technological improvements that allowed the company to further reduce piece rates stirred dissatisfaction as well. A new form of cutting steel, permitting faster lathe speeds, provoked an agitational campaign among the metal turners at M.A.N. in 1901–1902, though without short-term results. Piece-rate cuts were also used to force speedups; according to H.-J. Rupieper this resulted in growing dissatisfaction among older skilled workers, because they had difficulty sustaining their earnings at accustomed levels. By 1904–1905 many had become less timid about airing their grievances, which fueled the movements of those years.[67]

The unintended effects of work intensification and rationalization were reinforced by other factors. Under Rieppel's leadership Klett / M.A.N. diversified and expanded, thoroughly transforming in the process the age structure and company experience of the work force. The core (*Stamm*) of older skilled workers closely tied to the firm was overwhelmed by large numbers of younger workers. Turnover jumped correspondingly, so that in 1900 only 30 percent of M.A.N. workers in Nuremberg had been with the firm five years or more. Simultaneously, Schuckert undertook a reckless expansion that catapulted it into the position of being the third-largest German electrotechnical firm after AEG and Siemens. But bad planning in the shops, an "army" of well-paid and arrogant foremen and managers, and piece-rate cuts juxtaposed with astounding sums of money earned by the officers of the company all stirred unrest at an earlier stage at Schuckert than at M.A.N. Worker dissatisfaction came into the open when the 1900 recession nearly bankrupted the company. Massive layoffs became unavoidable, but the workers, with DMV help, mobilized themselves enough to force the company to accept short time (eight hours per day) in October 1901 instead of accelerating layoffs further. In order to salvage its position the company was forced to give up its independence to the Siemens empire. From April 1, 1903, it was combined with the high-voltage sections of Siemens to form a new company, the Siemens-Schuckertwerke (SSW), with headquarters in Berlin.[68]

Almost immediately the new company directors attempted to rationalize wage payment in the Nuremberg plant by installing an American premium-wage system. For a particular piece of work a time norm was laid down; if the worker finished it faster he or she received a bonus (which usually still amounted in toto to less money than would have been earned under a straight piece rate); if the worker was slow, deductions were made. The DMV roused the workers to protest and the system was not instituted. Thereafter the SSW workers were relatively inactive until 1905, but the movements of 1901–1903 doubtlessly strengthened the DMV's position in the plant.[69]

In the new M.A.N. factory in southern Nuremberg, to which most production had been shifted by 1900, the workers took somewhat longer to mobilize themselves. In June 1904, a movement began among the blacksmiths. Despite a record of apathy and narrow craft consciousness, complaints and agitation among this group regarding piece-rate cuts, speedups, and arrogant foremen can nonetheless be found as far back as 1898. The 1904 movement appears to have drawn impetus from the victory in the toy industry that year. DMV district leader Enßner, as the representative of the blacksmiths, wrote to Rieppel to remind him of the formal recognition the union had received in the toy-industry contract negotiations. But Rieppel refused to admit that the Metal Industrialists' Association had ever officially accepted the union as the legitimate representative of the workers. He claimed that he had acted only as a private mediator at the request of the toy-industry employers. He therefore refused to consider Enßner's request for a 15 percent raise for the blacksmiths.[70]

Thwarted, the union leaders directed their campaign through the firm's workers' committee, which they had often earlier dismissed as useless. Since those elected to this body had to be over thirty years of age with ten years' service to the company, they were naturally disinclined to risk their jobs. But as the character of the work force changed and as the trade-union commitment of all workers rose, the committee became more assertive. During 1904–1905 the DMV tacitly admitted the committee's usefulness by starting a campaign to lower the minimum requirement for representatives to two years' service. The committee itself cooperated closely with the DMV and other socialist unions during 1904 and 1905, and within a few years was de facto controlled by the unions—itself a symbol of the drastic change in the position of the unions within M.A.N. in Nuremberg.[71]

Through workshop meetings called by the workers' committee, new demands were presented to Rieppel for a fifty-seven-hour week and wage improvements. Agitation by this time (August–September 1904) had spread from the blacksmiths to the iron molders, locksmiths, metal turners, and machinists, and Rieppel feared that a strike was "very near." An older worker reported that the meetings were largely controlled by the "young workers" and that his intervention left him exposed to "the strongest insults." The strong emotions of this newly aroused section of the M.A.N. workers did not suffice, however, to make a strike possible. Pointing out the approaching winter, the lack of adequate money or depth of organization (unionized workers were still in the minority), and the likely opposition of DMV headquarters, on September 19 the metalworkers' union leaders in the plant persuaded a workshop meeting to call off the movement. Citing intensification of the work pace as a reason, the workers made one further request for shorter hours, but it too was ignored.[72]

The short-term results of the 1904 movement may have been minimal, but its long-term importance was considerable. Outside of the foundry it was the first large movement among the Klett / M.A.N. workers since 1871. It also paved the way for the strike of 1905 by preparing and organizing many previously unreachable skilled workers and a few unskilled and semiskilled ones as well. The year 1904 was thus an important one for the DMV at M.A.N., but its significance was still minor compared to 1905. The strike at the Nuremberg plant followed a successful movement at Schuckert and strikes in Munich, and it provided the final excuse for the employers to lock out fourteen thousand metalworkers across Bavaria.

The origins of the great lockout of 1905 go back to the fall of the previous year. In September 1904 the Nuremberg-Fürth metal industrialists' organization incorporated Munich and Augsburg to become the VBM. In spite of this unification, the Maffei locomotive factory in Munich still conceded a six-month contract in October to certain sections of its work force. During the months preceding the expiration of this contract on May 1, 1905, the DMV began an offensive movement in the Bavarian capital for the nine-hour day and formal labor contracts. Three strikes in late May and a total lockout of the machine industry in that city on June 3 resulted.[73]

Meanwhile the workers of Siemens-Schuckert and M.A.N. in Nuremberg had begun to stir themselves. The proximate cause for the movement at SSW was an examination of the wages and working conditions at the Nuremberg, Berlin, and Vienna factories of the firm, which was published by the Nuremberg DMV, based upon questionnaires distributed in the shops. From this booklet the workers in the local plant discovered that the other two factories had higher wages and shorter hours. "With a storm of outrage, the local leadership was asked to call a factory meeting."[74] This meeting, held on April 10, 1905, produced demands for a formal contract stipulating a fifty-four-hour week and wage increases. The firms eventually offered fifty-seven hours (a reduction of one and a half hours per week) and a 5 percent wage increase. The workers were not satisfied but were convinced by the DMV leadership to continue negotiations before initiating a strike. Finally on April 28 the company's last offer of fifty-seven hours, a 10 percent raise for hourly wages, and corresponding adjustments to piece rates was accepted by a meeting of Siemens-Schuckert workers. Participating in the movement were some 1,700 workers, of whom 1,475 were organized. This latter figure was only 30 percent of the 5,020 workers at the factory, but it proved significant enough to move the company to make concessions.[75]

The Siemens-Schuckert success emboldened the organized workers at the Nuremberg plant of M.A.N. Preparations for a movement had been made since at least February, but this new achievement at SSW inspired the workers' committee to present a proposed labor contract to the company on May 1. A fifty-six-hour week, a 15 percent raise, minimum hourly wages, and open lists of piece rates were the chief demands. These conditions were unacceptable to Rieppel and the other directors of the company, who wanted to hold the line against further changes in wages and hours. They also wanted to avoid undercutting the Munich members of the VBM in their struggle with the DMV. If these demands were unacceptable, the demand for a contract was unspeakable, because of its implied formal recognition of the unions as representatives of the workers. In an attempt to quell the movement Rieppel publicly revealed a decision already made by the company directors on April 4 in anticipation of further agitation and trouble. The work week was lessened to fifty-eight hours in Nuremberg, an hour-and-a-half decrease.[76]

The workers, over 2,500 of whom came to a meeting May 14, were not satisfied. They demanded that they at least receive the concessions given to their counterparts at SSW. By this time it is clear that the movement was no longer under the control of the union leadership. Enßner's cautionary words about an open struggle with the company were ignored, and one speaker even demanded an immediate strike if the company did not surrender. That the campaign had reached many previously unorganized workers unaccustomed to trade-union discipline is also shown by a number of anonymous and rather illiterate threatening letters sent to

Rieppel. All further compromises were rejected by the company, and a strike began on the morning of May 20. For tactical reasons a total strike was avoided by the DMV and the woodworkers' union; 1,215 workers marched out of the targeted shops and into the street—primarily metal turners, locksmiths, blacksmiths, and joiners. "The unbelievable thing is that many people with up to eighteen years of service are gone," reported a surpised manager to Rieppel.[77]

Since there was no immediate agreement, the rest of the some three thousand workers in the Nuremberg plant were locked out three weeks later, on June 10. Meanwhile it was becoming clear to the DMV and its allied unions (in a rare moment of cooperation, the Hirsch-Duncker and Christian unions worked together with the socialist unions throughout the Bavarian lockout) that the VBM was going to link the Munich and Nuremberg movements with a statewide lockout to defeat the unions. Through a director of SSW, negotiations were initiated by the employers. Two workers each from Nuremberg, Munich, and Augsburg formed the official negotiating committee, but their "advisor," the vice-chairman of the DMV, Reichel, from headquarters in Stuttgart, was the real leader of the negotiations on the workers' side.[78] The VBM carefully avoided formal recognition of the unions as the representatives of the workers, but the admission of Reichel constituted de facto recognition and a great victory. The DMV at least was treated by the employers as the voice of labor, something that even the disappointing results of the lockout could not obscure.

The lockout was postponed to June 22 to allow further negotiations. The VBM representatives refused, however, to concede more than a fifty-eight-hour week and small wage increases. The workers were not satisfied, and those at a meeting for M.A.N.-Nuremberg employees rejected these conditions outright as "unacceptable." The rank and file was now more militant than the DMV leadership, who were urging a retreat from earlier demands. The VBM's minor concessions rejected, its member firms put 14,158 workers on the street on the twenty-second. In Nuremberg there were now close to nine thousand metalworkers and woodworkers striking or locked out, including those earlier out at M.A.N. and Siemens-Schuckert, and virtually all the smaller machine factories and foundries in the city were closed down.[79]

The lockout was to be relatively brief. The financial burden for the union was considerable; in Nuremberg alone the DMV was supporting about five thousand workers, and the total cost of the Bavarian struggle for the union was later figured at half a million marks. Since Enßner,

Reichel, and most of the other leaders had little enthusiasm for this confrontation in the first place and since the VBM was unwilling to make further significant concessions, eventual acceptance of the employers' conditions was unavoidable. After M.A.N.-Nuremberg and Maffei in Munich upgraded and clarified their wage concessions, an agreement was signed between the negotiating parties on July 3 that set the fifty-eight-hour week as standard. Convincing the rank and file was the last hurdle. The workers of Munich and Augsburg were weary of the struggle and voted strongly to accept the settlement. Only in Nuremberg was there significant resistance; the shop stewards voted 131 to 94 to oppose the settlement, and only after heated debates at a number of meetings was a return to work narrowly accepted by the rank and file by a vote of 1,571 to 1,303. Work resumed slowly after July 8.[80]

For the DMV and the Nuremberg metalworkers the results of this conflict were clearly mixed. The settlement itself was made on the employers' terms and could in no way be construed as a union victory. The lockout was sufficiently effective to make the DMV's leadership almost excessively cautious in the future. Major conflicts in the Nuremberg machine industry were avoided before 1918, and a breakthrough to formal labor contracts and union recognition proved impossible to achieve under the Empire. Yet the 1905 conflict did produce some concessions, and in 1906 the VBM granted the fifty-seven-hour week to forestall further disruption.[81] The de facto recognition of the DMV in the negotiations was in itself an important step. Although disappointment over the results of the M.A.N. strike and the lockout inevitably created some recriminations between the more militant members and the leadership of the local DMV, the prestige of the organization grew as well. There was a quantum jump in local membership during 1905—from eight to twelve thousand in one year (see Figure 5.1).

Not all of this, of course, can be attributed to the strike and lockout. There was vigorous strike activity during the year in a heterogeneous collection of firms and trades (see Appendix B). But no conflict was as important as the struggle with M.A.N., Siemens-Schuckert, and the VBM. The mobilization of a significant fraction of the machine-industry labor force qualitatively transformed the importance of the major metalworkers' organization in the city. By 1909 the metalworkers' union together with other socialist unions claimed to have organized 63 percent of the M.A.N. workers and 60 percent of those at SSW.[82] As an industrial union the Nuremberg DMV had indeed reached maturity. It had succeeded in penetrating all the important sectors of the metal industries of greater Nuremberg. Some inroads had been made into the ranks of the semiskilled and unskilled in the machine industry and, even more significantly, into the ranks of women workers in the toy and light metal industries. Craft unionism was essentially defunct, both within and outside of the DMV. Competing unions, whether socialist or nonsocialist, were insignificant. And a large minority (40 percent in 1905) of the city's metalworkers were members of the organization. Many could not be held to membership for long periods of time, but precisely because of this turnover, many more than two-fifths were members at one time or another.

Thus a trade-union activism shaped by class-conscious socialism had touched the lives of most metalworkers in Nuremberg in one way or another, and within a few years, half would be DMV members at any one time. The union had grown into a gigantic bureaucratic organization that towered over its members. Yet the organization still ultimately rested on the power its skilled-worker membership wielded as a result of their craftsmanship and labor market position. The dialectic of craft and class continued, albeit in a disguised form. There would always be tensions between trades and between apprenticed and unapprenticed workers within the union, and without some sense of craft pride and power among the skilled no effective union would have been possible. The interests of craft and class would not always coincide. Nonetheless, essentially gone were the craft-conscious snobbishness, the self-identity as a member of an artisanal estate, and the disinterest in politics that had marked the mentality of preindustrial journeymen. Skilled metalworkers had recognized their inferior social status and their common identity with other skilled and unskilled workers, and many had joined an industrial union or had voted for the SPD to do something about it. In the seventy years since 1835 their world was transformed and they with it. The metalworking artisan had become the skilled metalworker.

# CONCLUSION

Two different worlds: no other phrase better encapsulates the drastically different social, economic, and political environments in which Nuremberg skilled metalworkers lived and labored in 1835 and 1905. In the first world, metalworking journeymen were artisans: they worked in small-scale production in an economic system regulated by the guilds, the city government, and the state bureaucracy; they were normally unmarried and lived under the patriarchal authority of their employers; and they possessed a self-identity as future masters, and therefore as part of an honorable but subordinate estate in a hierarchical, authoritarian society. In the second world, metalworking journeymen were workers: they labored in a heterogeneous variety of enterprises within an energetically capitalist economic system; they often had families and lived in the sprawling suburbs of a city seven times as populous as in 1835; they possessed a working-class identity, usually voted socialist, and were frequently members of an industrial metalworkers' union.

So much is clear. But how did the transformation from artisan journeymen to skilled workers take place? It is convenient to distinguish two separate phases: the dissolution of the old artisanal order from 1835 to 1868, and the rise of a new identity as workers, as expressed through trade unions and socialism, from 1869 to 1905. The first phase was the product of at least four factors—capitalism, industrialization, population growth, and political repression—of which capitalism was the most important.

As far back as the eighteenth century, putting-out capitalism organized by Nuremberg merchants intruded into the artisanal production process, thereby reducing many masters to dependency. Manufactories appeared as well, but their importance was not great. Intermittently throughout the early and mid-nineteenth century—depending upon the political climate—the control of the city and state bureaucracies over the economy

167

loosened further, allowing greater competition among masters, the more extensive use of technological and organizational innovations, and more capital investment in mechanized factories. These developments were resisted bitterly by the conservative majority of masters, who wished to uphold the quasi-guild system as it had been adapted from the pre-Napoleonic period. In the end this resistance proved futile as the ruling classes of Nuremberg and Bavaria slowly accepted economic liberalism and reluctantly undertook the destruction of the old economic order. The reforms of 1868–1869 culminated the process of transformation of the legal relations of production.

In the first few decades after 1835 industrialization—narrowly defined as the growth of mechanized industrial production—had less impact upon the Nuremberg metalworkers. Many light metalworking crafts like the beating trades and the toy industry mechanized slowly or not at all, and even in the machine industry the production process at mid-century did not differ sharply from that in artisanry. It was only after the old economic system had disappeared that factory work in medium-sized or large firms became typical for most Nuremberg metalworking journeymen. Even then skilled labor remained central to the production process in virtually all branches of the industrial use of metals. The first signs of the erosion of the position of skilled metalworkers through technological change, piece rates, and the reorganization of work surfaced at the end of the century, but the importance of apprenticed workers in metalworking and machine manufacture was still unquestioned in 1905.

The impact of capitalism and capitalist industrialization was nonetheless profound. Together they undermined whatever sense of community was left within the artisan estate, separated masters and men into employers and workers, and opened up new employment opportunities for metalworking journeymen outside the traditional crafts, but also condemned the great majority to lifelong wage work. The dream of economic independence and social status as a master artisan had already been undermined before 1835 by economic stagnation and the third factor, rapid population growth. For all but a fortunate few that dream now disappeared entirely. Those working in industry might hope to become foremen instead, but there, too, the odds were poor. The number of positions was so limited as to make the possibility "extremely small" for workers at M.A.N., according to Rupieper.[1]

The gradual acceptance by journeymen of their lifelong status as workers reinforced many ongoing social processes—not the least of which were the rise of working-class consciousness and the decline in the authority of artisan masters over their men. With some help from the restrictive Bavarian marriage and residence laws prior to 1868, the prohibitions on marriage and living-out that had still been upheld in the early nineteenth century simply collapsed by the 1860s. Master-journeymen relations were further worsened by conflicts over the supervision of the journeymen's associations and by a new emphasis on work and time discipline, which the masters were forced to accept because of the pressure of competition from other masters and the new factories. The diverging interests of masters and journeymen became apparent during the Revolution of 1848–1849, when the two groups pursued different goals, although they did not clash directly over how to reshape artisanal institutions to cope with economic change. By the 1870s, however, metalworking journeymen were much more willing to accept organizations and ideologies that directly opposed them to all but masters with few or no employees.

The interlocking processes of growing working-class consciousness, declining master-journeymen relations, and the dissolution of the old artisanal order were reinforced by the final factor: political repression. The fear which haunted German and Bavarian ruling groups following the French revolutionary era and the events of 1848–1849 caused them to repress all signs of independence by journeymen and workers energetically. The eighteenth-century "brotherhoods," which had linked together the journeymen's associations, were suppressed, and the local associations were limited to basic welfare functions. Harmless artisanal customs were hunted down and stamped out by the city and state authorities largely out of fear of the conspiratorial activities of the revolutionary secret societies, which, ironically, had no foothold in Nuremberg. The hostility of journeymen toward the authorities grew, and this was further exacerbated by slow economic growth before 1850, a rapidly increasing population, the hunger crisis of the mid-forties, and the effects of early industrialization. Metalworking artisans, like all artisans, became politicized. The process of politicization culminated finally in the collapse of the leadership that the bourgeois liberals had exercised over Nuremberg artisans between 1848 and 1868, and in the rise of the Social Democratic movement in the second phase of the transformation from artisans to workers from 1869 to 1905. The relaxation of repression in the 1860s and 1870s did not suffice to reconcile journeymen and workers to the existing social and political system. The city government remained too clearly based upon the minority rule of a bourgeois elite, and the various discriminatory laws that remained on the books after 1868–1869, like the residence and marriage laws, only furthered class conflict. The Nuremberg liberals, disoriented by Bismarck's "revolution from above" and fearful of working-class independence, squandered their hold over workers and artisans and thereby helped destroy the possibility of a liberal-reformist labor movement.

Emerging from the dissolution of the old artisanal order was thus a consciousness, or at least a vague sense, of working-class identity and of opposition to the interests and power of masters, employers, and ruling authorities. But it was much more difficult to translate this feeling into concrete political and economic organizations to challenge existing power relations within the city and workshop. On the one hand, with the highly favorable circumstances of an ethnically homogeneous, mostly Protestant, and predominantly skilled working class, a city government dominated by the interests of the employers, and a charismatic leader (Grillenberger), the Social Democrats easily won the votes of Nuremberg workers. On the other hand, it was difficult to establish permanent political and auxiliary organizations, especially in view of the renewed repression before and during the Socialist Law, and there were even more obstacles to the creation of effective and stable trade unions.

The obstacles to unionization were indeed manifold. The first unions in the Nuremberg metal trades were in principle industrial organizations, but only a few ideologically committed journeymen/skilled workers accepted this principle before 1890. The early craft unions, in both the seventies and the eighties, appeared largely independently of the small band of socialist party activists. But because of the rapid emergence of a virtual socialist monopoly in working-class politics, most of the craft unions either associated themselves from the outset with the Social Democrats or evolved in that direction from neutral or Hirsch-Duncker origins. Socialist votes did not, however, translate automatically into union membership— unions of all types met considerable worker apathy, especially in view of the poorer economic climate and the renewed repression beginning in the mid-seventies. The dissolution of the old journeymen's associations obstructed the development of new organizations as well, because this marked a decline in the internal cohesion and solidarity of the crafts. Only with the new economic boom after 1895 were something approaching half of all Nuremberg metalworkers recruited into unions. Crucial to this development was the rise of the DMV as a large, bureaucratic industrial union, able to offer an increasingly comprehensive benefit system as well as effective representation in confrontations with employers.

Although it was difficult to overcome the passivity and instability of working-class lives in order to organize even the skilled, the development of the unions in this period nonetheless demonstrates the existence of a dialectic of craft consciousness and class consciousness among Nuremberg metalworkers. On the one side, the development of socialist industrial unionism reflected the growth of working-class consciousness. Industrialization, resulting in a further concentration of production into larger and increasingly rationalized factory units, contributed to the underlying socioeconomic formation of the working class in Nuremberg. Metalworking craftsmen were brought more and more into employment that exposed them to other trades and the unskilled, and the craftsmen's control of the work process began to be threatened, as we have seen, especially after the 1890s. Class formation at the social and economic levels was strongly reinforced by renewed political repression, which encouraged working-class formation at the political-ideological level. As I mentioned in the Introduction, the role of the state must be seen as one of the most important factors leading to the creation of a united and fairly radical socialist movement in Germany. This political context was crucial to the growth of industrial unionism, because the SPD consciously fostered a working-class identity, and many movement activists saw industrial unionism as the form of union most consistent with socialist principles. The other two factors from the first phase—population growth and capitalism—had less significance, as economic growth outstripped population growth and as the growth of capitalism became increasingly synonymous with the growth of industrial production.

But the development of Nuremberg metalworkers' unions also shows the other side: the continuing importance of craft consciousness and its complex interaction with class consciousness. There was no linear decline of the first with the rise of the second. As we have seen, the craft section system was crucial to the early growth of the DMV, and even the submergence of the last sections in the General Local in 1905 did not eliminate craft identities in the union. By the same token, craft loyalties and craft traditions cannot be written off only as obstacles to the development of class identity. In some traditional trades, craft loyalties could certainly breed snobbery or resistance to change. Nor can it be denied that the adoption of a wider working-class identity was furthered by the dissolution of the bonds that held journeymen into tight social groups based upon craft. But craft traditions and craft consciousness had positive roles as well. The journeymen's associations were a model for the early unions, especially the pre-1891 craft unions. Traditions of intratrade cooperation and self-help—to the extent that they survived—aided the activists in their attempt to start new organizations. The labor-market power and self-identity springing from skill, moreover, were also the foundation of all organizations. And only through the construction of organizations and the execution of strikes could most skilled metalworkers be brought to a consciousness of their social position.

In the last analysis, the construction of a viable industrial union depended on the prior growth of craft unionism and its harnessing through the section system. It is therefore no contradiction that the city possessed both one of the strongest DMV organizations in Germany and one of the most vibrant craft traditions in the metal trades. Craft consciousness and class consciousness were linked in a dialectical process: in varying degrees they strengthened and weakened each other simultaneously. This process would not and could not disappear as long as skilled workers remained central to industrial production and the labor movement, that is, until at least 1933. In general terms, however, it may be said that craft consciousness obstructed class consciousness and industrial unionism more than it aided them up to the 1880s. Thereafter the relationship turned more toward one of mutual reinforcement.

The question remains why among German metalworkers the relationship between craft and class consciousness was, on balance, a reinforcing one, and therefore why socialist industrial unionism became so important in a labor movement based upon skilled workers. The cases of North American and British craft unionism remind us that this development was by no means inevitable. Of course craft unionism was also important in Germany, and indeed the central organization of the German socialist unions, the General Commission, was mostly controlled by craft unionists. Yet industrial unionism appeared at an earlier stage than in almost any other country—the 1890s—and it conquered prominent sectors of the working class: the metalworkers, the woodworkers, and the textile workers, to name only the earliest adherents of this organizational form. Why should this be the case?

Some answers may be drawn from the history of the DMV's formation and from the special case of the Nuremberg metalworkers. Two have already been mentioned in passing: the ability of the new union to integrate craft unionism through the section system, and the fact that socialist advocates of class-conscious industrial unionism controlled the metalworkers' movement locally and nationally by the end of the 1880s. In the national context it is also significant that German metal industrialists were united in their willingness to use aggressive lockout tactics to combat unionism, most notably in north Germany at the time of the union's founding, and that as a result of the Socialist Law, national craft unionism had not had a chance to become entrenched in the metal trades before 1890. All of these factors, but especially the first three, were ultimately products of the tendency to class polarization and unification of employers and workers into organized blocs that was inherent to the development of German society during industrialization. Naturally there were considerable regional variations, and in some areas, particularly the critical Rhine/Ruhr region, powerful employers' associations faced weak and divided labor organizations. In contrast, the case of Nuremberg shows that in some regions capital owners and wage workers became divided from each other economically, socially, and politically in ways that fit classical Marxist descriptions of the process, even if, as I have stressed, class consciousness among Nuremberg workers was always essentially reformist.[2] Although not every metalworker had a powerful working-class identity, and no metalworker was free of conflicting loyalties and identities, the strength of the class formation process in the city was such that craft consciousness did not fundamentally obstruct class consciousness. Instead they combined into a fruitful dialectic that allowed the deepening of socialist industrial unionism to such a degree that half of all metalworkers in Nuremberg were DMV members in the years before World War I.

# Appendixes

# Appendix A
# NUREMBERG
# METALWORKERS' UNIONS,
# 1869–1905

In this and following union tables, dates given are month/year. The following special abbreviations are used: SD–Social Democratic, HD–Hirsch-Duncker. For other acronyms see the Abbreviations list preceding the Notes.

Sources: *FDWB/SDWB/NFSD/FT*; *DMZ*; Stadtkomm. records (StadtAN, StaatsAN); Direktorium A (StadtAN); Vereinspolizeiakten (StadtAN, HR Vd15); Eckert, *Liberal- oder Sozialdemokratie*.

| Union | Dates | Membership | Remarks |
|---|---|---|---|
| *1. Unions Founded 1869–1878* | | | |
| International Metalworkers | 4/69–10/78 | 96 (8/69), 90–100 (?/78) | SD, founder of national union |
| Braziers | 1/70–?/73? | 34 (1/70) | neutral travel fund |
| Gold and Silver Workers | ?/70–? | ? | existence uncertain |
| Mach. Bldg. and Metal-workers | 6/70–1933? | 61 (1/80), 107 (1/04) | HD national union local |
| Tinsmiths | 8/71–9/78 | 70 (9/71), 30–40 (?/78) | HD, later SD, national union local 1873–76 |

| Union | Dates | Membership | Remarks |
|---|---|---|---|
| Metal Beaters | 9/71–8/82 | 28 (9/71), 20 (?/80) | HD, from 1877 local II of the Mach. Bldg. and Metalw. |
| Math. Inst. Makers | 2/72–2/79 | 59 (2/72) | neutral |
| Wire Drawers | 7/72–?/77 | c. 30 (3/77) | HD |
| Brass Molders | 2/73–?/74 | ? | neutral |
| Gold Beaters | 4/73–?/76 | 80 (4/73) | HD |
| Metal Pressers | 10/74–12/75 | ? | SD? |
| Filemakers | 7/75–? | ? | neutral travel fund |
| Metal Pressers | 4/76–4/78 | ? | SD |
| Locksmiths | 2/77–10/78 | ? | SD |
| *2. Unions Founded 1879–July 1891* | | | |
| Locksmiths | 9/80–6/82 | c. 50? | SD |
| Metal Pressers | 10/81–7/91 | 60 (2/85), 70 (10/86), 100 (4/91) | SD, joined DMV |
| Tin Molders | 12/82–11/97 | 10 (4/91) | neutral, leaning to SD, joined DMV |
| Fine Mechanics | 1/83–12/87 | ? | neutral, merged with national union |
| Metal Beaters | 4/83–8/91 | c. 200 (4/90, 66 (4/91) | neutral, later SD, joined DMV |
| Gold Beaters | 5/83–?/93 | ? | neutral, later SD, most joined DGSV |

| Union | Dates | Membership | Remarks |
|---|---|---|---|
| Tinsmiths | 9/83–8/91 | 53 (9/83), 120 (10/86), 265 (4/91) | SD, joined DMV |
| Filemakers | 1/84–7/91 | 17 (4/91) | SD, joined DMV |
| Braziers | 10/84–7/85 | 38 (4/85) | |
| Math. Inst. Makers | 11/84–2/90 | 35 (11/84) | SD, merged with Polishers |
| Metalworkers/ Locksmiths and Machinists | 12/84–7/91 | 60 (2/85), 175 (1/88), 300+ (12/88), 800(7/89), 904 (12/90), 800 (4/91) | SD, joined DMV |
| Iron Molders | 4/86–7/91 | 150 (10/86), 300 (1/90), 280 (4/91) | SD, majority joined DMV |
| Iron Rollers | 1/87–1935 | 40 (1/87) | neutral company union |
| Fine Mechanics (national union local) | 2/87–9/91 | 41 (4/87) | SD, joined DMV |
| Stokers and Machinists (Alter Verein) | 12/87–?/14 | 115 (3/89), 96 (1/04) | neutral, minority joined DMV |
| Brass and Bell Molders | 1/88–8/91 | 135 (4/91) | SD, joined DMV |
| Blacksmiths | 9/88–2/91 | ? | neutral, majority joined SD union |
| Fine Mechanics | 10/88–1/90 | 14 (10/88) | SD, splinter group |
| Tinsmiths and Metalworkers local | 12/88–3/06 | ? | HD national union, merged with Mach. Bldg. and Metalw. |

| Union | Dates | Membership | Remarks |
|---|---|---|---|
| Math. Instr. Polishers | 4/89–2/90 | ? | SD, merged with Math. Instr. Makers |
| Plumbers | 5/89–9/91 | ? (very small) | (*Installateure*) |
| Blacksmiths | 8/89–8/91 | 130 (4/91) | SD, joined DMV |
| Math. Instr. Workers | 2/90–7/91 | 190 (4/91) | merger of Makers and Polishers, joined DMV |
| Women Workers | 4/90–3/91 | 74 (4/90), 60 (8/90) | SD, merged with Tinsmiths |
| Machinists and Stokers (Anerkannter Verein) | 5/90–11/05 | 52 (7/94), 31 (8/96), 15 (11/05) | neutral, inactive |
| Metalworkers Schniegling-Doos | 5/90–8/91 | ? | SD, joined DMV, suburban |
| DGSV local | 3/91–9/99 | 429 (4/91) | SD, merged with DMV Gold Beaters |

*3. Nuremberg DMV Sections and Locals, July 1891–1905*

| Union | Dates | Membership | Remarks |
|---|---|---|---|
| Locksmiths and Machinists | 7/91–12/95 | 964 (12/91), 594 (12/92), 240 (12/93), 972 (12/94), 1292 (12/95) | formed Gen. Local |
| Iron Molders | 7/91–3/05 | 129 (12/92), 168 (12/94), 240 (12/96), 278 (12/98), 243 (12/00), 410 (12/04) | absorbed Central Assoc. local, joined Gen. Local |
| Metal Pressers | 7/91–?/02 | 118 (12/92), 139 (12/94), 160 (12/96), 142 (12/98), 174 (12/00) | joined Gen. Local |

| Union | Dates | Membership | Remarks |
|-------|-------|------------|---------|
| Math. Instr. Industry | 7/91–3/05 | 172 (12/92), 176 (12/94), 162 (12/96), 220 (12/98), 308 (12/00), 346 (12/04) | joined Gen. Local |
| Brass Molders (from 3/96 incl. Braziers and Metal Turners) | 8/91–4/00 | 119 (12/91), 143 (12/93), 219 (12/95), 293 (12/97), 485 (12/98), 295 (12/99) | joined Gen. Local |
| Tinsmiths and Women Workers | 8/91–3/05 | 191 (12/92), 232 (1/95), 446 (12/96), 540 (12/98), 576 (12/00), 1074 (12/04) | joined Gen. Local |
| Blacksmiths | 8/91–3/05 | 114 (12/92), 115 (12/94), 267 (12/96), 440 (12/98), 490 (12/00), 274 (12/02) | joined Gen. Local |
| Metal Beaters | 8/91–7/96 | 77 (12/91), 30 (12/92), 43 (12/93), 43 (12/94) | joined Gen. Local |
| Stokers and Machinists | 8/91–1/93 | 32 (12/91), 31 (12/92) | formed national union local |
| Tin Molders | 8/91–7/92 | 22 (8/91), 25 (12/91) | merged with Fine Mechanics' Section |
| File Industry | 8/91–9/93 | 24 (12/91), 19 (12/92) | dissolved |
| Schniegling-Doos Local | 8/91–10/02 | 45 (12/91), 86 (12/95), 145 (12/97), 182 (12/98), 70 (12/99), 108 (12/00) | joined Gen. Local |
| Fine Mechanics (from 7/92 "and Tin Molders") | 9/91–4/97 | 44 (12/91), 136 (12/93), 76 (12/94), 120 (12/96) | joined Gen. Local |
| Mögeldorf Local | 12/92–1/07 | 31 (12/92), 86 (12/96), 55 (12/97), 77 (12/99), 86 (12/01), 121 (12/05) | joined Gen. Local |

| Union | Dates | Membership | Remarks |
|---|---|---|---|
| Harmonica Makers | 7–12/95 | ? | formed Gen. Local |
| General Local | 1/96–1933 | 800 (1/96), 1471 (12/96), 2663 (12/98), 2715 (12/00), 3060 (12/02), 4817 (12/04), 11,897 (12/05) | formed by the Locksmiths and Machinists and by the Harmonica Makers |
| Tin Molders | 11/97–11/03 | 64 (12/97), 67 (12/99), 87 (12/00) | formed from local union, joined Gen. Local |
| Gold Beaters | 12/97–3/05 | 40 (12/97), 741 (12/99), 819 (12/00), 901 (12/02), 905 (12/03), 741 (12/04) | absorbed DGSV local 9/99, joined Gen. Local |
| Grinders and Polishers | 7/98–3/02 | 127 (12/98), 149 (12/99), 132 (12/00) | joined Gen. Local |

*4. Other New Unions, July 1891–1905*

| Union | Dates | Membership | Remarks |
|---|---|---|---|
| Iron Molders (Central Assoc. local) | 11/91–10/01 | 70 (4/98), 16 (9/01) | SD, merged with DMV Iron Molders |
| Blacksmiths | 10/92–12/99 | ? | local closed craft union, joined DMV Blacksmiths |
| Machinists and Stokers (national union local) | 1/93–1933? | 102 (5/03) | SD, formed from DMV Stokers Section |
| Metal Beaters | 3/97–7/98 | ? | neutral |
| Christian-Social Metalworkers | 7/98–1933? | 1084 (4/10) | became CMV local 2/1900 |

| Union | Dates | Membership | Remarks |
|---|---|---|---|
| Engravers (national union local) | 9/99–9/07 | ? | SD, merged with DMV |
| Blacksmiths (Central Union local) | 3/01–10/12 | ? | SD, merged with DMV |
| Goldsmiths | 10/01–c. 1930 | ? | neutral |
| Blacksmiths | 10/05–1913? | ? | neutral |

# Appendix B
## STRIKES AND LOCKOUTS OF NUREMBERG METALWORKERS, 1869–1905

The sources used in this appendix are the same as Appendix A, with the addition of strike reports in StaatsAN, Regg. KdI 1932, Tit. IX. Dates given are day/month/year. Maximum size is the maximum number of workers participating. Offensive strikes are defined as those initiated by the workers to gain better wages and working conditions. Defensive strikes are defined as those initiated by the workers primarily to sustain previous wages and working conditions against changes for the worse by employers. A successful strike is one where most or all of the stated objectives of the strikers are achieved. A failure is a strike in which the workers achieve few or none of their demands. A partial success is one where both sides were forced to compromise or where the workers achieved some of their objectives only at some of the firms struck. The following special abbreviations are used: off.–offensive; def.–defensive; part. succ.–partial success.

| Trades | Dates | Max. size | Location | Aim/Results |
|--------|-------|-----------|----------|-------------|
| | | *1. Job Actions, 1869–1878* | | |
| Locksmiths | 2/4–?/6?/72 | ? | many masters | off./part. succ.? |
| Metal beaters | 22–28/4/72 | 50 | 2 masters | off./success |
| Tinsmiths | 22/7–?/8/72 | ? | many masters | off./failure |
| Blacksmiths | 23–25/9/72 | 50 | 22 masters | off./success |
| Metal beaters | 2/2–2/3/74 | 120 | many masters | def./success |

*185*

| Trades | Dates | Max. size | Location | Aim/Results |
|---|---|---|---|---|
| Metal beaters and helpers | ?/6–?/8/74 | 200 | many masters | def./? |
| Tinsmiths | 27/7–?/8/74 | 30 | 1 factory | def./success |
| Metal beaters | 17/5–?/?/78 | 26 | 1 master | ?/? |
| *2. Job Actions, 1879–1890* | | | | |
| Metal pressers | 17–20/3/84 | 22 | metalwares factory | def./success |
| Metal pressers | 4(?)–20/12/84 | 12–15 | toy factory | def./failure |
| Filemakers | 10/6/85–? | ? | file factory | ?/? |
| Brass molders and turners | 3/9/88–? | c. 20 | brass foundry | def./unknown |
| Iron molders | 29–31/10/88 | c. 15 | foundry | def./success |
| Iron molders | 25(?)/11–22/12/88 | ? | foundry | def./failure |
| Tinsmiths, Metal pressers, fine mechanics, metal turners | 23/4–6/5/89 | 32 | toy factory | def./success |
| Tinsmiths | 7–9/5/89 | 20 | toy factory | off./success |
| Metal beaters | 12–19/6/89 | 12 | 1 master | off./failure |
| Tinsmiths and metal pressers | 24–25/6/89 | 23 | toy factory | off./part. succ. |
| Tinsmiths | 8–13/7/89 | c. 140 | many masters | off./succ. |
| Gold beaters and helpers | 6–30/8/89 | 422 | many masters | off./part. succ. |

| Trades | Dates | Max. size | Location | Aim/Results |
|--------|-------|-----------|----------|-------------|
| Locksmiths, mechanics, fine turners, and others | 23/9–15/10/89 | 292 | Schuckert | def./failure |
| Filemakers | 9–21/4/90 | 7 | 5 masters | off./success |
| Metal beaters and helpers | 2–7/6/90 | 16 | 1 master | off./success |
| Metal beaters and helpers | 2/6–1/7/90 | 11 | 1 master | off./part. succ. |
| Metal beaters and helpers | 9/6–1/7/90 | 54 | 2 masters | off./part. succ. |
| Gold beaters | 3–8/11/90 | 78 | 1 master | def./success |
| *3. Job Actions, 1891–1905* | | | | |
| Math. instr. makers | 6/1–20/2/93 | 17 | math. instr. factory | def./succ. |
| Iron molders | 15/1–12/2/94 | c. 225 | foundries and machine factories | def./part. succ. |
| Metal pressers | 5–6/4/94 | ? | metalwares factory | def./succ. |
| Gold beaters and helpers | 22/6–20/8/94 | 73 | 1 master | def./failure |
| Locksmiths, turners, and helpers | 17–21/1/95 | 184 | bicycle factory | def./part. succ. |
| Locksmiths, turners, and polishers | 22/3–29/4/95 | 141 | bicycle factory | off./part. succ. |
| Blacksmiths and helpers | 3/7–3/8/95 | 20 | machine factory | off./failure |

| Trades | Dates | Max. size | Location | Aim/Results |
|---|---|---|---|---|
| Tinsmiths, metal pressers, and others | 25/3–7(?)/4/96 | 109 | toy factory | off./part. succ. |
| Harmonica makers | 20/4–30/5/96 | 15 | 2 masters | off./failure |
| Brass molders, braziers, and others | 4–18/5/96 | 50 | brass foundry | off./failure |
| Blacksmiths | 5–9/4/97 | 29 | 12 masters | off./part. succ. |
| Filemakers | 16/5–15/6/98 | 37 | many masters | off./part. succ. |
| Iron molders | 6–15/8/98 | 31 | foundry | off./part. succ. |
| Iron molders and helpers | 19–20/8/98 | 150 | Schuckert | off./failure |
| Brass molders, turners, locksmiths, and braziers | 14–29/10/98 | 71 | brass foundry | off./part. succ. |
| Math. instr. polishers | 30/11–2/12/98 | 7 | math. instr. factory | def./success |
| Iron molders and helpers | 9/2–14/6/99 | 113 | Schuckert | off./failure |
| Math. instr. makers and helpers | 18/2–4/4/99 | 29 | math. instr. factory | def./success |
| Tinsmiths | 28/3–10/4/99 | 24 | lantern factory | off./success |
| Gold beaters and helpers | 6/5–24/7/99 | 618 (after lockout) | c. 25 masters | off./part. succ. |

| Trades | Dates | Max. size | Location | Aim/Results |
|---|---|---|---|---|
| Blacksmiths | 10/7–19/8/99 | 60 | 25 masters | off./success |
| Math. instr. polishers | 3–6/10/99 | 2 | 2 factories | off./success |
| Math. instr. polishers, turners, and justifiers | 3/10–4/12/99 | 43 | 1 factory | off./success |
| Tinsmiths | 22–26/3/00 | 12 | toy factory | def./success |
| Iron molders and helpers | 21/4–21/7/00 | 336 | foundries and machine factories | off./failure |
| Turners, brass molders, blacksmiths, and others | 5/5–14/7/00 | 116 | fire-fighting equip. factory | off./failure |
| Blacksmiths | 5–6/7/00 | 17 | machine factory | off./failure |
| Metal beaters and helpers | 6/10–28/11/00 | 65 | 6 masters | off./part. succ. |
| Gold beaters and helpers | 23–24/10/01 | 53 | 1 master | def./success |
| Math. instr. makers | 27/3–22/5/02 | 6 | 1 master | def./failure |
| Tinsmiths and helpers | 31/7–6/8/02 | 19 | toy factory | def./success |
| Metal beaters and helpers | 9–29/9/02 | 31 | 4 masters | off./part. succ. |
| Metal pressers | 15–22/9/02 | 4 | metalwares factory | off./part. succ. |
| Math. instr. polishers | 3/11/02–14/5/03 | 10 | math. instr. factory | off./failure |

| Trades | Dates | Max. size | Location | Aim/Results |
|---|---|---|---|---|
| Metal pressers | 23–28/2/03 | 3 | metalwares factory | off./success |
| Metal beaters and helpers | 20/4–23/6 or 7/8/03 | 102 | 10 masters | off./success (in 9 cases) |
| Tinsmiths and helpers | 4–8/6/03 | 14 | metalwares factory | def./failure |
| Tin molders | 8/6–28/7/03 | 45 | 4 masters | def./failure |
| Tinsmiths | 30/7–4/8/03 | 57 | toy factory | off./success |
| Brass molders, turners, and others | 25/9–12/11/03 | 51 | brass foundry | def./failure |
| Polishers | 13–15/7/04 | ? | oven factory | off./success |
| Const. tinsmiths | 23/7–13/8/04 | 134 | many masters | off./success |
| Metal pressers, tinsmiths, and others | 6–7/9/04 | 18 | metalwares factory | def./success |
| Auto workers | 25–31/10/04 | 13 | auto factory | off./? |
| Gold beaters and helpers | 1–4/11/04 | 62 | 1 master | def./success |
| Polishers | 24/1/05 | ? | toy factory | def./success |
| Toy workers | 4–13/2/05 | 24 | toy factory | def./success |
| Locksmiths, turners, blacksmiths, and others | 20/5–8/7/05 | 2773 (lockout from 10/6) | M.A.N. | off./part. succ. |
| Const. locksmiths | 5/6–3/7/05 | 207 | many masters | off. failure |

| Trades | Dates | Max. size | Location | Aim/Results |
|--------|-------|-----------|----------|-------------|
| Iron molders | 17/6–?/?/05 | 18 | foundry | def./failure |
| Bavarian lockout | 22/6–8/7/05 | 6008 | machine industry | part. succ. |
| Tinsmiths | 24/7–3/8/05 | 6 | toy factory | def./failure |
| Mach. ind. workers | 24–25/7/05 | 70 | machine factory | def./success |
| Math. instr. makers | 10–14/8/05 | 10 | math. instr. factory | off./? |
| Metal-workers | 21–24/8/05 | 9 | metalwares factory | off./success |
| Locksmiths and polishers | 23–29/8/05 | 110 | oven factory | off./part. succ. |
| Bicycle workers | 22–27/9/05 | ? | bicycle parts factory | off./part. succ. |
| Metal beaters | 11–14/10/05 | ? | 1 master | def./failure |
| Bronze workers | 12/10–28/11/05 | 54 | metalwares factory | def./failure |

# ABBREVIATIONS

ADAV    Allgemeiner Deutscher Arbeiterverein
BAA Frankfurt    Bundesarchiv Aussenstelle Frankfurt
BA Nbg.    Bezirksamt Nürnberg
CMV    Christlicher Metallarbeiter-Verband
DGSV    Deutscher Gold- und Silberarbeiter-Verband
DMV    Deutscher Metallarbeiter-Verband
DMZ    *Deutsche Metallarbeiter-Zeitung*
FDWB    *Fürther Demokratisches Wochenblatt*
FK    *Fränkischer Kurier*
fl.    Gulden
FT    *Fränkische Tagespost*
HR    Hauptregistratur, Stadtarchiv Nürnberg
HSA Munich    Hauptstaatsarchiv München (Munich)
Hwa.    Handwerksarchive (Stadtarchiv Nürnberg)
Kgl.    Königliche (royal)
kr.    kreutzer
M    mark (Reichsmark)
M.A.N.    Maschinenfabrik Augsburg-Nürnberg
Mf.    Mittelfranken (Middle Franconia)
MZ    *Metallarbeiter-Zeitung*
Nbg.    Nürnberg (Nuremberg)
NFSD    *Nürnberg-Fürther Sozialdemokrat*
Pf.    Pfennig
Rgg.    Regierung (regional government)
SAPD    Sozialistische Arbeiterpartei Deutschlands

*Skilled Metalworkers of Nuremberg*

| | |
|---|---|
| SDAP | Social-Demokratische Arbeiterpartei |
| *SDWB* | *Socialdemokratisches Wochenblatt* |
| SPD | Sozialdemokratische Partei Deutschlands |
| SSW | Siemens-Schuckertwerken |
| StaatsAN | Staatsarchiv Nürnberg |
| StadtAN | Stadtarchiv Nürnberg |
| Stadtkomm. | Stadtkommissariat Nürnberg |
| Stadtmag. | Stadtmagistrat Nürnberg (city council) |
| VBM | Verein Bayerischer Metallindustrieller |
| VMD | Vereinigung der Metallarbeiter Deutschlands |

Note: In 1903 the name of the *DMZ* was shortened to *MZ*. The *FDWB* (1871–1874), the *SDWB* (1874), and the *NFSD* (1874–1878) are the successive precursors of the *FT*. SDAP (1869–1875) and SAPD (1875–1891) were earlier names for the SPD.

# NOTES

Note: Unless otherwise indicated, archival sources cited in the notes are from the Stadtarchiv Nürnberg (Nuremberg City Archive).

## Introduction

1. It was only in the late 1970s that historians in West Germany began to touch on the central place of skilled workers in the German labor movement. See, e.g., Brockhaus, *Zusammensetzung und Neustrukturierung der Arbeiterklasse vor dem ersten Weltkrieg;* Schönhoven, *Expansion und Konzentration;* Renzsch, *Handwerker und Lohnarbeiter;* and the contributions in Conze and Engelhardt, eds., *Arbeiter im Industrialisierungsprozeß.* Samplings of more recent work are found in Engelhardt, ed., *Handwerker,* and in Mommsen and Husung, eds., *The Development of Trade Unionism.* A masterly analysis of the earlier inadequacies of the German literature on artisans and skilled workers is given in Kocka, "Craft Traditions."

2. Kocka, "The Study of Social Mobility," 114. A somewhat less skeptical assessment of the usefulness of "labor aristocracy" theories as applied to Germany is found in Breuilly, "The Labour Aristocracy in Britain and Germany." On Britain see Hobsbawm, "The Labour Aristocracy in Nineteenth-Century Britain," and the bibliography in McLennan, "'The Labour Aristocracy' and 'Incorporation.'" For a seminal article on the importance of skilled workers in Victorian industry see Samuel, "Workshop of the World." On American skilled workers see Montgomery, *Workers' Control in America.* For the historiography of skilled workers see Hanagan and Stephenson, "The Skilled Worker and Working-Class Protest."

3. Kocka, "The Study of Social Mobility," 115–116.

4. Among German and other West European workers class consciousness gradually increased up to the 1920s, but with the coming of mass culture, the dispersed suburbanized city, the welfare state, and a large number of white-collar workers, the process has generally run the other way since then. James Cronin, in "Labor Insurgency and Class Formation: Comparative Perspectives on the Crisis of 1917–1920 in Europe," 140–143, emphasizes the development of extensive working-class neighborhoods in European cities with intricate social networks, a process which reached its apogee between 1890 and 1920 and then was reversed by suburbanization and the automobile.

5. Jürgen Kocka, "Problems of Working-Class Formation in Germany," in *Working-Class Formation,* ed. Katznelson and Zolberg, 280–283. A longer version

of the same work has been published as *Lohnarbeit und Klassenbildung*. I find Kocka's four stages of class formation to be inherently clearer than those in the introduction to the book by Ira Katznelson, "Working-Class Formation: Constructing Cases and Comparisons," 14–20. See also Kocka, "The Study of Social Mobility," 104–109, especially his critique of the Marxist-Leninist assumptions of Hartmut Zwahr's useful study of Leipzig, *Zur Konstituierung des Proletariats als Klasse*.

6. Aristide R. Zolberg, "How Many Exceptionalisms?" in *Working-Class Formation*, ed. Katznelson and Zolberg, 450.

7. Bernard Moss, in his *Origins of the French Labor Movement*, has shown how artisan traditions decisively shaped French socialist ideologies and utopias. The same has often been suggested recently for the popularity of producer cooperatives in the early German socialist movement.

8. On the impact of religion and secularization on the labor movement see Lidtke, "Social Class and Secularization in Imperial Germany," and McLeod, "Protestantism and the Working Class in Imperial Germany." The Düsseldorf information is drawn from Nolan, *Social Democracy and Society*, 113–117. The proportion of Catholics in Nuremberg comes from Eckert, *Liberal- oder Sozialdemokratie*, 90.

9. Fischer, *Industrialisierung*, 390–396.


1: Capitalism, Industrialization, and the Metalworking Artisans of Nuremberg

1. Pfeiffer, ed., *Nürnberg*, 303–324; Voit, *Nürnberger Gold- und Silberschlägerei*, 27–28; Grießinger and Reith, "Obrigkeitliche Ordnungskonzeptionen," 119–127. The population estimate comes from Gömmel, *Wachstum*, 22–23, 186, corrected for the presence of the 3,000-man garrison, which Gömmel excludes. The city's population in 1622 was "somewhat over 40,000." Ibid., 22n.

2. Wiest, *Entwicklung*, 39–41, 65–83; Lehnert, "Nürnberg—Stadt ohne Zünfte"; Voit, *Nürnberger Gold- und Silberschlägerei*, 8–13.

3. Wiest, *Entwicklung*, 89–100; Rosenhaupt, *Nürnberg-Fürther Metallspielwarenindustrie*, 18–20.

4. For descriptions of the Bavarian system see Eckert, *Liberal- oder Sozialdemokratie*, 52–56; Schwarz, "*Nahrungsstand*," 71–75; and Shorter, "Social Change," 95–131 and passim. Chapter 2 will discuss the system insofar as it applies to the difficulties of becoming a master.

5. Gömmel, *Wachstum*, 46–47, 162; Walker, *German Home Towns*, 309–310, 313, 338–340.

6. Quoted in Senst, *Metallspielwarenindustrie*, 20. Emphasis in the original. Unless otherwise noted all translations are my own.

7. Gömmel, *Wachstum*, 46–47, 162.

8. Volkov, *Rise of Popular Antimodernism*, 53–54.

9. Wiest, *Entwicklung*, 133; Reß, "Die Nürnberger 'Briefbücher,' " 2:801.

10. Schröder, *Entwicklung des Nürnberger Großgewerbes*, 26.
11. Wiest, *Entwicklung*, 30–31.
12. Schröder, *Entwicklung*, 30.
13. For example, most locksmith masters had zero to three journeymen in 1850–1851 but one had eight to ten (depending on the month), and another increased his helpers from one to eight in the space of eight months. Hwa., Schlosser Nr. 18e.
14. Soergel, "Zwei Nürnberger Metallgewerbe"; Eibert, *Maschinenbauer*, 40–43; Schröder, *Entwicklung*, 135.
15. Gömmel has shown that the normal workweek of Nuremberg artisans jumped from sixty-one to sixty-seven hours between 1845 and 1870. See *Wachstum*, 72. The problem of longer hours, work discipline and Blue Monday drinking will be treated in Chapter 2.
16. Stadtmag. decision of 6 Oct. 1837 in HR VIb7, R Nr. 4. An even greater variety of distinctions are listed by the molders themselves in the Protokoll of 12 Feb. 1844 in Hwa., Rotgießer Nr. 28.
17. Protokoll of 12 Feb. 1844 in Hwa., Rotgießer Nr. 28; Wiest, *Entwicklung*, 166; Gewerberat report of 1 June 1874 in Industrie- und Handelskammer Nr. 70. The description of brass molding is taken from the technically near-identical iron-molding trade.
18. Protokolle of 18 Apr. and 5 June 1837 and 29 Dec. 1845 in HR 12778.
19. Protokolle of 29 Dec. 1845 in HR 12778.
20. Protokoll of 11 Sept. 1846 in HR VIb7, R Nr. 4; clipping from *FK*, 25 Oct. 1851, in Hwa., Rotgießer Nr. 28.
21. *FK*, 12 Feb. 1844.
22. Protokolle of 18 and 21 July 1843 in HR VIb7, R Nr. 4.
23. Protokoll of 23 July 1858 in HR VIb7, R Nr. 15.
24. Gömmel, *Wachstum*, 111–112. These figures have been converted from Gulden to marks. See the Note on Currency.
25. Senst, *Metallspielwarenindustrie*, 15–16, 21–22; Rosenhaupt, *Nürnberg-Fürther Metallspielwarenindustrie*, 18–20, 26–27, 30–31, 44–47.
26. Appeal to the king of 23 Jan. 1852 in Hwa., Flaschner Nr. 9.
27. Police senate decision of 1 Mar. 1847, Protokoll of 29 Oct. 1850, Rgg. Mf. decision of 11 Dec. 1850, appeal of 11 Jan. 1851, and appeal to king of 23 Jan. 1852 in Hwa., Flaschner Nr. 19.
28. Protokoll of 19 Nov. 1839 and Gutachten of 29 Dec. 1858 in HR VIb7, G Nr. 1; Dr. Beeg to Rgg. Mf., 29 Feb. 1860 in HR 12765; Beeg, "Der Nürnberg-Fürther Industriedistrikt," 1064–1065.
29. Senst, *Metallspielwarenindustrie*, 21–22; Protokolle of 22 Apr., 3 July, and 25 Aug. 1844, and police senate decision of 23 Sept. 1844 in HR VIb7, F Nr. 11.
30. Rosenhaupt, *Nürnberg-Fürther Metallspielwarenindustrie*, 46.
31. Voit, *Nürnberger Gold- und Silberschlägerei*, 7, 13–14, 84–91.
32. Ibid., 28–31; Morgenstern, *Fürther Metallschlägerei*, 3–6 and passim.
33. Protokolle of 17 Nov., 24 Nov., and 23 Dec. 1843 in HR VIb7, G Nr. 8.

34. Protokoll of 27 Apr. 1843 in HR VIb7, G Nr. 6; Morgenstern, *Fürther Metall-schlägerei*, 44–46, 189–192, 197–200.
35. Protokolle of 17 and 24 Nov. 1843 in HR VIb7, G Nr. 8.
36. Schröder, *Entwicklung*, 100, 116–118; Eibert, *Maschinenbauer*, 40–43.
37. Eibert, *Maschinenbauer*, 41, 57–71, 292–293; Schröder, *Entwicklung*, 121–125.
38. On the work process in the machine industry see especially Landes, *Unbound Prometheus*, 303–317, and Renzsch, *Handwerker und Lohnarbeiter*, 146–158.
39. Photocopy of clipping from Nov. 1857 in M.A.N.-Nbg. Werksarchiv, Nr. 111.
40. Based upon the 1872 production of some 4,000 cars in a year of about 300 workdays. Eibert, *Maschinenbauer*, 118; Gömmel, *Wachstum*, 189.
41. Eibert, *Maschinenbauer*, 117–118; Büchner, *Hundert Jahre Geschichte der Maschinenfabrik Augsburg-Nürnberg*, 80–82.
42. "Once upon a Shop Floor," 49.
43. M.A.N.-Nbg. Werksarchiv, Nr. 221.3.
44. Rupieper, "Regionale Herkunft," 108n.
45. Ibid., 109; Rupieper, *Arbeiter und Angestellte*, 109; Renzsch, *Handwerker und Lohnarbeiter*, 153, 155.
46. Renzsch, *Handwerker und Lohnarbeiter*, 154–155.
47. Foth, "Soziale Chronik aus 100 Jahren MAN," Anlage 10, 14.
48. Renzsch, *Handwerker und Lohnarbeiter*, 154–156.
49. Ibid., 153.
50. Gömmel, *Wachstum*, 111, 115.
51. Rupieper, "Regionale Herkunft," 100; Eibert, *Maschinenbauer*, 175; Rupieper, *Arbeiter und Angestellte*, 84–89.
52. Iron molder apprentices are found in Klett records of the 1840s and 1850s. M.A.N.-Nbg. Werksarchiv, Nr. 221.3.
53. 1844 shop rules in Biensfeldt, *Cramer-Klett*, 229–231; Renzsch, *Handwerker und Lohnarbeiter*, 18. On adaptation to work discipline generally see Thompson, "Time, Work-Discipline and Industrial Capitalism"; Pollard, *The Genesis of Modern Management*, ch. 5; Stearns, "Adaptation to Industrialization"; and Roberts, "Drink and Industrial Work Discipline."
54. Renzsch, *Handwerker und Lohnarbeiter*, 147–156.
55. Ibid., 147–158.
56. Ibid., 147–148; Rupieper, *Arbeiter und Angestellte*, 99–100.
57. Heron, "Crisis of the Craftsman," 10–11. Although this article draws on Canadian and American sources, its description of iron molding is excellent and applicable to Germany. For a foundry in Switzerland on the German border see Vetterli, *Industriearbeit*.
58. DMZ, 24 Aug. 1895; Renzsch, *Handwerker und Lohnarbeiter*, 148; Rupieper, *Arbeiter und Angestellte*, 100–102.
59. Rupieper, *Arbeiter und Angestellte*, 100–102; Renzsch, *Handwerker und Lohnarbeiter*, 148.
60. DMZ, 9 Jan. 1886 and 8 June 1895; Heron, "Crisis of the Craftsman," 10–

11. At M.A.N. the foundry was not properly heated before 1905, and it was not until 1926 that a solution was found to the dust problem created by cleaning the castings. Foth, "Soziale Chronik," 94–95.

61. Schröder, *Entwicklung*, 122; Biensfeldt, *Cramer-Klett*, 26–27.

62. Bavaria, Kgl. Statistisches Bureau, *Die Bevölkerung und die Gewerbe des Königreichs Bayern nach der Aufnahme vom Jahre 1861*, 80–81, 122–123.

63. Protokoll of 4 Oct. 1852, StaatsAN, BA Nbg., Stadtkomm. Nr. 18.

64. From Grillenberger's memoirs of his Wanderschaft, reprinted in Gärtner, *Grillenberger*, 17–18.

65. Protokoll of 8 Nov. 1858 in HR VIb7, Nr. 63.

66. M.A.N.-Nbg. Werksarchiv, Nr. 221.3.

67. "Zahlungsliste der Giesser Juli 1862–Decbr. 1865" from Spaeth, in the possession of Dr. Dieter Rossmeissl, Nuremberg. For the cost of living see Gömmel, *Wachstum*, 159.

68. *FT*, 21 June 1899; Stadtmag. to Rgg. Mf., 11 July 1899 in StaatsAN, Regg. KdI 1932, Tit. IX, Nr. 651(VI); Protokoll of 24 Jan. and poster of 5 Feb. 1853 in HR VIb7, H Nr. 3.

69. Rupieper, *Arbeiter und Angestellte*, 102–103; Renzsch, *Handwerker und Lohnarbeiter*, 148–149.

70. Foth, "Soziale Chronik," Anlage 10, 14. The differential is also considerable in the mid-1840s. See M.A.N.-Nbg. Werksarchiv, Nr. 221.3.

71. *FT*, 27 Feb. 1880; Soergel, "Zwei Nürnberger Metallgewerbe," 438, 446–460.

72. Appeal to Rgg. Mf., 6 Nov. 1843, in Hwa., Schlosser Nr. 69.

73. Appeal to king, 31 Jan. 1852, in Hwa., Schlosser Nr. 42.

74. Protokoll of 9 Apr. 1861 in HR VIb7, Nr. 65.

75. M.A.N.-Nbg. Werksarchiv, Nr. 221.3; Foth, "Soziale Chronik," Anlage 10, 14.

76. Rupieper, *Arbeiter und Angestellte*, 107.

77. Lüdtke, "Cash, Coffee-breaks, Horse-play," 68–69.

78. Schröder, *Entwicklung*, 34, 140–141.

79. Eibert, *Maschinenbauer*, 182–199, 372; Seubert, "Die Entstehung der Nürnberger Fahrzeugindustrie," 14–18; Rossmeissl, *Arbeiterschaft und Sozialdemokratie*, 37.


2: The Transformation of the Journeyman's World

1. Grießinger, *Das symbolische Kapital*, 302–307.

2. Until 1856, the purchaser of a Realrecht could not be denied a Konzession unless his indebtedness was large or his reputation poor. As a result the price of one was astronomical—often three or four hundred Gulden. In Nuremberg the only metal trades with Realrechte were the gold beaters and blacksmiths. Schwartz, "Nahrungsstand," 86–100; Schröder, *Entwicklung*, 21.

3. Walker, *German Home Towns*, 294–298; Eckert, *Liberal- oder Sozialdemokratie*, 30–38.

4. Walker, *German Home Towns*, 309–310, 313, 339–340; Held, *Arbeitsverhältnis*, 54–56, 79–84; Schröder, *Entwicklung*, 14–16; Schwarz, "*Nahrungsstand*," 71–72. Although the 1853 Vollzugsinstruktion contained some innovations, the assertion by Shorter that it was progressive is certainly incorrect. Shorter, "Social Change," 690–693.

5. Eckert, *Liberal- oder Sozialdemokratie*, 32–33, 44–45; Schwarz, "*Nahrungsstand*," 148.

6. It would be possible to quantify the Niederlassungsakten generated by Konzession and Ansässigmachung applications of Nuremberg artisans, but this huge project has already defeated one German graduate student. These records exist in the StadtAN for the years 1828–1861, 1877–1887, and 1906–1907. The others were destroyed in a World War II air raid.

7. Wiest, *Entwicklung*, 77–80; Held, *Arbeitsverhältnis*, 16–17. Grießinger, *Das symbolische Kapital*, treats the whole crisis in artisanry and the journeymen's brotherhoods in the eighteenth century. Although overloaded with sociological and social psychological jargon, the book is very important for having brought the strike movement of the 1700s to light. A useful summary, "Handwerkerstreiks in Deutschland während des 18. Jahrhunderts" is found in *Handwerker*, ed. Engelhardt, 407–434.

8. Gömmel, *Wachstum*, 56, 65, 175. Schröder, *Entwicklung*, 17, gives two examples of "overfilling" in the Nuremberg metal trades. Between 1830 and 1850, 157 compass-maker apprentices were graduated but only 32 became masters. The total number of masters scarcely grew. Only one new license was awarded to a nailsmith between 1840 and 1850.

9. Schwarz, "*Nahrungsstand*," 161–162.

10. Schröder, *Entwicklung*, 17. On the free trades see ibid., 21n; Schwarz, "*Nahrungsstand*," 157–160; and Stadtmag. to Rgg. Mf., 11 May 1837 and 19 Nov. 1838 in HR 12765.

11. Appeal of 8 July 1855 in HSA Munich, MH 7667. A translation does not capture the flavor of the original. The letter begins: "Unterzeichneter, fühlt sich zu Seiner Königlichen Majestät füßen gebeigt, um die Allerhögste Gnade, meines Großmächtigten Königs und Vaters, Fürsten und Herrn anzuflehe.

"Da ich als geborner Bürger Sohn zu Nürnberg das Handwerk meines verstorbenen Vaters als Schlosser erlernte, und mich heran bittete, um den beruffe späterer Jahre, als tauglicher Bürger, in der Gesellschaft, meiner mittbürger mich zu erfreuhen strebte, finde ich mich tief gebeigt vor seine königliche Mayestät tretent, da es mir bisher so sehr erschwert wurde, um das oben erwähnte Ziel von seite des Magisterraths zu erlangen."

12. Protokoll of 19 Dec. 1850 in HR VIb7, M Nr. 19.

13. Eckert, *Liberal- oder Sozialdemokratie*, 33, 40, 63; Shorter, "Social Change," 506, 655–657; Held, *Arbeitsverhältnis*, 9–10, 57; Gesellenordnung of 1834(?) in Hwa., Schlosser Nr. 84; "Gewerbs-Ordnung für die Huf- und Waffenschmieds-

Zunft" of 5 Feb. 1853 in HR VIb7, H Nr. 3; appeal to king by Schlossermeister of 31 Jan. 1852 in Hwa., Schlosser Nr. 42.

14. Shorter, "Social Change," 700–706; statement of Schlosser Vorgeher of 26 Apr. 1848 in HR VIb7, S Nr. 42; Wiessner, "Anfänge der Nürnberger Fabrikindustrie," 240–243; petition of 17 July 1848 in BAA Frankfurt, DB51, Nr. 120, Pet. 1224, and petition of 5 Jan. 1849 in BAA Frankfurt, DB51, Nr. 125, Pet. 5319; Klings, "Kampf um die Gewerbefreiheit," 104, 110; Schröder, *Entwicklung,* 18; Bonnet, "Anfänge der Arbeiterbewegung," 39–40n.

15. Grießinger, *Das symbolische Kapital,* passim; Wilfried Reininghaus, "Die Gesellenvereine am Ende des Alten Reichs" in *Handwerker,* ed. Engelhardt, 219–241; Schanz, *Gesellen-Verbände,* 129–140; Schoenlank, "Gesellenverbände"; Werner, "Travelling Journeymen," 211–212; Stürmer, ed., *Herbst des alten Handwerks,* 153–168; Held, *Arbeitsverhältnis,* 37–38. On compagnonnage see Truant, "Solidarity and Symbolism among Journeyman Artisans" and Sewell, *Work and Revolution,* ch. 3. For a discussion of the journeymen's associations in all Nuremberg trades in the nineteenth century, see my article, "German Artisans and Political Repression."

16. Protokoll of 6 Sept. 1842 in HR 17090; Protokoll of 3 June 1850 in HR 17094; Pilz, *Die 600jährige Geschichte des Nürnberger Schlosserhandwerks,* 33–35.

17. Held, *Arbeitsverhältnis,* 19–21, 71–73; order of Kgl. Handwerks-Gericht of 1 Feb. 1808 in Hwa., Schlosser Nr. 84; Protokolle of 29 Nov. and 14, 19, and 23 Dec. 1850 in HR VIb7, M Nr. 19; Protokolle of 22 Apr. 1846, 27 Sept. 1847, 28 Jan. 1850, 27 May 1850, and 1 May 1851 in HR 17094. See also the regulations of the stickpin makers of 21 Apr. 1837 and 5 Nov. 1848 in Hwa., Heftleinmacher Nr. 5 and Nr. 38 respectively, and of the blacksmiths of 4 Mar. 1861 in HR 16193.

18. Circular of Rgg. Mf. of 12 Dec. 1834 in StaatsAN, BA Nbg., Stadtkomm. Nr. 16.

19. Held, *Arbeitsverhältnis,* 63; Werner, "Travelling Journeymen," 212–218; Schraepler, *Handwerkerbünde,* 32–40; Ministry of Interior orders of 6 June and 3 Sept. 1834 and Rgg. Mf. order of 20 Feb. 1835, in Stadtkomm. XV B2a; Rgg. Mf. circulars of 4 Nov. 1840 and 26 Jan. 1841 in HR 16612. Further materials on the repression of the associations and revolutionaries between 1842 and 1846 may be found in HR 2726 and HR 3105, and in StaatsAN, Regg. KdI 1932, Tit. IX, Nr. 412.

20. Grießinger, *Das symbolische Kapital,* passim.

21. Grießinger and Reith, "Obrigkeitliche Ordnungskonzeptionen," 134.

22. Sitzungs-Protokolle of Stadtmag. of 1 and 4 May 1835, and Stadtmag. to Rgg. Mf., 2 May 1835 in HR 3104. See also Held, *Arbeitsverhältnis,* 48, 76–78, 87. For a hatmakers' strike in 1821 see Protokolle of 10, 13, and 15 Jan. 1821 in ÄMR 1069. For an 1865 tailors' strike see Protokolle of 8 and 14 May 1865, police senate decisions of 15 and 16 May 1865, Staatsanwaltschaft to Stadtmag., 16 May 1865 in HR 17160. The tailors also tried to start a movement in 1857 but were stopped by the masters and authorities. See Protokolle of 23 and 24 Mar. 1857 in HR 17155. This and a conflict between some glovemakers and their employer the same year

are erroneously reported in Eckert, *Liberal- oder Sozialdemokratie*, 298, as strikes. For the glovemakers see the Protokolle of 25 and 26 May 1857 in HR 16672.

23. Protokoll of 4 Nov. 1842, taken in Neuötting, in HR 17332; Protokoll of 15 Mar. 1852 in HR 16855.

24. Police senate decision of 24 June 1844 in Hwa., Flaschner Nr. 39; Protokolle of 8 Mar. 1848 and 7 July 1866 in HR VIb7, G Nr. 11.

25. Quoted in Margrit S. Beerbühl, "Kontinuität und Wandel der Londoner Gesellenorganisationen im 18. Jahrhundert," in *Handwerker*, ed. Engelhardt, 259n. On Germany see Werner, "Travelling Journeymen," 204–206, 213; Koeppen, *Anfänge*, 4.

26. Gesellenschein of 15 Mar. 1840, Zeugnis of 17 Oct. 1842, letters of 2 Nov. 1835 and undated [c. 1839], Protokolle of 5 Oct., 4 Nov., and 17, 21, and 29 Dec. 1842 in HR 17332; Gesellenscheine of 29 July 1839 and 23 June 1851, and Protokolle of 15, 22, and 29 Mar. 1852 in HR 16885; Stadtrat Chemnitz to Stadtmag., 8 Apr. 1842, Gesellenschein of 13 Feb. 1840, Kgl. Landgericht Altdorf to Stadtmag., 26 Feb. 1843, and police senate decision of 1 May 1843, Gesellenschein 1 Mar. 1859 in ÄMR 952; Polizei-Direktion Munich to Stadtmag., 11 Nov. 1844 in HR 3105; Protokolle of 15 Aug. and 6 Sept. 1842 in HR 17090. There is also a case of a forged Gesellenschein among the stickpin makers. See Protokoll of 22 Mar. 1843 in ÄMR 952.

27. These passes can be found in Stadtkomm. XV B2d. Included is one from the Munich coppersmiths, issued 19 June 1853. According to the Berlin police, Gesellenscheine were illegal but tolerated in Prussia because of their useful function in traveling. Kgl. Polizei-Präsidium Berlin to Stadtmag., 5 Jan. 1859 in ibid.

28. Protokoll of 13 Sept. and police senate decision of 27 Sept. 1848 in HR 16612; Protokoll of 14 Dec. 1859, police senate decision of 21 Dec. 1859 (refusal), and reversal of decision by Rgg. Mf. on 8 Mar. 1860 in HR 16855.

29. Protokoll of 20 May and police senate decision of 10 June 1846 in HR 16904; Protokoll of 12 Jan. 1852 in HR 17904; Protokoll of 18 May 1853 in HR 16193.

30. Protokolle of 13 and 19 Oct. 1858 in HR 16637; entries in Hwa., Schlosser Nr. 18a.

31. The full initiation ritual is much more complicated, and is detailed in Grießinger, *Das symbolische Kapital*, 211–222. On apprenticeship see ibid., 58–60, 64, 66–67; Held, *Arbeitsverhältnis*, 3–7, 52–53; Eckert, *Liberal- oder Sozialdemokratie*, 62–63; the rules to be read to new apprentices in the 1854–1862 Schlosser Lehrlingsbuch in Hwa., Schlosser Nr. 24; section 35 of the 1845 "Allgemeine Grundzüge zu einem Entwurf der Gewerbs-Vereins-Satzungen" in HR 12278; police senate decision of 7 Oct. 1873 in HR VIb7, S Nr. 82. The locksmiths' "Gewerbs-Ordnung" of about 1834 states: "The mishandling and hitting of apprentices is only a right of the master, and not of the journeyman." Hwa., Schlosser Nr. 84.

32. The latter verse runs: "ich wünsche die Glück zum Gesellenstand, / vom Gesellenstand ins fremde Land, / vom fremden Land zum Meisterstand, / vom Meisterstand in den Ehestand, / gedenke meiner auch dabei / daß ich dein Meß-

ner gewesen sei." Protokoll of 20 June 1828 in ÄMR 1137; Held, *Arbeitsverhältnis*, 8–9.

33. Protokolle of 15 and 22 Mar. 1852 in HR 16855; Protokoll of 6 Sept. 1842 in HR 17090; Protokoll of 29 Dec. 1842 in HR 17332; Werner, "Travelling Journeymen," 213.

34. Protokolle of 15 and 22 Mar. 1852 in HR 16855.

35. Ibid., and police senate decision of 5 May 1852 in HR 16855; Protokolle of 4 Nov., 17 Dec., 21 Dec., and 29 Dec. 1842 and police senate decision of 30 Jan. 1843 in HR 17332; Protokoll of 26 Jan. and police senate decision of 2 Feb. 1846 on the gold beaters in HR 16612; Ministry of Interior orders of 5 June 1834 and 3 Mar. 1837 in HR 16612; letter of master Morhardt (Bamberg), 6 May 1859, to Schlosser Vorgeher in HR 17126. The brass molders claimed that their 3 fl. charge for food and drink had "long since" been abolished as "gross mischief." See Protokoll of 6 Sept. 1842 in HR 17090.

36. Gärtner, *Grillenberger*, 12.

37. Grießinger, *Das symbolische Kapital*, 14, 108–111, 217–229, 355–356, 389–425, 443–456; Wissel, *Des Alten Handwerks*, 2:145–273.

38. Appeal of the Rotgiesser Vorgeher to Stadtmag., 20 Sept. 1837, in HR 3104.

39. Poster of 10 July 1850 in Stadtkomm. XV B2b.

40. Entry in Hwa., Schlosser Nr. 18a.

41. Circular of Rgg. Mf. of 30 Jan. 1854 in Stadtkomm. XV B2a.

42. From Grillenberger's memoirs quoted in Gärtner, *Grillenberger*, 15–20. On hostels see Gutachten of Dr. Beeg to Stadtmag., 16 June 1864 and Gewerberat to Stadtmag., 28 Nov. 1865 and 12 Dec. 1866 in HR 16635. Notices given to the police regarding changes of location of hostels show that at the very least there were still hostels for the turners and nailsmiths in 1864, the tin molders and coppersmiths in 1865, and the locksmiths in 1867. These moves were often accompanied by parades with music and flags in the old style. See notices of 11 Apr. and 28 Apr. 1864, 23 Jan. and 29 Mar. 1865, and 27 Aug. 1867 in ibid.

43. Protokoll of 15 May 1852 in HR 9328. Entries of travel money paid out in the account book of the gold beaters' journeymen's association were rare. See Hwa., Goldschläger Nr. 7. On the sentiment of those remaining see "Gehülfen-Versammlung" Protokoll of 10 Mar. 1850 in HR 9328. There are indications that a number of other former "closed" trades stubbornly stuck to not wandering in spite of the law. See Protokoll of 29 Dec. 1845 in HR 12778 (brass molders), Protokoll of 7 Nov. 1850 in HR VIb7, Nr. 29 (Scheibenzieher), and Protokolle of 22 and 29 Mar. 1852 in HR 16855 (filemakers).

44. Anonymous letter [c. 1847] in Hwa., Goldschläger Nr. 62.

45. Ibid.; entries for 1854 in account book, Hwa., Goldschläger Nr. 7; Protokolle of 10 Feb. and 9 Mar. 1846 and 30 Nov. 1849 and draft statutes of 1 Apr. 1846 in HR 16885; Protokolle of 4 Feb., 23 Feb., and 22 Apr. 1850, 4 Jan., 19 Feb., 14 May, 15 May, 21 Aug., 15 Sept., and 1 Oct. 1852, 2 Sept. 1861, and 19 Feb. 1863, draft statutes of Feb. 1850 and 21 June 1861, and "Gehülfen-Versammlung" Protokoll of 10 Mar. 1850 in HR 9328.

46. Grießinger, *Das symbolische Kapital*, 102.

47. Protokoll and draft statutes of 23 Feb. 1850 in HR 9324. On wandering see note 43. The journeymen metal beaters started an abortive sickness insurance fund in 1866, four years after the guild's dissolution. See Protokolle of 24 Dec. 1866 and 19 Mar. 1867 in HR 9420.

48. Protokoll and statutes of 29 May 1865 in HR Vd15, Nr. 231.

49. Koehne, "Blauen Montags," 268–287, 394–413; Reulecke, "Vom blauen Montag zum Arbeiterurlaub," 207–211; Wissel, *Des Alten Handwerks*, 2:415–439; Werner, "Travelling Journeymen," 213; Held, *Arbeitsverhältnis*, 87–88; Schanz, *Gesellen-Verbände*, 114–116; Reid, "The Decline of St. Monday"; Protokoll of 16 Aug. 1845 in HR VIb7, Nr. 27; Protokoll of 24 Mar. 1862 in HR VIb7, Z Nr. 13; "Gewerbs-Ordnung" [c. 1834] in Hwa., Schlosser Nr. 84; "Gewerbs-Ordnung of 24 Jan. 1853 in HR VIb7, H Nr. 3, and reply of journeymen of 14 Mar. 1853 in Hwa., Huf- und Waffenschmiede Nr. 21; Protokoll of 3 Oct. 1843 in HR VIb7, Nr. 35; Protokoll of 5 Mar. 1855 in HR 16636; Protokoll of 8 Nov. 1858 in HR 16637; Protokoll of 8 Mar. 1859 in HR VIb7, M Nr. 86; Wiest, *Entwicklung*, 115.

50. Decision of police senate of 12 Nov. 1863 in HR 16638.

51. Gömmel, *Wachstum*, 51.

52. Staatsanwaltschaft to Stadtmag., 31 Aug. 1864 in HR 16638; Foth, "Soziale Chronik," 39; 1844 work rules in Biensfeldt, *Cramer-Klett*, 229–232.

53. Stadtmag. orders of 27 May and 8 June 1858 in HR 16612.

54. Police senate decision of 10 Oct. 1842 in HR 16612; Stadtkomm. to Stadtmag., 13 July 1852 in HR 16636.

55. Rgg. Mf. to Stadtmag., 2 July 1858, police senate decision of 12 July 1858, Rgg. Mf. to Stadtmag., 2 Oct. 1858, police senate decision of 11 Apr. 1861, police officer's reports of 27 May 1861 and 9 Nov. 1863, police senate decisions of 30 Oct., 5 Nov., and 26 Nov. 1863 in HR 16612; Protokoll of 25 Aug. 1858 in Polizei-senats-Protokolle, Bd. 40; police officer's reports of 30 Aug., 20, 27, and 28 Sept., 12 and 18 Oct., and 22 Nov. 1858, 3, 17, and 31 Jan., 22 and 28 Mar., 4 Apr., and 21 Nov. 1859 in HR 16637; Staatsanwaltschaft to Stadtmag., 10 Nov. 1863, police senate decisions of 12 Nov. 1863 and 14 July 1864 in HR 16638; Armenpflegschafts-rat to Stadtmag., 1 Sept. 1863 in HR 9833; Koehne, "Blauen Montags," 413; *FK*, 18 May 1875; cases of 1875 and 1877 in HR VIb7, Nr. 68.

56. *FK*, 19 and 23 Aug., 12 Sept., 27 Oct., 4, 10, 14, and 19 Nov. 1863 and 21 June 1868; *Correspondent von und für Deutschland*, 9 Nov. 1863; Rgg. Mf. to Stadt-komm., 17 Aug. 1863, Stadtkomm. to Rgg. Mf., 19 Aug. 1863, transcript of police officer's report of 19 Aug. 1863, and Stadtkomm. to Stadtmag., 11 Aug. 1863, in StaatsAN, Regg. KdI 1932, Tit. II, Nr. 5451; police senate decision of 19 Nov. 1863 in HR VIb7, Nr. 29; Pfeiffer, ed., *Nürnberg*, 389; Pfeiffer, "Das Nürnberger Gemeindebevollmächtigtenkolleg"; Leitl, "Carl Crämer," 71; Stadtchronik, 23 June 1867.

57. Roberts, "Der Alkoholkonsum deutscher Arbeiter im 19. Jahrhundert," 226–227; Gömmel, *Wachstum*, 83, 211.

58. Gömmel, *Wachstum,* 72.
59. Protokoll of 10 Mar. 1857 in HR 16636.
60. Protokoll of 8 Nov. 1858 in HR 16637. The Munich *Fabrikrat* emphasized in 1860 the connections between living out and piece-rate payment and the weakening of the employer's authority, resulting in more Monday drinking. See his statement, quoted in Schwarz, *"Nahrungsstand,"* 169. Evidence for piece-rate payment among the brass molders can be found in the Protokoll of 25 Sept. 1858 in HR 16637.
61. Of seventy-two metalworkers convicted between 1843 and 1862, there were twenty-five metal beaters, thirteen locksmiths, six blacksmiths, six braziers, four iron molders, four unskilled laborers, and three tinsmiths. The remainder came from a wide variety of trades. For sources, see Figure 2.1.
62. Protokoll of 1 Sept. 1859 in HR VIb7, S Nr. 82. For numbers of convictions see note 61.
63. Rgg. Mf. to Stadtmag., 2 July 1858 in StaatsAN, Regg. KdI 1932, Tit. IX, Nr. 412.
64. Protokolle of 24 Jan. and 4 Apr. 1853, and poster of 5 Feb. 1853 in HR VIb7, H Nr. 3; Protokoll of 14 Mar. 1853 and undated letter of masters to journeymen in Hwa., Huf- und Waffenschmiede Nr. 21.
65. This presumption is based upon research into adaptation to work discipline already cited in Chapter 1, n. 53, especially Thompson's "Time, Work-Discipline and Industrial Capitalism" and Pollard's *Genesis of Modern Management.* Notwithstanding the justified critiques leveled at the thesis of adaptation by James Roberts in "Drink and Industrial Work Discipline," and by Daniel T. Rodgers in "Tradition, Modernity and the American Industrial Worker," I think that the idea that there was a gradual acceptance and internalization by workers of the work ethic as industrialization proceeded is still basically sound.
66. Gömmel, *Wachstum,* 71. For cases in the seventies and eighties see Protokoll of 31 July 1874 in HR VIb7, S Nr. 82; case of 7 Nov. 1877 in HR VIb7, Nr. 68; and *FT,* 3 Jul. and 1 Oct. 1888. On Monday drinking and other work discipline problems see Roberts, "Drink and Industrial Work Discipline," 26–33.
67. Koehne, "Blauen Montags," 404. Two 1865 cases are the first I have run across where the verb form "blau machen" is used. See Protokolle of 24 Apr. and 22 June 1865 in HR VIb7, Nr. 64. Usage in the seventies and late eighties increasingly seems to indicate that any day could be a "blauen." See *SDWB,* 5 Aug. 1874; Protokoll of 4 Dec. 1874 in HR 8681; Protokoll of 5 July 1875 in HR VIb7, M Nr. 94; and *FT,* 12 Apr. and 26 Oct. 1888.
68. Weber, "Comment la Politique Vint aux Paysans," 358. John Breuilly in "Artisan Economy, Artisan Politics, Artisan Ideology," 214–217, comments on the "unpolitical conception of politics" of European artisans in the nineteenth century.
69. Zimmmerman, *Einheits- und Freiheitsbewegung,* 55–56, 137; Koeppen, *Anfänge,* 24–25; Bundes-Central-Behörde lists sent by Rgg. Mf. on 1 and 16 Mar.

1841 in HR 3105 and on 25 Nov. 1842 in HR 2726; Arno Herzig, "Kontinuität und Wandel der politischen und sozialen Vorstellungen Hamburger Handwerker 1790–1870," in *Handwerker*, ed. Engelhardt, 310.

70. Stadtkomm. to Rgg. Mf., 27 Apr. and 6 May 1847 in StaatsAN, BA Nbg., Stadtkomm. Nr. 32; 2. Bürgermeister Seiler to Rgg. Mf., 8 and 16 May 1866 in StaatsAN, Regg. KdI 1932, Tit. II, Nr. 545I.

71. The term "moral economy" comes from E. P. Thompson's description of English food rioters in "The Moral Economy of the English Crowd in the Eighteenth Century."

72. Koeppen, *Anfänge*, 36, 40–46; Zimmermann, *Einheits- und Freiheitsbewegung*, 268–269; Meyer, *Vereinswesen*, 105–109; Brigade Nbg. to Kgl. Gendarmie-Corps, Compagnie von Mf., 8 Mar. 1848, HSA Munich, MInn 46058.

73. Shorter, "Social Change," 700–703. Shorter mistranslates Altgesellen as "elderly journeymen."

74. Presentation of Schlosser Vorgeher of 25 Apr. 1848 in HR VIb7, S Nr. 42; petition of 17 July 1848 in BAA Frankfurt, DB51, Nr. 120, Pet. 1224; petition of 5 Jan. 1849 in BAA Frankfurt, DB51, Nr. 125, Pet. 5319; Wiessner, "Anfänge der Nürnberger Fabrikindustrie," 241–243.

75. Koeppen, *Anfänge*, 59; Klings, "Kampf um die Gewerbefreiheit," 104, 110, 112; Meyer, *Vereinswesen*, 177–178; Brunner, *Politische Bewegungen*, 110–111; Balser, *Sozial-Demokratie*, 1:47–48; Kocka, "The Study of Social Mobility," 112.

76. Brigade Nbg. to Gendarmerie-Compagnie Mf., 28 June 1849 in HSA Munich, MInn 45538. According to Klings, "Kampf um die Gewerbefreiheit," 110, journeymen locksmith Köchert, who was Vorstand of the Arbeiterverein at the time of his arrest, had represented the Nuremberg "Fabrikarbeiter" at the April conference.

77. Vorstand list of 2 Apr. 1850 in Stadtkomm. IX 34a; Stadtkomm. to Rgg. Mf., 22 Aug. 1849, and Stadtkomm. to Polizei-Direktion Munich, 27 May 1850, in StaatsAN, BA Nbg., Stadtkomm. Nr. 33; Zimmermann, *Einheits- und Freiheitsbewegung*, 27, 109; Gärtner, *Nürnberger Arbeiterbewegung*, 6.

78. Protokoll of 3 May 1849 and report to Rgg. Mf. of 14 May 1849 in HSA Munich, MInn 45538; Stadtkomm. to Rgg. Mf., 24 Oct. 1848, and undated lists [c. Oct. 1848] of Politischer Verein and Volksverein Vorstände in StaatsAN, BA Nbg., Stadtkomm. Nr. 30; Meyer, *Vereinswesen*, 105–110; Zimmermann, *Einheits- und Freiheitsbewegung*, 268–269, 293, 300, 369; Brunner, *Politische Bewegungen*, 52, 70, 90, 97, 185–188.

79. Petition of 5 Jan. 1849 in BAA Frankfurt, DB51, Nr. 125, Pet. 5319. Signatures of metal trades journeymen identified as such included 18 awlsmiths, 19 filemakers, 26 goldsmiths, 6 needle and fish-hook makers, 30 nailsmiths, 70 brass molders, 4 bellmakers, 8 polishers, and 42 compass makers.

80. Protokoll of 4 Oct. 1852 in StaatsAN, BA Nbg., Stadtkomm. Nr. 18; Kalsing, who was questioned for left-wing political activity, was also present in Nuremberg in 1848 and therefore was probably a member of the Arbeiterverein then.

81. Klings, "Kampf um die Gewerbefreiheit," 62–63; Stadtkomm. to Stadt-

komm. Würzburg, 14 Nov. 1849, in StaatsAN, BA Nbg., Stadtkomm. Nr. 28; Kgl. Kreis-Commando der Landwehr to Rgg. Mf., 19 Apr. 1848, in HSA Munich, MInn 46058. Threats were apparently also made by journeymen carpenters against colleagues who were not native to Nuremberg, in order to create more work for locals. Kgl. Landgericht Nbg. to Stadtmag., 27 Apr. 1848, in HR 2727.

82. Noyes, *Organization and Revolution,* 72–73, 129–130, 134, 154–155, 199–202; Marquardt, "A Working Class in Berlin," 199 and passim; Zwahr, *Zur Konstituierung des Proletariats,* 106, 231–232, 249, 256, 268, and passim. See also Marquardt, "Sozialer Aufstieg, sozialer Abstieg."

83. Meyer, *Vereinswesen,* 106–108; Brunner, *Politische Bewegungen,* 69–70; Stadtkomm. to Rgg. Mf., 24 Oct. 1848, and undated Vorstände lists in StaatsAN, BA Nbg., Stadtkomm. Nr. 30.

84. Petition of 17 July 1848 in BAA Frankfurt, DB51, Nr. 120, Pet. 1224.

85. Walker, *German Home Towns,* 364.

86. Zimmermann, *Einheits- und Freiheitsbewegung,* 427; Koeppen, *Anfänge,* 72–79, Protokoll of 19 June 1849 in HR 2761; Regierungspräsident to King, ? July 1849, HSA Munich, MInn 45539; Balser, *Sozial-Demokratie,* 1:186–188; Schraepler, *Handwerkerbünde,* 423–424, 426; Staatsministerium des Innern to Stadtkomm., 30 May 1851 and Stadtkomm. report of 31 May 1851 in StaatsAN, BA Nbg., Stadtkomm. Nr. 17. The optimistic assessment of Herwig Förder in "Die Nürnberger Gemeinde des Bundes der Kommunisten" is not borne out by the evidence.

87. Stadtkomm. monthly reports in StaatsAN, BA Nbg., Stadtkomm. Nr. 34a; Protokoll of 15 Aug. 1853 in StaatsAN, BA Nbg., Stadtkomm. Nr. 41.

88. Meyer, *Vereinswesen,* 112–114, 187–188; Eckert, *Liberal- oder Sozialdemokratie,* 93–98; Bonnet, "Anfänge der Arbeiterbewegung," 73, 77, 112, 118–120; Protokoll and statutes of 12 Oct. 1861 and report of 4 Nov. 1862 in Stadtkomm. IX, Nr. 34a; report of 13 Oct. 1861 in StaatsAN, Regg. KdI 1932, Tit. II, Nr. 584I; reports of 29 Mar. 1863 and 30 Dec. 1865 in StaatsAN, BA Nbg., Stadtkomm. Nr. 46.

89. Eckert, *Liberal- oder Sozialdemokratie,* 98–106. A similar pattern of disinterest in the ADAV and growth of the People's Party is found in Württemberg. See Dowe, "Deutschland," 95–96.

90. Kocka, "Problems of Working-Class Formation," in *Working-Class Formation,* ed. Katznelson and Zolberg, 348; Breuilly, "Liberalism or Social Democracy," 27–28.

91. Eckert, *Liberal- oder Sozialdemokratie,* 106–108, 113–118; for a general discussion of liberalism's dilemmas and failures in this period see Sheehan, *German Liberalism,* pts. 3 and 4.

92. Eckert, *Liberal- oder Sozialdemokratie,* 118–128, 174–180.

93. Membership list of 4 June 1866 in Stadtkomm. IX Nr. 34b.

94. Eckert, *Liberal- oder Sozialdemokratie,* 242–245. There was also a strike or movement among the shoemakers in 1865, but I have been unable to find further information. See Protokolle of 23 and 27 Jan. 1866 and Stadtmagistrat Nürnberg to Regierung Mittelfranken, 27 Jan. 1866 in HR 16723. For other strikes and movements, see note 22 above.

3: The Hesitant Beginnings of Trade Unionism

1. Stadtchronik, 13–14 Aug. 1869.

2. Since the issue of whether a union is formally willing to accept unskilled members is an important indicator of consciousness, I have chosen to make this one of the two criteria (along with its openness to all trades in an industry) of an industrial union. This of course does not deal with the tricky problem of how unionists defined an "industry," or why in Germany from the outset industrial unions were determined by the material worked—wood, metal, etc. Virtually nothing is known about the history of this problem, in Germany or elsewhere. See Eric J. Hobsbawm, "The 'New Unionism' Reconsidered," in *The Development of Trade Unionism*, ed. Mommsen and Husung, 22.

3. Eckert, *Liberal- oder Sozialdemokratie*, 54–58.

4. Ibid., 30, 37, 40–42, 275. On the political context of the 1868–1869 reforms see Spindler, ed., *Handbuch der bayerischen Geschichte*, 4:261–267.

5. Eckert, *Liberal- oder Sozialdemokratie*, 37–43, 274–276.

6. Ibid., 45–47; Rossmeissl, *Arbeiterschaft und Sozialdemokratie*, 16–19; Fischer, *Industrialisierung*, 222–224.

7. Eckert, *Liberal- oder Sozialdemokratie*, 186–188, 242–243.

8. Schnorbus, *Arbeit und Sozialordnung*, 145–146, 149.

9. Eckert, *Liberal- oder Sozialdemokratie*, 183.

10. Engelhardt, *"Nur vereinigt sind wir stark,"* passim; Eckert, *Liberal- oder Sozialdemokratie*, 247.

11. Eckert, *Liberal- oder Sozialdemokratie*, 245–250, 302–303.

12. Protokoll and statutes of 10 Apr. 1869 in HR Vd15, Nr. 332.

13. Ibid.; agitators list of 6 Sept. 1878 in HR Vd15, Nr. 440e; membership list of 4 June 1866 and entry of 19 June 1868 in Stadtkomm. IX, Nr. 34b; Eckert, *Liberal- oder Sozialdemokratie*, 178.

14. *Nürnberger Anzeiger*, 12 June 1869. This advertisement was translated into English and French by J. Ph. Becker and published abroad. Eckert, *Liberal- oder Sozialdemokratie*, 257.

15. Eckert, *Liberal- oder Sozialdemokratie*, 257–258; *Nürnberger Anzeiger*, 20 Aug. 1869.

16. Hirschfelder, *Die bayerische Sozialdemokratie*, 1:130; undated poster and Protokoll of 30 Aug. 1869 in Stadtkomm. IX, Nr. 20.

17. Agitator list of 6 Sept. 1878 in HR Vd15, Nr. 440e; *FT,* 22 Sept. 1887; Eckert, *Liberal- oder Sozialdemokratie*, 178, 258.

18. Eckert, *Liberal- oder Sozialdemokratie*, 184–186, 258; IG Metall, ed., *Fünfundsiebzig Jahre Industriegewerkschaft*, 68; Protokoll of 19 Apr. 1870 in HR Vd15, Nr. 332.

19. Letter and statutes of 11 June 1870 and Vorstand list of 27 July 1870 in HR Vd15, Nr. 366; Eckert, *Liberal- oder Sozialdemokratie*, 255.

20. Protokoll of 21 Jan. 1870 and statutes of 22 Nov. 1869 in HR 9517; list of nonpolitical associations in StaatsAN, BA Nbg., Stadtkomm. Nr. 50. No record of

the gold and silver workers' union appears in the city archive. Eckert does not list it but lists a short-lived brass molders' union in 1870–1871. I have found no trace of such a union. Eckert, *Liberal- oder Sozialdemokratie*, 302. On Hamburg see Herzig, "Kontinuität und Wandel," in *Handwerker*, ed. Engelhardt, 318–319.

21. Protokolle of 3, 5, 12, 14 Aug. and 5 Sept. 1871 in Stadtkomm. IX, Nr. 4d; Protokolle of 3 and 18 Sept. 1871 in HR Vd15, Nr. 381; Protokoll of 16 Oct. 1871 in Stadtkomm. IX, Nr. 21.

22. Poster of 27(?) Oct. 1871 in Stadtkomm. IX, Nr. 17a.

23. *Nürnberger Anzeiger*, 21 Oct. 1871; Stadtkomm. to Min. of Interior, 7 Nov. 1871, in Stadtkomm. IX, Nr. 17a.

24. Poster of 27(?) Oct. 1871 in Stadtkomm. IX, Nr. 17a.

25. Protokoll of 28 Oct. 1871 in Stadtkomm. IX, Nr. 17a. On the significance of producer cooperatives in early German socialist ideology see Kocka, "Craft Traditions," 102–103. On the artisanal character of early French socialism see Moss, *Origins of the French Labor Movement*, and Sewell, *Work and Revolution*.

26. Transcript of 28 Oct. 1871 company declaration in Stadtkomm. IX, Nr. 17a; Mauersberg, "Die M.A.N.," 172.

27. Company declaration of 4 Nov. 1871 in Stadtkomm. IX, Nr. 17a. Work times were also set down. The factory did not literally have a ten-hour day because the workday varied, with a total workweek of sixty hours. In a concession perhaps to weekend drinking, Mondays and Saturdays were nine hours, the other days ten and a half. In the winter, work did not begin on Mondays until 8:00, instead of 6:00. Ibid.

28. Protokoll of 5 Nov. 1871 and Stadtkomm. to Rgg. Mf., 6 Nov. 1871, in ibid.

29. Eibert, *Maschinenbauer*, 88. On Klett's development see Ch. 1.

30. Investigation of factory welfare measures (1874) in HR 8740; Eibert, *Maschinenbauer*, 94–101; Eckert, *Liberal- oder Sozialdemokratie*, 27–28.

31. *FDWB*, 29 Nov. 1873.

32. Machtan, " 'Im Vertrauen,' " 59–60.

33. Weekly reports of 18 Nov. 1876 and 5 July 1875 in Direktorium A, Nr. 9; *NFSD*, 14 Aug. 1875 (anonymous letter).

34. Eibert, *Maschinenbauer*, 93; weekly reports of 3 Aug. 1874 and 9 Dec. 1876 in Direktorium A, Nr. 9; *NFSD*, 23 Oct. 1875 and 1 June 1876.

35. Eckert, *Liberal- oder Sozialdemokratie*, 216–218; Gärtner, *Grillenberger*, 60–62, 68. If he had been prominently involved he would have been among those fired. He only emerged as a leader in the union and party from mid-1872 on.

36. *FK*, 26 Nov. 1871.

37. Renzsch, *Handwerker und Lohnarbeiter*, 158–169.

38. Marquardt, "A Working Class in Berlin" and "Sozialer Aufstieg, Sozialer Abstieg."

39. Kocka, "Problems of Working-Class Formation," in *Working-Class Formation*, ed. Katznelson and Zolberg, 342–343. For an insightful discussion of sensitization to the market see Wolfgang Kaschuba, "Vom Gesellenkampf zum sozialen Protest," in *Handwerker*, ed. Engelhardt, 389–390. On France see Alain Cottereau,

"Working-Class Cultures, 1848–1900," in *Working-Class Formation*, ed. Katznelson and Zolberg, 132–135; on Britain, Price, "Structures of Subordination"; for the United States, Montgomery, "Workers' Control"; and for Canada, Palmer, *Culture in Conflict*.

40. Protokolle of 3 and 5 Aug. 1871 in Stadtkomm. IX, Nr. 4d.

41. Breuilly, "Liberalism or Social Democracy;" Kocka, "Problems of Working-Class Formation," 347–348.

42. Protokolle of 3 and 18 Sept. 1871 in HR Vd15, Nr. 381; Protokoll of 16 Oct. 1871 in Stadtkomm. IX, Nr. 21; Protokoll, statutes and membership list of 7(?) Apr. 1873 in HR Vd15, Nr. 435a.

43. Protokolle of 6 and 11 Nov. 1871 in Stadtkomm. IX, Nr. 17a.

44. Protokoll of 11 Nov. 1871 in Stadtkomm. IX, Nr. 17a; *FK*, 28 Nov. 1871; Protokolle of 3 June 1878 and 28 Feb. 1879 and Vorstand list and statutes of 5 Feb. 1872 in HR Vd15, Nr. 393.

45. *FK*, 11 and 25 Nov. 1871; Protokoll of 25 Nov. 1871 in HR Vd15, Nr. 378. On Social Democratic attitudes toward women see Protokoll of 26 June 1871 in Stadtkomm. IX, Nr. 17a and *FDWB*, 14 Dec. 1872 and 30 Aug. 1873 and *NFSD*, 9 May and 9 Sept. 1876.

46. Gömmel, *Wachstum*, 218–219.

47. Protokolle of 17 and 24 Mar. and 15 Apr. 1872 in Stadtkomm. IX, Nr. 33; Protokoll and statutes of 3 Feb. 1873 and Protokoll of 6 Sept. 1878 in HR Vd15, Nr. 428. See also *FK*, 15 Mar. 1872 and *FDWB*, 23 Nov. 1872.

48. *FDWB*, 17 and 24 Feb. and 9 Mar. 1872; note and Protokoll of 20 Mar. 1872, and Protokoll of 1 Apr. 1872 in Stadtkomm. IX, Nr. 17a; weekly reports of 6 and 13 Apr. and 25 May 1872 in Direktorium A, Nr. 9; *FDWB*, 20 Sept. 1873; *SDWB*, 23 Sept. 1874.

49. Notices from Stage of 22 and 28 Apr. 1872, and Protokoll of 25 Apr. 1872 in Stadtkomm. IX, Nr. 21; Protokoll of 15 Apr. 1872 in Stadtkomm. IX, Nr. 17a; Eckert, *Liberal- oder Sozialdemokratie*, 144.

50. Poster, 10 June 1872 and Protokoll of 15 June 1872 in Stadtkomm. IX, Nr. 4d; K. Feucht to Stadtmag. in HR Vd15, Nr. 378; weekly reports of 10 and 31 Aug. 1872 in Direktorium A, Nr. 9; *FDWB*, 7 Sept. 1872.

51. Stadtmag. to Stadtkomm., 24 Sept. 1872 in Stadtkomm. IX, Nr. 20; strike report of Stadtmag. in Industrie- und Handelskammer Nr. 146; weekly report of 5 Oct. 1872 in Direktorium A, Nr. 9; "Verwaltungsbericht des Magistrats . . . für das Jahr 1873" in HR 20; Protokoll of 16 Nov. 1872 in Stadtkomm. IX, Nr. 20. It should be noted that the closely related cartwrights (Wagner), 23 in all, struck simultaneously for the same demands and with the same results. Two other 1872 strikes are reported but have not been confirmed by other sources. Lothar Machtan reports a two-hour strike by blacksmiths in a Nuremberg factory over wage deductions made as a result of disturbances over poor beer in the factory. His source is *Der Volksstaat* (Leipzig). Machtan, " 'Im Vertrauen,' " 227. The mayor also reports that some filemakers (Feilenhauer) were striking simultaneously with

the locksmiths, but no other source mentions it. Weekly report of 6 Apr. 1872 in Direktorium A, Nr. 9.

52. *FDWB*, 30 Nov. 1872; Protokoll and statutes of 23 Sept. 1872 in HR Vd15, Nr. 418.

53. *FDWB*, 20 Sept. 1873.

54. Ibid.

55. Ibid.; *FDWB*, 31 May, 14 June and 9 Aug. 1873; *NFSD*, 23 Mar. 1876 and 22 May 1877. Grillenberger's artisanal values appear clearly in the 1873 articles, as well as in his memoirs quoted in Gärtner, *Grillenberger*, 14, 18–20, 43. His great skill enabled him to rise rapidly to the position of Werkmeister in a Forchheim gas plant after quitting Klett on 26 Mar. 1873. He only remained there until 1 Oct. 1873 because he was called to Nuremberg to edit the *FDWB*.

56. *FDWB*, 31 May 1873.

57. Protokolle of 28 Aug. 1873 and 15 June 1874, Hamburg police to Stadtmag., 13 May 1875, and Protokolle of 30 and 31 May 1875 in HR Vd15, Nr. 378; *NFSD*, 5, 24 and 26 June 1875; Eckert, *Liberal- oder Sozialdemokratie*, 268n.

58. Volkov, *Rise of Popular Antimodernism*, 12, 82–84.

59. Gömmel, *Wachstum*, 186.

60. Report for 1874–1876 in Industrie- und Handelskammer Nr. 72.

61. Protokoll of 15 Jan. 1876 in HR VIb7, S Nr. 82; *NFSD*, 15 Jan. 1876.

62. Protokoll and statutes of 7 July 1875 and Protokoll of 17 May 1879 in HR Vd15, Nr. 550; Protokoll and statutes of 21 Oct. 1874 and Protokoll of 23 Dec. 1875 in HR Vd15, Nr. 510; Protokoll and statutes of 19 Apr. 1876 and Protokoll of 29 Apr. 1878 in HR Vd15, Nr. 593; Protokoll and statutes of 16 Feb. 1877 and Protokoll of 15 May 1878 in HR Vd15, Nr. 631; *NFSD*, 10 Nov. 1877, 5 Mar. and 1 Sept. 1878.

63. Weekly reports of 9 Feb. and 29 June 1874 in Direktorium A, Nr. 9; "Verwaltungsbericht des Magistrats . . . für das Jahr 1874" in HR 21; *SDWB*, 8 and 29 July 1874; Morgenstern, *Fürther Metallschlägerei*, 171–174; Reich Dampfhammerwerk to Ind.- u. Handelskammer, 27 Jan. 1877 in Industrie- und Handelskammer Nr. 72; Eckert, *Liberal- oder Sozialdemokratie*, 255.

64. Eckert, *Liberal- oder Sozialdemokratie*, 225, 229–237; Hirschfelder, *Die bayerische Sozialdemokratie*, 1:197. See also the excellent Nuremberg party histories by Eckert and Rossmeissl. Useful information is also found in the old party history by Gärtner (1908).

65. Blos, "Grillenberger, Karl, sozialdemokratischer Politiker 1848–1897," 133–134.

66. Eckert, *Liberal- oder Sozialdemokratie*, 219–220, 224–225, 229–241. For a very useful discussion of Social Democratic ideology and the Gotha program of 1875 see Lidtke, *Outlawed Party*, ch. 2 and app. A.

67. See Fischer, *Industrialisierung*, and the comments in the Introduction.

68. Scherm was born in 1851 in the Oberpfalz (southeast of Nuremberg) and was the only Catholic among prominent Social Democrats in the seventies.

Agitator list of 6 Sept. 1878 in HR Vd15, Nr. 440e; Eckert, *Liberal- oder Sozialdemokratie*, 240.

**4: Repression, Revival, Unification**

1. Protokoll of 30 Sept. 1878, HR Vd15, Nr. 378; Protokoll of 28 Oct. 1878, HR Vd15, Nr. 631; written notice of J. Faaz of 21 Oct. 1878 in HR Vd15, Nr. 332.

2. Eckert, *Liberal- oder Sozialdemokratie*, 255; Protokoll of 12 Aug. 1882 in HR Vd15, Nr. 381; Protokoll of 10 Dec. 1888 in HR Vd15, Nr. 1336.

3. Lidtke, *Outlawed Party*, 146n; Hirschfelder, *Die bayerische Sozialdemokratie*, 2:363, 367; Gärtner, *Nürnberger Arbeiterbewegung*, 88–110, 126, 131.

4. Gärtner, *Nürnberger Arbeiterbewegung*, 97–110, 116–130; Eckert, *Liberal- oder Sozialdemokratie*, 237.

5. Lidtke, *Outlawed Party*, 176.

6. Protokolle of 26 Feb. and 16 Apr. 1884 and 22 July 1885 in HR Vd15, Nr. 913.

7. In the 1882 census there were twenty tin-molding shops, with eighty-one employees, and ten filemaking shops, with thirty employees, in the city. Bavaria, Kgl. Statistisches Bureau, *Die Ergebnisse der Berufszählung im Königreich Bayern vom 5. Juni 1882*, 384, 386.

8. Statutes of 1 Jan. 1884 in HR Vd15, Nr. 957; statutes of 10 Dec. 1882 and 30 Aug. 1890 in HR Vd15, Nr. 907; *DMZ*, 5 Feb. 1887.

9. Statutes of 11 Oct. 1886 in HR Vd15, Nr. 907; *DMZ*, 29 Nov. 1890, 30 Oct. 1886, 18 Oct. 1890, and 15 Aug. 1891.

10. Protokolle of 9 Jan. 1883 and 21 July 1886 in HR Vd15, Nr. 913.

11. Protokoll of 31 Aug. 1890 in HR Vd15, Nr. 1622.

12. *FT*, 5 Apr. 1888. See also *DMZ*, 29 Jan. 1887.

13. Protokoll of 17 Apr. 1887 in HR Vd15, Nr. 1177.

14. Kocka, "Problems of Working-Class Formation," in *Working-Class Formation*, ed. Katznelson and Zolberg, 342.

15. Stadtmag. to Rgg. Mf., 15 Apr. 1884, in StaatsAN, Regg. KdI 1952, Nr. 1844; *DMZ*, 20 Feb. 1885; Protokoll of 2 June 1885 in HR Vd15, Nr. 842; Protokoll of 28 July 1891 in HR Vd15, Nr. 1605.

16. There were twenty-six metal pressers with eighty-two employees in 1882. Bavaria, *Berufszählung*, 386; *DMZ*, 1 Dec. 1888.

17. *DMZ*, 31 July 1884.

18. Protokolle of 12 and 13 Aug. 1891 in HR 8682.

19. Anonymous letter of 30 May 1885 in HR 8756; *FT*, 10 Apr. 1888 and 7 July 1890; *DMZ*, 1 Dec. 1888.

20. *DMZ*, 11 Apr. 1891.

21. Protokolle of 24 Mar. and 8 Apr. 1882 in HR Vd15, Nr. 882.

22. IG Metall, *Fünfundsiebzig Jahre Industriegewerkschaft*, 91; *DMZ*, 15 Sept. 1883.

23. *FT*, 6 Aug. 1883; *DMZ*, 31 Aug. 1884.

24. Protokolle of 20 Dec. 1884 and 18 Jan. 1885 and police senate decision of 27

Feb. 1885 in HR Vd15, Nr. 1042; *DMZ*, "Beilage zu Nr. 1," 1885, and 20 Mar. 1885; Lütcke, ed., *Dokumentation zur Organisationsgeschichte*, 29. Inconsistently, the Stadtmagistrat did not force the metal pressers out of the VMD. That union quit shortly before the dissolution of the national organization. Protokolle of 2 June and 10 Aug. 1885, and Stadtmag. to Petrich, 22 July 1885, in HR Vd15, Nr. 842.

25. Statutes of 18 Jan. 1885 in HR Vd15, Nr. 1042.

26. *DMZ*, 16 Jan. 1886. Emphasis in the original.

27. Verwaltung lists of 18 Jan. 1885 and 11(?) Jan. 1886 in HR Vd15, Nr. 1042.

28. *DMZ*, 29 May 1886 and 7 May 1887; Protokoll of 21 Jan. 1888 in HR Vd15, Nr. 1042.

29. Protokoll of 3 Sept. 1887, statutes of 11 Sept. 1886 in HR Vd15, Nr. 1042; *FT*, 12 Feb. 1888. The union also held courses in the calculation of gear settings for screw cutting on the lathe, which reinforces the impression that its primary basis was skilled machine-industry workers. *DMZ*, 6 Aug. 1887; *FT*, 20 Oct. 1887.

30. *DMZ*, 6 Aug. 1887; Protokolle of 25 Feb. and 29 Sept. 1888 in HR Vd15, Nr. 1042; *FT*, 17 June 1884.

31. *FT*, 20 Apr. 1886.

32. *DMZ*, 9 Jan. 1886.

33. *DMZ*, 30 Oct. 1886; *FT*, 14 Apr. 1887; Protokoll of 11 Jan. 1890 in HR Vd15, Nr. 1119. In 1882 there were eight foundries with 367 workers in the city and suburbs together; not all of these workers were skilled. Bavaria, *Berufszählung*, 386–387.

34. *DMZ*, 16 Feb. 1889, 4 Apr. 1891.

35. *FT*, 9 Apr. 1888, 14 Apr. 1887.

36. *FT*, 9 Apr. 1888. The original runs: "Wo sich Männer finden, / Die für Ehr und Recht / Muthig sich verbinden / Weilt ein frei Geschlecht."

37. *FT*, 17 Feb. 1888.

38. *DMZ*, 17 Nov. 1888; *FT*, 7 Aug. 1889; Protokoll of 29 July 1890 in HR Vd15, Nr. 1119.

39. Protokoll of 11 Jan. 1890 in HR Vd15, Nr. 1119; *FT*, 16 Jan. 1890 and 13 July 1891; *DMZ*, 3 Jan. and 4 Apr. 1891.

40. Protokolle of 20 Aug. 1884 and 24 July 1885 in HR Vd15, Nr. 691; *FT*, 20 Apr. 1883.

41. Gömmel, *Wachstum*, 187, 219.

42. Protokoll of 11 Jan. 1890 in HR Vd15, Nr. 1119.

43. *DMZ*, 7 Sept. 1889.

44. *DMZ*, 27 Apr. 1889; *FT*, 23 Apr. and 6, 8, 10, 15, 18, and 22 May 1889; Protokoll of 28 Apr. 1889 in HR Vd15, Nr. 1330; Stadtmag. to Rgg. Mf., 8 and 26 June 1889 in StaatsAN, Regg. KdI 1952, Nr. 1844.

45. Protokoll of 3 Oct. 1888 in HR Vd15, Nr. 1042; *FT*, 5 Oct. 1888, 30 Mar. 1889.

46. Protokolle of 2 and 22 June and 6 July 1889 in HR Vd15, Nr. 940; *FT*, 3, 8, 9, 17 July 1889; Stadtmag. to Rgg. Mf., 9 and 20 July 1889 in StaatsAN, Regg. KdI 1952, Nr. 1844; *DMZ*, 20 July 1889.

47. Protokolle of 22 June, 6 July, and 7 Dec. 1889 in HR Vd15, Nr. 940; *FT*, 17 July and 14 Sept. 1889; Stadtmag. to Rgg. Mf. in StaatsAN, Regg. KdI 1952, Nr. 1844.

48. Thönnesen, *Emancipation of Women*, 39–45; Protokoll of 27 Nov. 1889 in StaatsAN, Regg. KdI 1952, Nr. 1844.

49. Meyer, *Vereinswesen*, 196; Rgg. Mf. to Stadtmag., 28 Apr. 1890, and Protokolle of 21 and 28 Apr. and 17 Mar. 1891 in HR Vd15, Nr. 1462; Protokoll of 31 Aug. 1890 in HR Vd15, Nr. 1622; statutes of 7 Mar. 1891 in HR Vd15, Nr. 940; *FT*, 13 Dec. 1890.

50. Protokolle of 21–23 Apr. 1889 in StaatsAN, Regg. KdI 1952, Nr. 1844; *FT*, 26 Apr. 1889.

51. A brief description of the work process is found in Chapter 1. For more detailed descriptions see Voit, *Nürnberger Gold- und Silberschlägerei*, 78–82, 84–91, and Morgenstern, *Fürther Metallschlägerei*, 198–203.

52. Protokoll of 1 May 1889 in StaatsAN, Regg. KdI 1952, Nr. 1844; *FT*, 8 and 10 May 1889.

53. Each union, like every association, should have a file in the Stadtarchiv as part of the Vereinspolizeiakten (HR Vd15). However, I have found none for the gold and metal beaters' unions of 1883–1891, although copies of Protokolle in Staatsarchiv sources indicate that the files once existed.

54. In the early twentieth century close to 80 percent of married gold beaters were married to female helpers in the same trade. Voit, *Nürnberger Gold- und Silberschlägerei*, 159–160.

55. BA Nbg. to Rgg. Mf., 6 and 28 Aug. 1889, Stadtmag. to Rgg. Mf., 7, 24, and 30 Aug. 1889, and Protokoll of 17 Aug. 1889 in StaatsAN, Regg. KdI 1952, Nr. 1844; weekly reports of 17 and 24 Aug. 1889 in Direktorium A, Nr. 14; *FT*, 8, 10, and 31 Aug. 1889; undated note (1889) in Hwa., Goldschläger Nr. 3; Voit, *Nürnberger Gold- und Silberschlägerei*, 80; *FT*, 18 Sept. 1889, 1 and 3 Nov. 1890, 24 Apr., 26, 27, and 30 May 1891; *DMZ*, 6 Dec. 1890 and 14 Feb. 1891; Protokolle of 30 Apr. and 4 May 1890 in StaatsAN, Regg. KdI 1932, Tit. IX, Nr. 651(I); Protokolle of 24, 29, and 31 Oct. 1890, 6 and 9 Nov. 1890, and 15 Mar. 1891, and Stadtmag. to Rgg. Mf., 3 and 8 Nov. 1890 in StaatsAN, Regg. KdI 1932, Tit. IX, Nr. 651(II).

56. Morgenstern, *Fürther Metallschlägerei*, 180–185; *FT*, 6, 13, and 20 June and 25 Oct. 1889, 21 and 24 Apr., 25, 29, and 31 May, 4, 11, and 16 June and 6 Aug. 1890; BA Nbg. to Rgg. Mf., 15, 19, and 21 June 1889 in StaatsAN, Regg. KdI 1952, Nr. 1844; *DMZ*, 24 Aug. 1889, 7 June 1890, and 11 Apr. 1891; Protokolle of 21 Apr., 19 and 24 May, 2, 20, and 28 June 1890, and Stadtmag. to Rgg. Mf., 2, 7, 10, and 28 June and 3 July 1890 in StaatsAN, Regg. KdI 1932, Tit. IX, Nr. 651(I).

57. The membership list was 521 locksmiths, 208 metal turners, 37 unskilled helpers, 36 fine mechanics, 30 iron molders, 15 blacksmiths, 9 polishers, 7 sievemakers, 7 glass polishers, 5 filemakers, 5 weightmakers, 5 nickel platers, 4 boiler makers, 3 brass molders, 3 toolmakers, 3 braziers, 3 mathematical instrument makers, 1 needle maker, 1 tinsmith, and 1 watchmaker. *DMZ*, 31 Jan. 1891. Ear-

lier membership figures: official Protokoll of the Weimar metalworkers' congress, 1888, in HR Vd15, Nr. 1042; *FT*, 6 July 1889.

58. Protokolle of 3 and 29 June, 13 and 25 July 1889 in HR Vd15, Nr. 1042; *FT*, 22 June, 3, 6, 16, and 23 July and 6 Aug. 1889.

59. Protokoll of 3 June 1889 in HR Vd15, Nr. 1042.

60. *FT*, 22 May and 9 July 1889; Cohen, *Schuckert*, 5, 37.

61. *FT*, 12, 25, and 26 Sept., 9, 15, and 16 Oct. 1889; Stadtmag. to Rgg. Mf., 24 and 28 Sept., 5 and 12 Oct. 1889 in StaatsAN, Regg. KdI 1952, Nr. 1844; supplement to weekly report, 25 Sept., and weekly report of 28 Sept. in Direktorium A, Nr. 14; Cohen, *Schuckert*, 25–26; Protokoll of 26 Sept. 1889 in HR Vd15, Nr. 1177; Protokoll of 26 Sept. 1889 in HR Vd15, Nr. 1042; *DMZ*, 5 Oct. 1889; Protokoll of 27 Nov. 1889 in StaatsAN, Regg. KdI 1952, Nr. 1844; Protokoll of 31 Aug. 1890 in HR Vd15, Nr. 1622.

62. Official Protokolle of Weimar congresses, 1888 and 1890, in HR Vd15, Nr. 1042; IG Metall, *Fünfundsiebzig Jahre Industriegewerkschaft*, 93–96; Lütcke, *Dokumentation zur Organisationsgeschichte*, 29–30; Hommer, *Entwicklung und Tätigkeit*, 12–13.

63. Eric Hobsbawm, "The 'New Unionism' Reconsidered," in *Development of Trade Unionism*, ed. Mommsen and Husung, 25.

64. Hommer, *Entwicklung und Tätigkeit*, 12–13.

65. Protokolle of 27 Apr. 1891 in HR Vd15, Nr. 1622; *FT*, 28 Apr. and 15 June 1891; *FK*, 17 June 1891; Lütcke, *Dokumentation zur Organisationsgeschichte*, 30, 34–35.

66. Keith Burgess, "New Unionism for Old? The Amalgamated Society of Engineers in Britain," in *Development of Trade Unionism*, ed. Mommsen and Husung, 174, 180.

67. Protokoll of 10 June 1890 in StaatsAN, Regg. KdI 1932, Tit. IX, Nr. 651(I); Protokolle of 22 Mar. and 20 Apr. 1891 in StaatsAN, Regg. KdI 1932, Tit. IX, Nr. 651(II); *DMZ*, 10 Jan. and 10 Oct. 1891; *FT*, 3 and 31 Mar. 1891; Protokoll of 2 Mar. 1891 in HR Vd15, Nr. 1551. A small minority appears to have carried on the old gold beaters' local union. *FT*, 4 Mar. and 22 Apr. 1891, 17 Mar. 1892.

68. *FT*, 6 Aug. 1891; Protokolle of 10 May, 2 June, and 15 Aug. 1891 in HR Vd15, Nr. 1119; *DMZ*, 11 Apr., 27 June, 18 July, and 8 Aug. 1891; *FT*, 13 May 1891; Protokoll and statutes of 13 Nov. 1891 in HR Vd15, Nr. 1629.

69. In April 1891 eleven major local unions had collectively 2,422 members (see Appendix A). *DMZ*, 11 Apr. 1891. To this must be added the Fine Mechanics' Union with perhaps 50 members. Other unions, each with probably about 50 members, or perhaps as many as 100, were the iron rollers, the second stokers and machinists' union, and the two Hirsch-Duncker unions (metalworkers and tinsmiths). The plumbers had perhaps 25, but soon folded.

5: The Maturation of Industrial Unionism

1. Bavaria, *Berufszählung . . . I. Theil: Die bayerische Bevölkerung nach ihrer Berufsthätigkeit*, 238; Germany, Kaiserliches Statistisches Amt, *Statistik des deutschen*

Reiches, N.F., 107:284, 207:257; Schwab, *Verschiebungen in den beruflichen Gliederung*, 2–3; Rossmeissl, *Arbeiterschaft*, 14–15, 62–72.

2. Germany, *Statistik*, 107:284–289, 207:257–261.

3. Ibid., 210.2:314.

4. Ibid., 207:260–261.

5. Ibid., 116:71–75, 217:277–281.

6. Rossmeissl, *Arbeiterschaft*, 133–135, 141–143, 174–185, 280; Gärtner, *Nürnberger Arbeiterbewegung*, 155–159; Hirschfelder, *Die bayerische Sozialdemokratie*, 2: 555–565; Meyer, *Vereinswesen*, 135–137, 155–170, 197–198. On Social Democratic cultural organizations see Lidtke, *Alternative Culture*.

7. Rossmeissl, *Arbeiterschaft*, 144–147, 154–173, 202–203, 207–221, 247–271.

8. Schönhoven, *Expansion und Konzentration*, 313–319, 357–365.

9. Protokolle of 27 July 1898 and 11 Feb. 1900, and "Geschäftsbericht des Bezirks Nürnberg" of CMV, 1910–1911 in HR Vd15, Nr. 2378; DMV-Nbg., "Jahresbericht der Verwaltungsstelle Nürnberg," 1910, in Vereinsarchiv Nr. 190; Germany, *Statistik*, 207:627–628.

10. Weekly report of 30 Mar. 1889 in Direktorium A, Nr. 14, and same of 26 Dec. 1896 in Direktorium A, Nr. 16; Nolan, *Social Democracy and Society*, 113–117.

11. *DMZ*, 2 June and 13 Oct. 1900. Hans Dieter Denk estimates that there were perhaps 800 CMV members in all Bavaria in 1904 and maybe 1,600 in 1905. See his *Die christliche Arbeiterbewegung*, 413.

12. DMV-Nbg., "Allgemeine Zahlstelle Nürnberg Jahresbericht, 1904" in Vereinsarchiv Nr. 190; Schönhoven, *Expansion und Konzentration*, 167–174; Hommer, *Entwicklung und Tätigkeit*, 18, 152; *DMZ*, 17 Oct. 1896.

13. For "Lebensverdienstkurven" of workers in the Esslingen (Württemberg) locomotive factory see Schomerus, *Die Arbeiter der Maschinenfabrik Esslingen*, 148–150.

14. Domansky-Davidsohn, "Arbeitskämpfe," 45; Schönhoven, *Expansion und Konzentration*, 68.

15. The estimate was reached as follows: there were 2,665 DMV members at the end of 1895. The census lists 11,066 workers in sectors V and VI. If there were 30,000 people in the suburbs incorporated in 1898–1899, there may have been about 25,000 in 1895. If we estimate that 10 percent were metalworkers that adds another 2,500 to the total. The organization rate would be about 19 percent. *DMZ*, 16 May 1896; Germany, *Statistik*, 107:286–289.

16. DMV-Vorstand, *Der Deutsche Metallarbeiter-Verband im Jahre 1905*, 298. Goulden, "Growth and Conflict," 45, estimates an organization rate for the Nuremberg DMV of 49.0 percent in 1912 and 48.5 percent in 1925. However, this is based upon the total work force in the metal industries (including white-collar workers, managers and owners). Rates calculated on the basis of workers only would be slightly higher.

17. *FT*, 18 Apr. 1896.

18. *DMZ*, 13 Oct. 1900; *FT*, 16 Feb. 1906; weekly report of 10 June 1905 in Di-

rektorium A, Nr. 18; DMV-Nbg., "Jahresberichten der Verwaltungsstelle Nürnberg," 1912, 1913, in Vereinsarchiv Nr. 190; Quataert, *Reluctant Feminists*, 62.

19. *DMZ*, 28 Aug., 3 Oct. and 5 Dec. 1891, 2 Jan. and 17 Sept. 1892, 2 Dec. 1893, 17 Oct. 1896; *FT*, 25 Jan. 1895.

20. *DMZ*, 3 Sept. 1892 and 2 Dec. 1893; *FT*, 18 Jan. and 20 Dec. 1894, 1 and 29 Nov. and 6 Dec. 1895, 20 Mar. 1897; Protokoll of 15 Dec. 1895 in HR Vd15, Nr. 1622; Protokolle of 30 Mar. 1896 and 21 and 22 Mar. 1897 in HR Vd15, Nr. 2036.

21. Entries of Aug.(?) 1888, 2 Aug. 1890, 25 Sept. and 25 Nov. 1895 in HR 2881; weekly report of 3 Sept. 1898 in Direktorium A, Nr. 16; Fischer, *Industrialisierung*, 332–333; Rossmeissl, *Arbeiterschaft*, 371; *FT*, 23 Mar. 1918.

22. *FT*, 14 Apr. 1899; note of 1 Feb. 1900 in HR Vd15, Nr. 2036.

23. Domansky-Davidsohn, "Arbeitskämpfe," 48–49, 251–258; Opel, *Deutsche Metallarbeiter-Verband*, 30–31; *DMZ*, 25 Apr. 1896, 13 Mar. 1897, 10 Dec. 1898.

24. *DMZ*, 16 Nov. 1901; *FT*, 26 and 28 Oct. 1901, 28 July 1903; entries of Oct. 1900 in HR 2913.

25. *DMZ*, 25 Mar. 1893.

26. *DMZ*, 27 May 1899.

27. Goulden, "Growth and Conflict," passim. Goulden's dissertation is a comparison of the successful DMV organization in Nuremberg to the weak one in Cologne, from 1900 to 1925.

28. Weekly report of 2 Oct. 1897 in Direktorium A, Nr. 16.

29. DMV-Vorstand, *Der Deutsche Metallarbeiter-Verband im Jahre 1903*, 7, and *Der Deutsche Metallarbeiter-Verband im Jahre 1904*, 10; *FT*, 3 Feb. 1905; DMV-Nbg., "Bericht der Verwaltungsstelle Nürnberg," 1905, 3, in Vereinsarchiv Nr. 190.

30. *DMZ*, 10 Apr. 1897.

31. Weekly report of 5 May 1900 in Direktorium A, Nr. 17.

32. *FT*, 22 Nov. 1901, 31 Jan., 14 Mar., 23 May, and 31 Oct. 1902, 22 May, 23 June, and 31 July 1903.

33. Domansky-Davidsohn, "Großbetrieb als Organisationsproblem," 95–116; "Arbeitskämpfe," 393–395.

34. *FT*, 20 Apr. and 27 June 1900.

35. Domansky-Davidsohn, "Arbeitskämpfe," 393–394.

36. Klaus Schönhoven, "Localism—Craft Union—Industrial Union," in *Development of Trade Unionism*, ed. Mommsen and Husung, 231.

37. Friedhelm Böll, "International Strike Waves," in ibid., 86.

38. Gömmel, *Wachstum*, 187, 219–220.

39. The one strike I have found that was refused full strike support for violation of the statutes was that of the polishers at the Rießner oven factory in 1904. DMV-Nbg., "Allgem. Zahlstelle Jahresbericht 1904" in Vereinsarchiv Nr. 190.

40. Protokolle of 28 June, 2 July, and 23 Nov. 1892 in HR Vd15, Nr. 1609; Protokoll of 10 Jan. 1894 in HR Vd15, Nr. 1629; *DMZ*, 9 July and 22 Oct. 1892 and 11 Mar. 1893; *FT*, 20 and 26 Aug. 1892, 24 Nov. 1892, 10 Feb., 29 Aug. and ? Sept. 1893 (unidentified in HR Vd15, Nr. 1609); Protokoll of Aufsichtsrat meeting of 18

Aug. 1893 in M.A.N.-Nbg. Werksarchiv, Nr. 221.5; Foth, "Soziale Chronik," 337.

41. Rieppel to Stadtmag., 29 Dec. 1893 and statutes of 30 Nov. 1893 in HR Vd15, Nr. 1840; Jegel, *Die wirtschaftliche Entwicklung*, 171–172; *FT*, 13, 15, 17, and 18 Jan. 1894; *DMZ*, 13 Jan. 1894; Protokolle of 10 and 16 Jan. 1894 in HR Vd15, Nr. 1629; Stadtmag. to Rgg. Mf., 15 Jan., and BA Nbg. to Rgg. Mf., 17 Jan. 1894, in StaatsAN, Regg. KdI 1932, Tit. IX, Nr. 651(III).

42. *FT*, 26 Jan. 1894.

43. *FT*, 22 and 25 Jan., 1, 2, 6, 7, 12, and 15 Mar. 1894; Rieppel to Erster Bürgermeister von Schuh, 23 Jan. 1894 in M.A.N.-Nbg. Werksarchiv, Nr. 221.4; weekly report of 27 Jan. 1894 in Direktorium A, Nr. 15; BA Nbg. to Rgg. Mf., 24, 27, and 30 Jan., 9 and 13 Feb. 1894 and Stadtmag. to Rgg. Mf., 27 Jan., 3, 7, and 12 Feb. 1894 in StaatsAN, Regg. KdI 1932, Tit. IX, Nr. 651 (III); *DMZ*, 17 Feb. 1894.

44. *FT*, 29 Aug. 1893; weekly report of 25 Feb. 1899 in Direktorium A, Nr. 16.

45. *FT*, 2 July 1894, 9, 19, 20, and 30 Aug. 1898, 13, 14, 16, and 21 Feb., 1 and 28 Mar., and 13 May 1899; *FK*, 14 Feb. 1899; *DMZ*, 13 Aug., 26 Nov., and 24 Dec. 1898, 25 Feb. and 4 Mar. 1899; Protokolle of 28 June 1894, 12 Jan. 1896, 6 Mar. 1899 in HR Vd15, Nr. 1609; Stadtmag. to Staatsmin. d. Innern, 8 and 17 Aug. 1898 in HSA Munich, MArb. 255; Protokoll, 12 Feb. 1899, in HR Vd15, Nr. 1622; weekly reports of 20 Aug. 1898, 11, 18, and 25 Feb., 4, 11, and 25 Mar. 1899 in Direktorium A, Nr. 16; Stadtmag. to Regg. Mf., 10, 18, and 26 Feb., and 14 June 1899 in StaatsAN, Regg. KdI 1932, Tit. IX, Nr. 651(VI).

46. *FT*, 21, 23, and 26 Apr., 3, 10, 11, 25, and 31 May, 2 and 25 June, 5, 14, 24, and 28 July 1900; *DMZ*, 31 Mar., 2 and 23 June, 21 July, 11 Aug. 1900; weekly reports of 21 Apr., 19 and 26 May, 2 June, 21 and 28 July 1900 in Direktorium A, Nr. 17; report of DMV Vorstand to the 1901 Nbg. Generalversammlung, 100–101, in HR Vd15, Nr. 1622; H. Buz to Stadtmag. Aug. (copy), 16 May 1900, in M.A.N.-Nbg. Werksarchiv Nr. 221.4; Foth, "Soziale Chronik," 339–342; Stadtmag. to Rgg. Mf., 30 Apr., 30 May, 6 June, and 24 July 1900 in StaatsAN, Regg. KdI 1932, Tit. IX, Nr. 651(VI); Rupieper, *Arbeiter und Angestellte*, 158–159.

47. Fischer, *Industrialisierung;* Vetterli, *Industriearbeit*.

48. Weekly report of 7 June 1890 in Direktorium A, Nr. 14.

49. *FT*, 3 Jan., 24 and 29 May, and 4 June 1894. See Montgomery's classic article, "Workers' Control of Machine Production in the Nineteenth Century." Evidence for output restriction at M.A.N.-Nbg. is given in an unpublished 1913 study cited in Rupieper, *Arbeiter und Angestellte*, 111. Skilled workers who allowed their piece-rate earnings to exceed their nominal day wage by 60 percent or more were looked upon as "stupid and clumsy" because they risked provoking rate reductions.

50. *FT*, 23, 25, 27, 28, and 30 Mar., 1, 5, 10, and 17 Apr., and 2 May 1895, 27 Feb. 1896; *DMZ*, 1 June 1895; Protokoll of 27 Mar. 1895 in HR Vd15, Nr. 1622; weekly reports of 30 Mar., 6, 13, and 20 Apr., and 20 July 1895, and 29 Feb. 1896

in Direktorium A, Nr. 16; BA Nbg. to Rgg. Mf., 22 Mar., 5 and 12 Apr., and 3 May 1895 in StaatsAN, Regg. KdI 1932, Tit. IX, Nr. 651(IV).

51. Seubert, "Entstehung der Nürnberger Fahrzeugindustrie," 21–24, 28; Protokoll of 16 Dec. 1897 in HR Vd15, Nr. 2036; *FT*, 4 Feb. 1898, 19 Mar. 1900, 1 Feb. and 29 Oct. 1901, 20 and 25 Mar., and 1 Apr. 1902; Paller, *Die bayerische Fahrrad-Industrie*, 50–51.

52. Voit, *Nürnberger Gold- und Silberschlägerei*, 104–105.

53. *FT*, 13, 22, 25, and 26 Apr., 12 and 24 May, 5 and 21 June, 20, 25, and 26 July 1899; *DMZ*, 1 and 26 July 1899; weekly report of 15 July 1899 in Direktorium A, Nr. 16; Report of DMV Vorstand to 1901 Nbg. Generalversammlung, 99–100, in HR Vd15, Nr. 1622; Stadtmag. to Rgg. Mf., 9 and 14 May, 26 June, 26 July 1899 in StaatsAN, Regg. KdI 1932, Tit. IX, Nr. 651(VI).

54. *FT*, 4 May 1892; Protokoll of 24 Oct. 1892 (copy) in StaatsAN, Regg. KdI 1932, Tit. IX, Nr. 651(III).

55. *FT*, 2 Oct. and 22 Dec. 1899, 9 Mar., 22 Sept., 8, 12, and 16 Oct., 28 Nov. 1900, 8 Feb. 1901, 27 Jan. and 9 Sept. 1902; weekly reports of 1 Dec. 1900 and 13 Sept. 1902 in Direktorium A, Nr. 17; report of the DMV Vorstand to the 1901 Nbg. Generalversammlung, 102–103, in HR Vd15, Nr. 1622; Stadtmag. to Rgg. Mf., 9 Oct. and 30 Nov. 1900, in StaatsAN, Regg. KdI 1932, Tit. IX, Nr. 651(VII).

56. Voit, *Nürnberger Gold- und Silberschlägerei*, 103–125; *FT*, 9 July 1900, 15 July and 21 Sept. 1901, 13 June 1902, 26 Mar., 7 and 9 Apr., 23 June, 28 July, and 7 Sept. 1903; weekly reports of 28 Apr. and 12 May 1900 in Direktorium A, Nr. 17; Stadtmag. Fürth to Rgg. Mf., 8 Apr. 1903, and Stadtmag. Nbg. to Rgg. Mf., 21 Apr. and 24 June 1903 in StaatsAN, Regg. KdI 1932, Tit. IX, Nr. 651(VII); DMV-Vorstand, *DMV im Jahre 1903*, 34, 61–63, and *DMV im Jahre 1905*, 134–136.

57. *DMZ*, 5 Jan. 1895; Protokolle of 18 May, 13 June, and 11 July 1896, and 17 May 1897 in HR Vd15, Nr. 1610; *FT*, 8 July 1896, 9 Apr. 1897.

58. *DMZ*, 23 Apr. 1904; *FT*, 1 and 22 Aug. 1903; DMV-Nbg., "Allgemeine Zahlstelle Jahresbericht 1904" in Vereinsarchiv Nr. 190; weekly report of 6 June 1903 in Direktorium A, Nr. 17; Stadtmag. to Rgg. Mf., 6 and 15 June and 1 and 4 Aug. 1903 in StaatsAN, Regg. KdI 1932, Tit. IX, Nr. 651(VII).

59. *FT*, 27 Mar. and 31 May 1904; DMV-Nbg. "Allgem. Zahlstelle Jahresbericht 1904," 5–6, in Vereinsarchiv Nr. 190.

60. *FT*, 14 June, 15 July, 8 Aug. 1904; DMV-Vorstand, *DMV im Jahre 1904*, 73, 88, 93; weekly reports of 6 Aug. 1904 in Direktorium A, Nr. 18.

61. DMV-Nbg., "Allgem. Zahlstelle Jahresbericht 1904," 6, in Vereinsarchiv Nr. 190; weekly report of 10 Sept. 1904 in Direktorium A, Nr. 18; DMV-Vorstand, *DMV im Jahre 1905*, 65.

62. A fascinating description of the work process in a small firm making mechanized toy ships is contained in the city records relating to the Tinsmiths' Guild. By 1913 this firm had so rationalized the work process that there were only five or six skilled workers left out of fifty-seven. Most of the rest were women. K. Arnold & Co. to Stadtmag., 5 June 1913, in HR VIb7, F Nr. 23.

63. *FT,* 3 Mar., 20 and 21 Apr., and 20 May 1896, 4, 17, and 21 June, 11 and 13 Aug. 1897; weekly reports of 26 June and 10 July 1897; Protokoll of 12 July 1897 in HR Vd15, Nr. 2036.

64. *FT,* 13 July and 13 Aug. 1898.

65. *FT,* 10 and 21 Dec. 1897; Protokoll of 19 Dec. 1897 in HR Vd15, Nr. 2036; weekly report of 18 Dec. 1897 in Direktorium A, Nr. 16.

66. Arbeitsordnung of 1893, "Dienst Anweisung" (undated) and Arbeitsordnung of 17 Dec. 1900 (valid 1 Jan. 1901) in M.A.N.-Nbg. Werksarchiv Nr. 221.1; Rupieper, *Arbeiter und Angestellte,* 111–112; *FT,* 13 Nov. 1897, 23 Mar. 1901; Protokoll of 19 Dec. 1897 in HR Vd15, Nr. 2036.

67. Rupieper, *Arbeiter und Angestellte,* 103, 110–111, 148; *FT,* 11 Dec. 1901; memo of G. Lipphardt of 6 June 1902 in M.A.N.-Nbg. Werksarchiv Nr. 221.2.

68. Rupieper, *Arbeiter und Angestellte,* 77; *FT,* 23, 27, and 29 Mar., 12 Sept., 7, 17, and 25 Oct. and 7 Dec. 1901; Protokoll of 6 Aug. 1901 in HR Vd15, Nr. 2036; weekly report of 6 Dec. 1902 in Direktorium A, Nr. 17; Eibert, *Maschinenbauer,* 189–198, 230–241, 280–281.

69. *FT,* 16 May, 10 and 30 July 1903; weekly report of 4 July 1903 in Direktorium A, Nr. 17.

70. *DMZ,* 30 July 1898; *FT,* 26 Nov. 1898, 24 Apr. and 30 June 1900, and 29 July 1902; meeting report of 27 June 1904, Enßner to Rieppel, 20 and 23 July 1904, and Rieppel to Enßner 21 and 25 July 1904 in M.A.N.-Nbg. Werksarchiv Nr. 221.5.

71. Rupieper, *Arbeiter und Angestellte,* 141–152; Foth, "Soziale Chronik," 369–370.

72. Arbeiterausschuß to mgmt., 9 and 10 Aug., and Rieppel to Arbeiterausschuß, 8 Sept. 1904, meeting reports of 14 and 20 Sept. 1904, and Rieppel to Buz (director in Augsburg), 19 Sept. 1904 in M.A.N.-Nbg. Werksarchiv Nr. 221.5; "Vorstandsprotokoll" of 2 Sept. 1904 in M.A.N.-Nbg. Werksarchiv Nr. 221.2; *FT,* 14 Sept. 1904; *DMZ,* 17 Sept. and 29 Oct. 1904.

73. VBM to Stadtmag., 6 Oct. 1904, in HR Vd15, Nr. 1840; DMV-Vorstand, *DMV im Jahre 1905,* 69–72; Rupieper, *Arbeiter und Angestellte,* 161–164.

74. Braun, *Die Lohn- und Arbeitsverhältnisse in den Siemens-Schuckertwerken;* DMV-Nbg., "Bericht der Verwaltungsstelle Nürnberg," 1905, 6, in Vereinsarchiv Nr. 190.

75. DMV-Nbg., "Bericht," 1905, 6–8 in Vereinsarchiv Nr. 190; *FK,* 20 Apr. 1905; *FT,* 22 and 29 Apr. 1905; weekly reports of 22 and 29 Apr. 1905 in Direktorium A, Nr. 18; DMV-Vorstand, *DMV im Jahre 1905,* 55; Werner von Siemens to Rieppel, 26 Apr. 1905, in M.A.N.-Nbg. Werksarchiv Nr. 221.5.

76. Questionnaire of 27 Feb. 1905 in M.A.N.-Nbg. Werksarchiv Nr. 221.4; Protokoll of 4 Apr. 1905 Vorstandssitzung in M.A.N.-Nbg. Werksarchiv Nr. 221.5; "Tarifvertrag" of 1 May and "Mitteilung an unsere Arbeiter" of 13 May 1905 in M.A.N.-Nbg. Werksarchiv Nr. 221.2; DMV-Nbg., "Bericht," 1905, in Vereinsarchiv Nr. 190.

77. Direktor G. Lipphardt to Rieppel, 15 and 20 May 1905, and anonymous letters of 29 May, 1 June, and 11 July (received) 1905 in M.A.N.-Nbg. Werksarchiv

Nr. 221.5; *FT*, 20 May 1905; weekly reports of 20 and 27 May 1905 in Direktorium A, Nr. 18; leaflets by DMV, ? May, and M.A.N.-Nbg., 7 June, in HR Vd15, Nr. 2036; Goulden, "Growth and Conflict," 91–93; DMV-Nbg., "Bericht," 1905, 8–9, in Vereinsarchiv Nr. 190.

78. DMV-Nbg., "Bericht," 1905, 10–11, in Vereinsarchiv Nr. 190; *FT*, 14 June 1905; weekly reports of 3 and 10 June 1905 in Direktorium A, Nr. 18; DMV-Vorstand, *DMV im Jahre 1905*, 79–81.

79. DMV-Vorstand, *DMV im Jahre 1905*, 81–82; *FT*, 21 and 22 June 1905; weekly report of 24 June 1905 in Direktorium A, Nr. 18; DMV-Nbg., "Bericht," 1905, 11–12, in Vereinsarchiv Nr. 190.

80. DMV-Nbg., "Bericht," 1905, 12–14, in Vereinsarchiv Nr. 190; DMV-Vorstand, *DMV im Jahre 1905*, 82–84; *FT*, 27 June and 6 July 1905; *FK*, 5 and 8 July 1905; *Vorwärts* (Berlin), 8 July 1905 (found in HR Vd15, Nr. 2036); weekly reports of 8 and 15 July 1905 in Direktorium A, Nr. 18.

81. DMV-Vorstand, *DMV im Jahre 1905*, 84; DMV-Nbg., "Bericht der Verwaltungstelle Nürnberg," 1906, 3–5.

82. Rupieper, *Arbeiter und Angestellte*, 149, 237n.


Conclusion

1. Rupieper, *Arbeiter und Angestellte*, 80–81.

2. Since I originally wrote these words Ira Katznelson has written: "The German case, in short, is the one that came closest in consciousness and organization to the classic Marxist model." See his "Working-Class Formation: Constructing Cases and Comparisons," in *Working-Class Formation*, ed. Katznelson and Zolberg, 27. I would agree with the implication of this statement that in other countries the model needs heavier revision.

# BIBLIOGRAPHY

## Archival Sources

Unless otherwise indicated, all archival sources cited in the notes are from the Stadtarchiv Nürnberg. Here I will omit a lengthy list of file numbers and names and instead will comment briefly on the usefulness of the various archives and of the main document groups in the Stadtarchiv Nürnberg.

### STADTARCHIV NÜRNBERG (STADTAN)

*Hauptregistratur (HR).* This source, the principal one for this study, includes most of the material generated by the city administration in the nineteenth and early twentieth centuries. Most of the files in the Hauptregistratur have been renumbered in a simple numerical sequence, for example, HR 12778. But the majority of the material I used fell into two groups that still had their old numbers at the time of my original research in 1980–1981. (A few files that I reused or discovered in later research are cited in the notes by their new numbers.) The first, HR VIb7, contains the city files relating to the guilds and artisans, primarily before 1868, although there is a limited amount of useful material on the new Innungen after 1881. This voluminous material includes the most interesting archival sources I found, namely documents concerning guilds and journeymen's associations, artisanal customs, Blue Monday drinking, etc. The holdings of the Stadtarchiv are fairly rich in these materials. The second major group is HR Vd15, the Vereinspolizeiakten (which the Stadtarchiv does not plan to renumber). All associations had to be registered with the city police, and most formed only after freedom of association was instituted in 1868–1869. HR Vd15 is primarily useful for the study of the unions and the socialist movement. Although many files contain little except lists of leaders, the files for the largest socialist organizations, which were watched closely by the police, contain much more information, including Protokolle (transcripts) of meetings taken by policemen present and newspaper clippings. The Vereinspolizeiakten are invaluable, even if they inevitably provide little insight into the the attitudes of average workers, because they include much otherwise inaccessible information on local union leaders, membership, and the level of activity.

223

*Skilled Metalworkers of Nuremberg*

*Stadtkommissariat Nürnberg (Stadtkomm.).* The Stadtkommissar was an official of the state bureaucracy assigned until 1873 to supervise the city's administration of the police and public order. This document group is particularly useful for the early labor movement (1861–1872). Another part of the old Stadtkommissariat records is found in the Staatsarchiv Nürnberg.

*Handwerksarchive (Hwa.).* The Handwerksarchive contain a motley collection of materials left to the city by the guilds. In general this material was less useful to me than the city's own records in HR VIb7, but there were a few fascinating items, especially in the records of the locksmiths, brass molders, tinsmiths and gold beaters.

*Direktorium A.* Each week the mayor or deputy mayor sent a report to the Regierung Mittelfranken in Ansbach. These reports are particularly useful for information on strikes, elections, and disturbances of public order.

*Vereinsarchiv Nr. 190.* This file contains publications of the local DMV after 1903 that are often unavailable in the Stadtbibliothek Nürnberg or in the IG-Metall Bibliothek in Frankfurt a. M., whose publications are listed below.

*Miscellaneous Sources.* Polizeisenats-Protokolle; Stadtchronik; Industrie- und Handelskammer; Ältere Magistrats-Registratur.

STAATSARCHIV NÜRNBERG (STAATSAN)

This is the archive of the Regierung Mittelfranken (the Bavarian state administration for the Middle Franconian region). The Nuremberg city administration stood directly under this bureaucracy, unlike the small villages around the city, which were controlled by an intermediate authority, the Bezirksamt Nürnberg. Two main record groups were useful: the remaining Stadtkommissariat records (BA Nbg., Stadtkomm.), helpful particularly for the Revolution of 1848–1849; and Regg. KdI 1932, Tit. IX, especially the many volumes of Nr. 651, containing reports by the city and the Bezirksamt on unions and strikes.

M.A.N.-NÜRNBERG WERKSARCHIV

The Nuremberg M.A.N. archive is much less useful than its Augsburg counterpart, mostly because of extensive war losses. There is some material in the record group Nr. 221, especially on the events of 1904–1905. Also helpful are the unpublished manuscripts by Foth and Mauersberg (see secondary sources). The limited resources of this archive have been fully exploited by H.-J. Rupieper in his book, *Arbeiter und Angestellte im Zeitalter der Industrialisierung.*

HAUPTSTAATSARCHIV MÜNCHEN (HSA MUNICH)

In the Ministry of Interior records (MInn) there are some materials on the Revolution of 1848–1849, and MArb. (Ministry of Labor) 255 contains strike reports for a period missing from the StaatsAN records.

224

BUNDESARCHIV AUSSENSTELLE FRANKFURT (BAA FRANKFURT)
The records of the Frankfurt parliament contain two petitions from Nuremberg artisans with signatures from the metal trades: DB 51, Nr. 120, Pet. 1224; and DB51, Nr. 125, Pet. 5319.

Newspapers

*Correspondent von und für Deutschland*, 1858, 1863
*Deutsche Metallarbeiter-Zeitung/Metallarbeiter-Zeitung*, 1883–1905
*Fränkische Tagespost* (and its predecessors: *Fürther Demokratisches Wochenblatt, Social-demokratisches Wochenblatt*, and *Nürnberg-Fürther Sozialdemokrat*), 1872–1905
*Fränkischer Kurier*, 1851, 1858, 1863, 1868, 1871–1872, 1875
*Nürnberger Anzeiger*, 1869, 1871

DMV Publications

*Allgemeine Zahlstelle Jahresbericht 1904*. Nuremberg: Fränkische Verlagsanstalt, 1905.
*Bericht der Verwaltungstelle Nürnberg des Deutschen Metallarbeiterverbandes für das Jahr 1905*. Nuremberg: Fränkische Verlagsanstalt, 1906.
*Bericht der Verwaltungstelle Nürnberg des Deutschen Metallarbeiter-Verbandes für das Jahr 1906*. Stuttgart: Alexander Schlicke, 1907.
Braun, Adolf. *Die Lohn- und Arbeitsverhältnisse in den Siemens-Schuckertwerken Nürnberg, Berlin, Wien*. 2nd rev. ed. Nuremberg: DMV, Verwaltungsstelle Nürnberg, 1905.
Vorstand des Deutschen Metallarbeiter-Verbandes. *Die Arbeitsverhältnisse der Feilenarbeiter. Statistische Zusammenstellung für Deutschland*. Stuttgart: DMV, 1905.
———. *Der Deutsche Metallarbeiter-Verband im Jahre 1903, . . . 1904, . . . 1905. Jahr- und Handbuch für Verbandsmitglieder*. Stuttgart: DMV, 1904, 1905, 1906.
———. *Statistische Erhebungen über die Lage der Berufe der Feinmechanik, Optik und verwandter Gewerbe*. Stuttgart: Alexander Schlicke, 1909.
———. *Statistische Erhebungen über die Lohn- und Arbeitsverhältnisse der Bauklempner und Installateure Deutschlands*. Stuttgart: Alexander Schlicke, 1907.

Statistical Sources

Arbeitersekretariat Nürnberg, ed. *Lohn-, Arbeits- und Wohnverhältnisse der Arbeiter Nürnbergs*. Nuremberg: Wörlein & Comp., 1898.
Bavaria. Königliches Statistisches Bureau. *Die Bevölkerung und die Gewerbe des Königreichs Bayern nach der Aufnahme vom Jahre 1861, die Gewerbe in Vergleichung mit deren Stande im Jahre 1847*. Munich: 1862.
———. *Die Ergebnisse der Berufszählung im Königreich Bayern vom 5. Juni 1882. I. Theil: Die bayerische Bevölkerung nach ihrer Berufsthätigkeit*. Beiträge zur Statistik des Königreichs Bayern, Heft 48. Munich: E. Mühlthaler, 1885.
———. *Die Ergebnisse der Berufszählung im Königreich Bayern vom 5. Juni 1882. III.*

## Skilled Metalworkers of Nuremberg

Theil: *Die bayerische Bevölkerung nach ihrer gewerblichen Thätigkeit.* Beiträge zur Statistik des Königreichs Bayern, Heft 50. Munich: G. Franz, 1886.

Germany. Kaiserliches Statistisches Amt. *Statistik des Deutschen Reiches*, N.F., vols. 107, 108, 116, 207, 210.2, 217. Berlin: Verlag für Sozialpolitik, Wirtschaft und Statistik, 1897–1910.

Secondary Sources

Aminzade, Ronald. *Class, Politics, and Early Industrial Capitalism: A Study of Mid-Nineteenth-Century Toulouse, France.* Albany: State University of New York Press, 1981.

————. "French Strike Development and Class Struggle: The Development of the Strike in Mid-Nineteenth Century Toulouse." *Social Science History* 4 (1980): 57–79.

Aretin, K. O. Freiherr von. "Das katholische Bayern im preussischen-deutschen Kaiserreich." *Zeitschrift für bayerische Landesgeschichte* 37 (1974): 546–551.

Bade, Klaus J. "Altes Handwerk, Wanderzwang und Gute Policey: Gesellenwanderung zwischen Zunftökonomie und Gewerbereform." *Vierteljahrsschrift für Sozial- und Wirtschaftsgeschichte* 69 (1982): 1–37.

Bagwell, Philip S., and Mingay, G. E. *Britain and America 1850–1936: A Study of Economic Change.* London: Routledge and Kegan Paul, 1970.

Balser, Frolinde. *Sozial-Demokratie 1848/49–1863. Die erste deutsche Arbeiterorganisation "Allgemeine deutsche Arbeiterverbrüderung" nach der Revolution.* 2 vols. Industrielle Welt, Bd. 2. Stuttgart: Ernst Klett, 1962.

Beckh, Max. *Die Nürnberger echte und leonische Gold- und Silberdrahtindustrie.* Diss., University of Munich, 1917. Munich: A. Heindl, 1917.

Beeg, J. G. "Der Nürnberg-Fürther Industriedistrikt." In *Bavaria*, 3.2:1059–77. Munich: Literarisches Anstalt, 1865.

Biensfeldt, Johannes. *Freiherr Dr. Th. von Cramer-Klett, erblicher Reichsrat der Krone Bayern. Sein Leben und sein Werk, ein Beitrag zur bayerischen Wirtschaftsgeschichte des 19. Jahrhunderts.* Leipzig and Erlangen: A. Deichertsche Verlagsbuchhandlung Dr. Werner Scholl, n.d. [1922].

Bitterauf, Otto. *Die Maschinenfabrik Augsburg-Nürnberg A.G., ihre Bedeutung und Entwicklung bis zum Anschluß an der Konzern der Gutehoffnungshütte.* Nuremberg: n.p. [M.A.N.], n.d. [1924].

Blos, Wilhelm. "Grillenberger, Karl, sozialdemokratischer Politiker 1848–1897." In *Lebensläufe aus Franken*, edited by Anton Chroust. Munich and Leipzig: Duncker and Humblot, 1919.

Bonnet, W. "Die Anfänge der Arbeiterbewegung in Nürnberg." Diss., University of Erlangen, 1925.

Bösch, Hans. *Geschichte der Maschinenbau-Aktiengesellschaft Nürnberg mit Filiale Gustavsburg und der Nürnberger Drahtstiftenfabrik Klett und Co.* Nuremberg: n.p., 1895.

Breuilly, John. "Artisan Economy, Artisan Politics, Artisan Ideology: The Artisan Contribution to the Nineteenth-Century European Labour Movement." In *Artisans, Peasants and Proletarians 1760–1860: Essays Presented to Gwyn Williams*, edited by Clive Emsley and James Walvin, 187–225. London: Croom Helm, 1985.

———. "The Labour Aristocracy in Britain and Germany: A Comparison." *Bulletin of the Society for the Study of Labour History* 48 (1984): 58–71.

———. "Liberalism or Social Democracy: A Comparison of British and German Labour Politics, c. 1850–75." *European History Quarterly* 15 (1985): 3–42.

Brockhaus, Eckhard. *Zusammensetzung und Neustrukturierung der Arbeiterklasse vor dem ersten Weltkrieg. Zur Krise der professionallen Arbeiterbewegung.* Munich: Trikont, 1975.

Brunner, Ludwig. *Politische Bewegungen in Nürnberg 1848/49.* Heidelberger Abhandlungen, Heft 17. Heidelberg: Carl Winters Universitätsbuchhandlung, 1907.

Büchner, Fritz. *Hundert Jahre Geschichte der Maschinenfabrik Augsburg-Nürnberg.* Frankfurt a. M.: n.p. [M.A.N.], 1940.

Cohen, R. *Schuckert 1873–1923.* Nuremberg: n.p. [SSW], 1923.

Conze, Werner, and Engelhardt, Ulrich, eds. *Arbeiter im Industrialisierungsprozeß. Herkunft, Lage und Verhalten.* Industrielle Welt, Bd. 28. Stuttgart: Klett-Cotta, 1979.

Crew, David F. *Town in the Ruhr: A Social History of Bochum, 1860–1914.* New York: Columbia University Press, 1979.

Cronin, James E. "Labor Insurgency and Class Formation: Comparative Perspectives on the Crisis of 1917–1920 in Europe." *Social Science History* 4 (1980): 125–152.

Crossick, Geoffrey, and Heinz-Gerhard Haupt, eds. *Shopkeepers and Master Artisans in Nineteenth-Century Europe.* London: Methuen, 1984.

Denk, Hans Dieter. *Die christliche Arbeiterbewegung in Bayern bis zum Ersten Weltkrieg.* Mainz: Matthias Grünewald, 1980.

Domansky-Davidsohn, Elisabeth. "Arbeitskämpfe und Arbeitskampfstrategien des Deutschen Metallarbeiterverbandes von 1891 bis 1914." Diss., Ruhr University Bochum, 1981.

———. "Der Großbetrieb als Organisationsproblem des Deutschen Metallarbeiter-Verbandes vor dem Ersten Weltkrieg." In *Arbeiterbewegung und industrieller Wandel*, edited by Hans Mommsen. Wuppertal: Peter Hammer, 1980.

Dowe, Dieter. "Deutschland: Das Rheinland und Württemberg im Vergleich." In *Europäische Arbeiterbewegungen im 19. Jahrhundert: Deutschland, Oesterreich, England und Frankreich im Vergleich*, edited by Jürgen Kocka, 77–105. Göttingen: Vandenhoeck und Ruprecht, 1983.

Eberlein, Alfred, ed. *Die Presse der Arbeiterklasse und der sozialen Bewegungen. Von den dreissiger Jahren des 19. Jahrhunderts bis zum Jahre 1967.* 5 vols. Archivale Forschungen zur Geschichte der Deutschen Arbeiterbewegung, Bd. 6. Berlin (East): Akademie-Verlag, 1968, 1970.

Eckert, Hugo. *Liberal- oder Sozialdemokratie. Frühgeschichte der Nürnberger Arbeiterbewegung.* Industrielle Welt, Bd. 9. Stuttgart: Ernst Klett, 1968.

Eibert, Georg. *Unternehmenspolitik Nürnberger Maschinenbauer (1835–1914)*. Beiträge zur Wirtschaftsgeschichte, Bd. 3. Stuttgart: Klett-Cotta (in Kommission), 1979.

Engelhardt, Ulrich. *"Nur vereinigt sind wir stark." Die Anfänge der deutschen Gewerkschaftsbewegung 1862/63 bis 1869/70*. 2 vols. Industrielle Welt, Bd. 23. Stuttgart: Klett-Cotta, 1977.

————. "Zur Entwicklung der Streikbewegungen in der ersten Industrialisierungsphase und zur Funktion von Streiks bei der Konstituierung der Gewerkschaftsbewegung in Deutschland." *Internationale wissenschaftliche Korrespondenz zur Geschichte der deutschen Arbeiterbewegung* 15 (1979): 547–569.

————, ed. *Handwerker in der Industrialisierung. Lage, Kultur und Politik vom späten 18. bis ins frühe 20. Jahrhundert*. Industrielle Welt, Bd. 37. Stuttgart: Klett-Cotta, 1984.

Evans, Richard J., ed. *The German Working Class 1888–1933: The Politics of Everyday Life*. New York: Barnes and Noble, 1981.

————, ed. *Society and Politics in Wilhelmine Germany*. New York: Barnes and Noble, 1978.

Fischer, Ilse. *Industrialisierung, sozialer Konflikt und politische Willensbildung in der Stadtgemeinde. Ein Beitrag zur Sozialgeschichte Augsburgs 1840–1914*. Abhandlungen zur Geschichte der Stadt Augsburg, Bd. 24. Augsburg: Hieronymus Mühlberger, 1977.

Fischer, Walter. *Die Fürther Arbeiterbewegung von ihren Anfängen bis 1870*. Diss., University of Erlangen-Nuremberg, 1965. Nuremberg: privately printed, 1965.

Förder, Herwig. "Die Nürnberger Gemeinde des Bundes der Kommunisten und die Verbreitung des Manifestes der Kommunistischen Partei im Frühjahr 1851." *Beiträge zur Geschichte der deutschen Arbeiterbewegung*. Sonderheft: Beiträge zur Marx-Engels-Forschung in der DDR, 4 (1962): 165–188.

Foth, Werner. "Soziale Chronik aus 100 Jahren MAN." Manuscript. M.A.N.-Nbg. Werksarchiv, 1943.

Gärtner, Georg. *Karl Grillenberger. Lebensbild eines Kämpfers für Volksrecht und Volksfreiheit*. Nuremberg: Fränkische Verlagsanstalt, 1930.

————. *Die Nürnberger Arbeiterbewegung 1868–1908*. 1908. Reprint. Bonn-Bad Godesberg: J.H.W. Dietz, 1977.

Glaser, Hermann; Ruppert, Wolfgang; and Neudecker, Norbert, eds. *Industriekultur in Nürnberg: Eine deutsche Stadt im Maschinenzeitalter*. Munich: C. H. Beck, 1980.

Gömmel, Rainer. *Wachstum und Konjunktur der Nürnberger Wirtschaft (1815–1914)*. Beiträge zur Wirtschaftsgeschichte, Bd. 1. Stuttgart: Klett-Cotta (in Kommission), 1978.

Goulden, Steven L. "Growth and Conflict in the German Metal Workers' Union: The Experience of Two German Cities, 1900–1925." Ph.D. diss., University of Chicago, 1976.

Gray, Robert Q. *The Labour Aristocracy in Victorian Edinburgh*. Oxford: Clarendon Press of Oxford University Press, 1976.

Grießinger, Andreas. *Das symbolische Kapital der Ehre. Streikbewegungen und kollek-

*tives Bewußtsein deutscher Handwerksgesellen im 18. Jahrhundert.* Frankfurt, Berlin, and Vienna: Ullstein, 1981.

Grießinger, Andreas, and Reith, Reinhold. "Obrigkeitliche Ordnungskonzeptionen und handwerkliches Konflitverhalten im 18. Jahrhundert. Nürnberg und Würzburg im Vergleich." In *Deutsches Handwerk im Spätmittelalter und Früher Neuzeit: Sozialgeschichte—Volkskunde—Literaturgeschichte*, edited by Rainer S. Elkar, 117–180. Göttingen: Otto Schwarz & Co., 1983.

Groh, Dieter. "Intensification of Work and Industrial Conflict in Germany, 1896–1914." *Politics and Society* 8 (1978): 349–397.

Hanagan, Michael P. *The Logic of Solidarity: Artisans and Industrial Workers in Three French Towns, 1871–1914.* Champaign: University of Illinois Press, 1981.

Hanagan, Michael P., and Stephenson, Charles. "The Skilled Worker and Working-Class Protest." *Social Science History* 4 (1980): 5–13.

Held, Max. *Das Arbeitsverhältnis im Nürnberger Handwerk.* Münchener Volkswirtschaftliche Studien, Bd. 97. Diss., University of Munich, 1909. Stuttgart and Berlin: J. G. Cotta'sche Buchhandlung Nachfolger, 1909.

Heron, Craig. "The Crisis of the Craftsman: Hamilton's Metal Workers in the Early Twentieth Century." *Labour/Le Travailleur* 6 (1980): 7–48.

Hirschfelder, Heinrich. *Die bayerische Sozialdemokratie 1864–1914.* 2 vols. Erlangen: Palm und Enke, 1979.

Hobsbawm, Eric. "The Labour Aristocracy in Nineteenth-Century Britain." In *Labouring Men: Studies in the History of Labour*, by E. Hobsbawm, 272–315. London: Weidenfeld and Nicolson, 1964.

Hommer, Otto. *Die Entwicklung und Tätigkeit des Deutschen Metallarbeiterverbandes: Ein Beitrag zum Gewerkschaftsproblem.* Berlin: Carl Heymann, 1912.

Huck, Gerhard, ed. *Sozialgeschichte der Freizeit. Untersuchungen zum Wandel der Alltagskultur in Deutschland.* Wuppertal: Peter Hammer, 1980.

IG Metall, ed. *Fünfundsiebzig Jahre Industriegewerkschaft 1891 bis 1966. Vom Deutschen Metallarbeiter-Verband zur Industriegewerkschaft Metall. Ein Bericht in Wort und Bild.* 3rd ed. Frankfurt a. M.: Europäische Verlags-Anstalt, 1966.

Jegel, August. *Die wirtschaftliche Entwicklung von Nürnberg-Fürth, Stein und des Nürnberger Raumes seit 1806. Mit Berücksichtigung des allgemeinen Geschehens.* Nuremberg: Lorenz Spindler, 1952.

Katznelson, Ira, and Zolberg, Aristide R., eds. *Working-Class Formation: Nineteenth-Century Patterns in Western Europe and the United States.* Princeton: Princeton University Press, 1986.

Kaufhold, Karl Heinrich. "Die 'moral economy' des alten Handwerks und die Aufstände der Handwerksgesellen. Überlegungen zu einer neuen Veröffentlichung." Review of *Das symbolische Kapital der Ehre*, by A. Grießinger. *Archiv für Sozialgeschichte* 22 (1982): 514–522.

Keller, Kurt. *Das messer- und schwertherstellende Gewerbe in Nürnberg von den Anfänge bis zum Ende der reichstädtischen Zeit.* Nürnberger Werkstücke zur Stadt- und Landesgeschichte, Bd. 31. Nuremberg: Stadtarchiv Nürnberg, 1981.

Kern, Horst, and Schumann, Michael. *Industriearbeit und Arbeiterbewußtsein. Eine empirische Untersuchung über den Einfluß der aktuellen technischen Entwicklung auf die industrielle Arbeit und das Arbeiterbewußtsein*. 2 vols. Frankfurt a. M.: Europäische Verlags-Anstalt, 1970.

Klings, Jochen. "Der Kampf um die Gewerbefreiheit in Nürnberg in den Jahren 1848–1850." Diss., University of Erlangen, 1951.

Kocka, Jürgen. "Craft Traditions and the Labour Movement in Nineteenth-Century Germany." In *The Power of the Past: Essays for Eric Hobsbawm*, edited by Pat Thane, Geoffrey Crossick, and Roderick Floud, 95–117. Cambridge: Cambridge University Press/Paris: Editions de la Maison des Sciences de l'Homme, 1984.

————. *Klassengesellschaft im Krieg. Deutsche Sozialgeschichte 1914–1918*. Kritische Studien zur Geschichtswissenschaft, Bd. 8. Göttingen: Vandenhoeck und Ruprecht, 1973.

————. *Lohnarbeit und Klassenbildung. Arbeiter und Arbeiterbewegung in Deutschland 1800–1875*. Berlin (West) and Bonn: J.H.W. Dietz Nachf., 1983.

————. "Sozialstruktur und Arbeiterbewegung: Die Entstehung des Leipziger Proletariats." Review of *Die Konstituierung des Proletariats als Klasse*, by H. Zwahr. *Archiv für Sozialgeschichte* 20 (1980): 584–592.

————. "The Study of Social Mobility and the Formation of the Working Class in the 19th Century." *Le Mouvement Social*, no. 111 (1980): 97–117.

————. "Traditionsbindung und Klassenbildung. Zum sozialhistorischen Ort der frühen deutschen Arbeiterbewegung." *Historische Zeitschrift* 243 (1986): 333–376.

Koehne, Karl. "Studien zur Geschichte des blauen Montags." *Zeitschrift für Sozialwissenschaft*, n.f., 11 (1920): 268–287, 394–413.

Koeppen, Werner. *Die Anfänge der Arbeiter- und Gesellenbewegung in Franken (1830–1852). Eine Studie zur Geschichte des politischen Sozialismus*. Erlanger Abhandlungen zur mittleren und neueren Geschichte, Bd. 21. Erlangen: Palm und Encke, 1935.

Landes, David S. *The Unbound Prometheus: Technological Change and Industrial Development in Western Europe from 1750 to the Present*. Cambridge: Cambridge University Press, 1969.

Lee, W. Robert. *Population Growth, Economic Development and Social Change in Bavaria, 1750–1850*. New York: Arno Press, 1977.

Lehnert, Walter. "Nürnberg—Stadt ohne Zünfte. Die Aufgaben des reichsstädtischen Rugamts." In *Deutsches Handwerk Im Spätmittelalter und Früher Neuzeit: Sozialgeschichte—Volkskunde—Literaturgeschichte*, edited by Rainer S. Elkar, 71–81. Göttingen: Otto Schwarz & Co., 1983.

Leitl, Edith. "Carl Crämer. Ansätze zu einer politischen Biographie." Zulassungsarbeit, University of Erlangen-Nürnberg, 1975.

Lidtke, Vernon L. *The Alternative Culture: Socialist Labor in Imperial Germany*. New York and Oxford: Oxford University Press, 1985.

————. *The Outlawed Party: Social Democracy in Germany, 1878–1890*. Princeton: Princeton University Press, 1966.

————. "Social Class and Secularization in Imperial Germany: The Working Classes." *Yearbook of the Leo Baeck Institute* 25 (1980): 21–40.

Lüdtke, Alf. "Arbeitsbeginn, Arbeitspause, Arbeitsende. Skizze zu Bedürfnisbe-friedigung und Industriearbeit im 19. and und frühen 20. Jahrhundert." In *So-zialgeschichte der Freizeit*, edited by Gerhard Huck. Wuppertal: Peter Hammer, 1980.

———. "Cash, Coffee-breaks, Horse-play: *Eigensinn* and Politics among Factory Workers in Germany around 1900." In *Confrontation, Class Consciousness, and the Labor Process: Studies in Proletarian Class Formation*, edited by Michael P. Hanagan and Charles Stephenson, 65–95. New York: Greenwood Press, 1986.

Lütcke, Klaus-Peter, ed. *Dokumentation zur Organisationsgeschichte des Deutschen Metallarbeiter-Verbandes*. Quellensammlung zur Geschichte der deutschen So-zialpolitik 1867–1914, Beiheft II.2.12. Wiesbaden: Franz Steiner, 1978.

Machtan, Lothar. " 'Im Vertrauen auf unsere gerechte Sache . . .': Streikbeweg-ungen der Industriearbeiter in den 70er Jahren des 19. Jahrhunderts." In *Streik*, edited by Klaus Tenfelde and Heinrich Volkmann. Munich: C. H. Beck, 1981.

———. "Zum Innenleben deutscher Fabriken im 19. Jahrhundert: Die formelle und die informelle Verfassung von Industriebetrieben, anhand von Beispielen aus dem Bereich der Textil- und Maschinenbauproduktion (1869–1891)." *Archiv für Sozialgeschichte* 21 (1981): 179–236.

———. "Zur Streikbewegung der deutschen Arbeiter in den Gründerjahren (1871–1873)." *Internationale wissenschaftliche Korrespondenz zur Geschichte der deutschen Arbeiterbewegung* 14 (1978): 419–442.

McLennan, Gregor. " 'The Labour Aristocracy' and 'Incorporation': Notes on Some Terms in the History of the Working Class." *Social History* 6 (1981): 71–81.

McLeod, Hugh. "Protestantism and the Working Class in Imperial Germany." *European Studies Review* 12 (1982): 323–344.

Marquardt, Frederick D. "A Working Class in Berlin in the 1840s?" In *Sozialge-schichte Heute: Festschrift für Hans Rosenberg zum 70. Geburtstag*, edited by H.-U. Wehler. Göttingen: Vandenhoeck und Ruprecht, 1974.

———. "Sozialer Aufstieg, sozialer Abstieg und die Entstehung der Berliner Ar-beiterklasse, 1806–1848." *Geschichte und Gesellschaft* 1 (1975): 43–77.

Mauersberg, Hans. "Die M.A.N. (1840–1965)." Manuscript, M.A.N.-Nbg. Werks-archiv, 1965.

Meyer, Wolfgang. *Das Vereinswesen der Stadt Nürnberg im 19. Jahrhundert*. Nürnber-ger Werkstücke zur Stadt- und Landesgeschichte, Bd. 3. Nuremberg: Stadtar-chiv Nürnberg, 1970.

Michels, Robert. "Die deutsche Sozialdemokratie: I. Parteimitgliedschaft und so-ziale Zusammensetzung." *Archiv für Sozialwissenschaft und Sozialpolitik* 23 (1906): 471–556.

Möckl, Karl. *Die Prinzregentenzeit. Gesellschaft und Politik während der Ära des Prinzre-genten Luitpold in Bayern*. Munich: R. Oldenbourg, 1972.

Mommsen, Hans, ed. *Arbeiterbewegung und industrieller Wandel. Studien zu gewerk-schaftlichen Organisationsproblemen im Reich und an der Ruhr*. Wuppertal: Peter Hammer, 1980.

Mommsen, Wolfgang J., and Husung, Hans-Gerhard, eds. *The Development of Trade Unionism in Great Britain and Germany, 1880–1914.* London: George Allen & Unwin, 1985.

Montgomery, David. *Workers' Control in America: Studies in the History of Work, Technology, and Labor Struggles.* Cambridge: Cambridge University Press, 1979.

————. "Workers' Control of Machine Production in the Nineteenth Century." *Labor History* 17 (1976): 485–509.

Morgenstern, Friedrich. *Die Fürther Metallschlägerei. Eine mittelfränkische Hausindustrie und ihre Arbeiter.* Tübingen: H. Laupp'schen Buchhandlung, 1890.

Moses, John A. *German Trade Unionism from Bismarck to Hitler, 1869–1933.* 2 vols. New York: Barnes and Noble, 1981.

Moss, Bernhard H. *The Origins of the French Labor Movement: The Socialism of Skilled Workers, 1830–1914.* Berkeley: University of California Press, 1976.

Neufeld, Michael J. "German Artisans and Political Repression: The Fall of the Journeymen's Associations in Nuremberg, 1806–1868." *Journal of Social History* 19 (1986): 491–502.

Nolan, Mary. *Social Democracy and Society: Working-class Radicalism in Dusseldorf, 1890–1920.* New York: Cambridge University Press, 1981.

Noll, A. *Sozio-ökonomischer Strukturwandel des Handwerks in der Zweiten Phasen der Industrialisierung unter besonderer Berücksichtigung der Regierungsbezirken Duisberg und Münster.* Göttingen: Vandenhoeck und Ruprecht, 1975.

Noyes, P. H. *Organization und Revolution: Working-Class Associations in the German Revolution of 1848–1849.* Princeton: Princeton University Press, 1966.

"Once upon a Shop Floor: An Interview with David Montgomery." *Radical History Review*, no. 23 (1980): 37–53.

Opel, Fritz. *Der Deutsche Metallarbeiter-Verband während des Ersten Weltkrieges und der Revolution.* Hanover: O. Goedel, 1962.

Paller, R. Ritter von. *Die bayerische Fahrrad-Industrie: Eine geschichtlich-statistische Betrachtung.* Nuremberg: G. Heydolf, 1908.

Palmer, Bryan D. *A Culture in Conflict: Skilled Workers and Industrial Capitalism in Hamilton, Ontario, 1860–1914.* Montreal: McGill-Queen's University Press, 1979.

Penn, Roger. "Trade Union Organization and Skill in the Cotton and Engineering Industries in Britain, 1850–1960." *Social History* 8 (1983): 37–55.

Pfeiffer, Gerhard. "Das Nürnberger Gemeindebevollmächtigtenkolleg 1818–1919." *Mitteilungen des Vereins für die Geschichte der Stadt Nürnberg* 65 (1978): 350–396.

————, ed. *Nürnberg: Geschichte einer europäischen Stadt.* Munich: C. H. Beck, 1972.

Pilz, Kurt. *Die 600jährige Geschichte des Nürnberger Schlosserhandwerks.* Nuremberg: Schlosser-Innung Nürnberg, 1965.

Pollard, Sidney. *The Genesis of Modern Management: A Study of the Industrial Revolution in Great Britain.* London: Edward Arnold, 1965.

Price, Richard. "The Labour Process and Labour History." *Social History* 8 (1983): 57–75.

————. "Structures of Subordination in Nineteenth-Century British Industry." In

*The Power of the Past: Essays for Eric Hobsbawm*, edited by Pat Thane, Geoffrey Crossick, and Roderick Floud, 119–142. Cambridge: Cambridge University Press/Paris: Editions de la Maison des Sciences de l'Homme, 1984.

Quataert, Jean H. *Reluctant Feminists in German Social Democracy, 1885–1917*. Princeton: Princeton University Press, 1979.

Reid, Douglas A. "The Decline of St. Monday 1766–1876." *Past and Present*, no. 71 (1976): 76–101.

Renzsch, Wolfgang. *Handwerker und Lohnarbeiter in der frühen Arbeiterbewegung. Zur sozialen Basis von Gewerkschaften und Sozialdemokratie im Reichsgründungjahrzehnt.* Kritische Studien zur Geschichtswissenschaft, Bd. 43. Göttingen: Vandenhoeck und Ruprecht, 1980.

Reß, Franz-Michael. "Die Nürnberger 'Briefbücher' als Quelle zur Geschichte des Handwerks, der eisen- und metallverarbeitende Gewerbe sowie der Sozial- und Wirtschaftsgeschichte." In *Beiträge zur Wirtschaftsgeschichte Nürnbergs*, 2:800–829. Nuremberg: Stadtarchiv Nürnberg, 1967.

Reulecke, Jürgen. "Vom blauen Montag zum Arbeiterurlaub. Vorgeschichte und Entstehung des Erholungsurlaubs für Arbeiter vor dem Ersten Weltkrieg." *Archiv für Sozialgeschichte* 16 (1976): 205–248.

Ritter, Gerhard A., and Tenfelde, Klaus. "Der Durchbruch der Freien Gewerkschaften zur Massenbewegung im letzten Viertel des 19. Jahrhunderts." In *Arbeiterbewegung, Parteien und Parlamentarismus*, by G. A. Ritter. Kritische Studien zur Geschichtswissenschaft, Bd. 23. Göttingen: Vandenhoeck und Ruprecht, 1976.

Roberts, James S. "Der Alkoholkonsum deutscher Arbeiter im 19. Jahrhundert." *Geschichte und Gesellschaft* 6 (1980): 220–242.

———. "Drink and Industrial Work Discipline in 19th-Century Germany." *Journal of Social History* 15 (1981–1982): 25–38.

Rodgers, Daniel T. "Tradition, Modernity and the American Worker: Reflections and Critique." *Journal of Interdisciplinary History* 7 (1976–1977): 655–681.

Rosenberg, Nathan. "Technological Change in the Machine Tool Industry, 1840–1910." *Journal of Economic History* 23 (1963): 414–443.

Rosenhaupt, Karl. *Die Nürnberg-Fürther Metallspielwarenindustrie in geschichtlicher und sozialpolitischer Bedeutung*. Diss., University of Munich, 1907. Stuttgart: Union Deutsche Verlagsgesellschaft, 1907.

Rossmeissl, Dieter. *Arbeiterschaft und Sozialdemokratie in Nürnberg 1890–1914*. Nürnberger Werkstücke zur Stadt- und Landesgeschichte, Bd. 22. Nuremberg: Stadtarchiv Nürnberg, 1977.

Rupieper, Hermann-Josef. *Arbeiter und Angestellte im Zeitalter der Industrialisierung. Eine sozialgeschichtliche Studie am Beispiel der Maschinenfabriken Augsburg und Nürnberg (MAN) 1837–1914*. Frankfurt and New York: Campus, 1982.

———. "Regionale Herkunft, Fluktuation und innerbetriebliche Mobilität der Arbeiterschaft der Maschinenfabrik Augsburg-Nürnberg (MAN), 1844–1914." In *Arbeiter im Industrialisierungsprozeß*, edited by W. Conze and U. Engelhardt, 94–112. Industrielle Welt, Bd. 28. Stuttgart: Klett-Cotta, 1979.

Ruppert, Wolfgang, ed. *Lebensgeschichten: Zur deutschen Sozialgeschichte 1850–1950.* Nuremberg: Ausstellungskatalog des Centrums Industriekultur, 1980.

Samuel, Raphael. "Workshop of the World: Steam Power and Hand Technology in Mid-Victorian Britain." *History Workshop: A Journal for Socialist Historians,* no. 3 (1977): 6–72.

Schäfer, Hermann. "Arbeitsverdienst im Lebenszyklus: Zur Einkommensmobilität von Arbeitern." *Archiv für Sozialgeschichte* 21 (1981): 237–267.

Schanz, Georg. *Zur Geschichte der deutschen Gesellen-Verbände.* Leipzig: Duncker und Humblot, 1877.

Schnorbus, Axel. *Arbeit und Sozialordnung in Bayern vor dem Ersten Weltkrieg (1890–1914).* Miscellanea Bavarica Monacensia, Heft 19. Munich: Stadtarchiv München, 1969.

Schoenlank, Bruno. "Gesellenverbände." In *Handwörterbuch der Staatswissenschaften,* edited by J. Conrad, L. Elster, W. Lexis, and E. Loening, 3:820–833. Jena: Gustav Fischer, 1893.

————. *Zur Lage der arbeitenden Klasse in Bayern. Eine volkswirtschaftlichen Skizze.* 1887. Reprint. Olching: Extra-Verlag, 1979.

Schomerus, Heilwig. *Die Arbeiter der Maschinenfabrik Esslingen. Forschungen zur Lage der Arbeiterschaft im 19. Jahrhundert.* Industrielle Welt, Bd. 24. Stuttgart: Klett-Cotta, 1977.

Schönhoven, Klaus. *Expansion und Konzentration. Studien zur Entwicklung Freien Gewerkschaften im Wilhelminischen Deutschland.* Industrielle Welt, Bd. 30. Stuttgart: Klett-Cotta, 1980.

Schraepler, Ernst. *Handwerkerbünde und Arbeitervereine 1830–1853. Die politische Tätigkeit deutscher Sozialisten von Wilhelm Weitling bis Karl Marx.* Veröffentlichungen des Historischen Kommission zu Berlin, Bd. 34. Berlin (West) and New York: De Gruyter, 1972.

Schröder, Peter. *Die Entwicklung des Nürnberger Großgewerbes 1806–1870. Studien zur Frühindustrialisierung.* Nürnberger Werkstücke zur Stadt- und Landesgeschichte, Bd. 8. Nuremberg: Stadtarchiv Nürnberg, 1971.

Schröder, Wilhelm-Heinz. *Arbeitergeschichte und Arbeiterbewegung. Industriearbeit und Organisationsverhalten im 19. und frühen 20. Jahrhundert.* Frankfurt and New York: Campus, 1978.

Schwab, Karl. *Verschiebungen in der beruflichen Gliederung der Bevölkerung Nürnbergs von 1852 bis 1907.* Diss., University of Erlangen, 1914. Munich: J. B. Lindl, 1914.

Schwarz, Gerhard. *"Nahrungsstand" und "erzwungener Gesellenstand." Mentalité und Strukturwandel des bayerischen Handwerks im Industrialisierungsprozeß um 1860.* Berlin (West): Duncker und Humblot, 1974.

Schwarz, Klaus-Dieter. *Weltkrieg und Revolution in Nürnberg. Ein Beitrag zur Geschichte der deutschen Arbeiterbewegung.* Kieler Historische Studien, Bd. 13. Stuttgart: Ernst Klett, 1971.

Scott, Joan W. *The Glassworkers of Carmaux: French Craftsmen and Political Action in a Nineteenth-Century City.* Cambridge, Mass.: Harvard University Press, 1974.

Seiler, Karl, and Hildebrandt, Walter. *Die Landflucht in Franken*. Berichte zur Raumforschung und Raumordnung, Bd. 3. Leipzig: K. F. Koehler, 1940.

Senst, Otto. *Die Metallspielwarenindustrie und der Spielwarenhandel von Nürnberg und Fürth*. Diss., University of Erlangen, 1901. Erlangen: Fr. Junge, 1901.

Seubert, Josef. "Die Entstehung der Nürnberger Fahrzeugindustrie." Diss., University of Erlangen, 1924.

Sewell, William H., Jr. *Work and Revolution in France: The Language of Labor from the Old Regime to 1848*. Cambridge and New York: Cambridge University Press, 1980.

Sheehan, James J. *German Liberalism in the Nineteenth Century*. Chicago and London: University of Chicago Press, 1978.

Shorter, Edward L. "Social Change and Social Policy in Bavaria, 1800–1860." 2 vols. Ph.D. Diss., Harvard University, 1967.

Smith, Steven A. "Craft Consciousness, Class Consciousness: Petrograd 1917." *History Workshop: A Journal of Socialist Historians*, no. 11 (1981): 33–56.

———. *Red Petrograd. Revolution in the Factories 1917–18*. Cambridge: Cambridge University Press, 1983.

Soergel, H. T. "Zwei Nürnberger Metallgewerbe." In *Untersuchungen über die Lage des Handwerks in Deutschland*, 3:484–495. Schriften des Vereins für Sozialpolitik, Bd. 64. Leipzig: Duncker und Humblot, 1895.

Spindler, Max, ed. *Handbuch der bayerischen Geschichte*, vol. 4. Munich: C. H. Beck, 1974.

Stearns, Peter N. "Adaptation to Industrialization: German Workers as a Test Case." *Central European History* 3 (1970): 303–331.

Steglich, Walter. "Eine Streiktabelle für Deutschland 1864–1880." *Jahrbuch für Wirtschaftsgeschichte* (1960), pt. 2:247–283.

Stürmer, Michael, ed. *Herbst des Alten Handwerks. Zur Sozialgeschichte des 18. Jahrhunderts*. Munich: DTV, 1979.

Tenfelde, Klaus, and Volkmann, Heinrich, eds. *Streik. Zur Geschichte des Arbeitskampfes in Deutschland während der Industrialisierung*. Munich: C. H. Beck, 1981.

Thompson, E. P. "The Moral Economy of the English Crowd in the Eighteenth Century." *Past and Present*, no. 50 (1971): 76–136.

———. "Time, Work-Discipline and Industrial Capitalism." *Past and Present*, no. 38 (1967): 56–97.

Thönnessen, Werner. *The Emancipation of Women: The Rise and Decline of the Women's Movement in German Social Democracy 1863–1933*. Translated by Joris de Bres. London: Pluto Press, 1973.

Truant, Cynthia M. "Solidarity and Symbolism among Journeymen Artisans: The Case of *Compagnonnage*." *Comparative Studies in Society and History* 21 (1979): 214–226.

Vetterli, Rudolf. "Arbeitssituation und Organisationsverhalten Schweizer Metallarbeiter." In *Arbeiter im Industrialisierungsprozeß*, edited by W. Conze and U. Engelhardt, 336–361. Stuttgart: Klett-Cotta, 1979.

————. *Industriearbeit, Arbeiterbewußtsein und gewerkschaftliche Organisation. Darge-stellt am Beispiel der Georg Fischer AG (1890–1930)*. Kritische Studien zur Ge-schichtswissenschaft, Bd. 28. Göttingen: Vandenhoeck und Ruprecht, 1978.

Voit, Hans. *Die Nürnberger Gold- und Silberschlägerei in historischer und sozialpoliti-scher Beleuchtung*. Nuremberg: Kommissionsverlag von Benedikt Hilz, 1912.

Volckmann, Erwin. *Alte Gewerbe und Gewerbegassen. Deutsche Berufs-, Handwerks-und Wirtschaftsgeschichte älterer Zeit.* 1921. Reprint. Hildesheim: Dr. H. A. Ger-stenberg, 1976.

Volkmann, Heinrich. "Modernisierung des Arbeiterkampfes? Zum Formwandel von Streik und Aussperrung in Deutschland 1864–1975." In *Probleme der Moder-nisierung in Deutschland. Sozialhistorische Studien zum 19. und 20. Jahrhundert*, ed-ited by H. Kaelble, et al. Opladen: Westdeutscher Verlag, 1978.

————. "Möglichkeiten und Aufgaben quantitativer Arbeitskampfforschung in Deutschland." *Internationale wissenschaftliche Korrespondenz zur Geschichte der deut-schen Arbeiterbewegung* 17 (1981): 141–154.

Volkov, Shulamit. *The Rise of Popular Antimodernism in Germany: The Urban Master Artisans, 1873–1896*. Princeton: Princeton University Press, 1978.

Walker, Mack. *German Home Towns, 1648–1871: Community, State and General Es-tate*. Ithaca and London: Cornell University Press, 1971.

Weber, Eugen. "Comment la Politique Vint aux Paysans: A Second Look at Peas-ant Politicization." *American Historical Review* 87 (1982): 357–389.

Weiss, Wilhelm. "Die Reisszeugindustrie Nürnbergs." Diss., University of Er-langen, 1924.

Werner, George S. "Travelling Journeymen in Metternichian South Germany." *Proceedings of the American Philosophical Society* 125 (1981): 190–219.

Wiessner, Paul. "Die Anfänge der Nürnberger Fabrikindustrie." Diss., University of Frankfurt, 1929.

Wiest, Ekkehard. *Die Entwicklung des Nürnberger Gewerbes zwischen 1648 bis 1806*. Forschungen zur Sozial- und Wirtschaftsgeschichte, edited by Fr. Lütge, Bd. 12. Stuttgart: Gustav Fischer, 1968.

Wissel, Rudolf. *Des Alten Handwerks Recht und Gewohnheit*. 2 vols. Enlarged and edited by Ernst Schraepler. Berlin (West): Colloquim, 1971.

Zimmermann, Ludwig. *Die Einheits- und Freiheitsbewegung und die Revolution von 1848 in Franken*. Veröffentlichungen der Gesellschaft für fränkische Geschichte, IX. Reihe, Bd. 9. Würzburg: Kommissionsverlag Ferdinand Schöningh, 1951.

Zorn, Wolfgang. "Zur Nürnberger Handels- und Unternehmensgeschichte des 19. Jahrhunderts." In *Beiträge zur Wirtschaftsgeschichte Nürnbergs*, 2:851–864. Nuremberg: Stadtarchiv Nürnberg, 1967.

Zwahr, Hartmut. *Zur Konstituierung des Proletariats als Klasse: Strukturuntersuchung über das Leipziger Proletariat während der industriellen Revolution*. Berlin (East): Aka-demie-Verlag, 1978.

# INDEX

ADAV, *see* Lassalleans
alcohol consumption, rates of, 53, 57. *See also* journeymen, drinking by
apprentices, 17, 36, 105, 107, 117–119, 151, 156; numbers of, 14–15
apprenticeship, 32, 47, 50, 86, 105, 107, 111; in the machine industry, 26
artisans, *see* apprentices; apprenticeship; capitalism; craft consciousness; industrialization; journeymen; journeymen's associations; master artisans; political repression; population growth; quasi-guild system; skilled workers; Trades Law (1825)
Association Law (1850), 76, 133
Augsburg, 20, 142, 153, 162, 164, 165; character of the working class in, 6, 99
*Augsburger Allgemeine Zeitung*, 23
awlsmiths, 12, 14

Bavaria, 13, 53, 56; citizenship and political rights in, 38, 74–76, 133; emigration from, 39; Heimat, marriage and settlement laws of, 37–40, 49, 73–74, 169; Landtag of, 61, 133; laws on striking in, 65, 70, 76; reforms of 1868–1869 in, 73–75; regulation of wandering artisans

in, 43, 45–46, 51; socialist movement in, 6
Bebel, August, 69, 76–77, 134
Belgium, 43
bellmakers, 14, 17
Berg foundry, 150
Berlin, 6, 65–66, 85, 87, 126, 160, 162
bicycle industry, 33, 135; workers in, 132, 149, 152–154
Bismarck, Otto von, 4, 68, 76, 97, 98, 101, 102, 170
blacksmiths, 14, 27, 55, 68, 199n2; DMV section of, 124, 134, 144; German terms for, 30; history, work process, and technology of, 30; journeymen's association of, 46, 47; strikes and wage movements by, 86, 91–92, 149, 161, 162, 164, 210n51; unions of, 113, 122, 123, 135; wages and hours of, 30, 53, 59
Blue Monday, 29; history of, in Nuremberg, 52–60
boilermakers, 30
Born, Stefan, 64
brass molders, 14, 61, 65, 68, 69, 72, 78, 79; DMV section of, 124, 134, 144, 145; German terms for, 16; history and technology of, 16–17; journeymen's association of, 42, 44, 45, 46, 52; strikes and wage movements by, 44, 49, 62, 115, 145;

*237*